Performance Intervention Maps

36 Strategies for Solving Your Organization's Problems

ASTD

*Linking People,
Learning & Performance*

ISPI

Improving Performance
Since 1962

*Ethan S. Sanders and
Sivasailam "Thiagi" Thiagarajan*

Ordering information: Books published by ASTD can be ordered by calling 800.628.2783 or 703.683.8100, or via the Website at www.astd.org.

Library of Congress Catalog Card Number: 2001117678

ISBN: 1-56286-293-6

Printed by Victor Graphics, Baltimore, MD.
www.victorgraphics.com

TABLE OF CONTENTS

Preface *by Ethan S. Sanders* v

Introduction *by Ethan S. Sanders and Sivasailam Thiagarajan*.................vii
    The HPI Mindset vii
    A Single Process for Multiple Interventions.............................viii
    Classifying Interventions x
    A Caveat xii
    How to Use the Intervention Selection Maps xvii
    Multiple Variables xix
    Reference xix

Chapter One—Tell Me How: Improving Knowledge and Skills 1
    1. Accelerated Learning *by Lou Russell* 5
    2. Action Learning *by Michael J. Marquardt*........................17
    3. Coaching *by Andrew Kimball* 23
    4. Electronic Performance Support Systems *by Kim E. Ruyle*..............31
    5. Job Aids *by Paul H. Elliott* 39
    6. On-the-Job Training *by Rick Sullivan*............................47
    7. Training Games *by Sivasailam Thiagarajan* 53
    8. Self-Directed Learning *by George Piskurich* 59

Chapter Two—Tell Me Why: Improving Motives.....................63
    9. Rewards and Recognition *by Linda Beck Halliburton*.......67
    10. Compensation Systems *by Ethan S. Sanders*
        and Jacqueline B. Visnius 73
    11. Playfulness *by Sivasailam Thiagarajan* 79
    12. Motivation Systems *by Matthew S. Richter* 85
    13. Team Building *by Sivasailam Thiagarajan*.......................93

Chapter Three—Give Me Tools: Improving Physical Resources 101
    14. Ergonomics and Human Factors *by Ethan S. Sanders*
        and Jacqueline B. Visnius 105
    15. Automation and Computerization *by Ralph Sanders* 111
    16. Physical Resource Management *by Ralph Sanders*.....................115

Chapter Four—Tell Me Who Does What and When:
Improving Structure and Process **121**
   17. Conflict Management *by Sivasailam Thiagarajan* 125
   18. Culture Reshaping *by Tom Devane* 131
   19. Process Leadership *by Andrew Kimball* 137
   20. Performance Appraisal *by Stewart Hickman*
       and Jacqueline B. Visnius 143
   21. Staffing *by Margo Prator* 149
   22. Process Redesign *by Tom Devane* 155
   23. Job Interviews *by Matthew S. Richter and Andrew Kimball*............161

Chapter Five—Tell Me: Improving Information **167**
   24. Knowledge Management *by Mark Van Buren* 171
   25. Networks for Information *by Patti Shank*...............................177
   26. Balanced Scorecard *by Stewart Hickman*
       and Jacqueline B. Visnius 185
   27. Meetings and Dialogue *by Ethan S. Sanders*
       and Jacqueline B. Visnius 191
   28. Newsletters *by Ethan S. Sanders* 197
   29. Public Relations Campaigns *by Jennifer Homer* 205
   30. Debriefing *by Sivasailam Thiagarajan* 211

Chapter Six—Get Well Soon: Improving Health **217**
   31. Energy Management *by Mark L. Berman* 221
   32. Work-Life Balance *by Mark L. Berman* 227
   33. Employee Assistance Programs *by Ethan S. Sanders*
       and Jacqueline B. Visnius 233
   34. Counseling *by Kathy Kelly* 239
   35. Win-Win Negotiation *by Kat Koppett*......................................245
   36. Violence Prevention *by Todd Packer* 251

Conclusion *by Sivasailam Thiagarajan* 259

Glossary 261

About the Authors 271

About the Contributors..273

PREFACE

Perhaps the most damaging words performance consultants use today are *other interventions*. While we have come a long way in explaining to our clients the need to take a more holistic approach toward analyzing organizational problems, somehow we have left the topic of solutions virtually uncharted. While we have become proficient at producing long lists of knowledge interventions (such as mentoring, coaching, training, and job aids) and provide examples of a few nonlearning interventions (such as ergonomics and compensation systems), we fail to spell out the range of interventions available and the benefits and limitations that each type of intervention possesses. When it comes to understanding interventions as a whole, the human performance improvement (HPI) literature gets thin.

Recently, some excellent resource books have captured a piece of this puzzle. Books such as *The Intervention Resource Guide* by Danny Langdon have made an important step forward in starting to document what these other interventions might be. However, as an instructor of HPI courses for ASTD, I have noticed one pervasive problem that exists when it comes to using these resources. Students are baffled about how they go from understanding the root cause of the problem to recommending interventions that have a high probability of success. What many HPI practitioners long for is a methodology for helping them recommend appropriate interventions. It is this problem that this book is intended to directly address.

The first step in tackling this problem was to put together a comprehensive classification system. My co-author, Sivasailam Thiagarajan ("Thiagi"), and I, together with many other people, worked for months on the classification system in this book. Some noted experts in the field oppose such classifications. Their reasons for this opposition vary, but in general they fear that such a system oversimplifies the considerations that go into selecting interventions, thereby trivializing the selection process. They also fear that a classification system will rapidly become outdated as the method of delivering these interventions continues to evolve.

Although we appreciate these concerns, the alternative of leaving this topic uncharted and undefined has far more potential for damaging the evolution of the field. The field of HPI has reached a point in its maturation process at which we simply must find ways of teaching emerging performance consultants how to produce the same results that the founders of this profession have produced. It is no longer good enough to cite the success records of noted performance consultants as evidence that HPI works. Instead, we need to demonstrate how these principles and methodologies are scalable, reproducible, and transferable regardless of who is using them. This book will allow all performance professionals to get a toehold into understanding the connection between root causes and available solutions. In no way is it intended to be the definitive source on how to select interventions. Rather, it is intended to be a road map from which a practitioner can begin investigating the most appropriate solutions for his or her clients.

As for the concern that this classification system may become rapidly outdated, we accept that the delivery method for these interventions may change, but the basic interventions are not nearly as fluid as some people believe. Coaching has basically been coaching since the time of Aristotle. While online coaching presents some legitimate logistical issues, the content of the intervention remains constant. The same goes for compensation, ergonomics, process improvement, and most other interventions listed in this book.

Finally, we are grateful to the numerous contributing authors who have lent their expertise, their ideas, and their energies to this book. Early in the development of this book, Thiagi and I deliberately chose practitioners who have a grassroots level of understanding about the types of interventions we are focusing on. We avoided the temptation of only contacting known experts in the field and searched vigorously for people who were in the trenches of performance improvement. In many ways this book is a family composition. We were unabashedly willing to contact friends, relatives, loved ones, and past colleagues who have impressed us with their ability to implement certain types of interventions. In other cases, we decided to contact the best-known person in the field because it was impossible to verify that others were successfully carrying out these interventions. This turned out to be one of the wisest decisions we made. While it was at times difficult pulling people out of their daily lives long enough to write their sections, the wisdom they were able to impart was well worth the effort. Too often in books such as this, the articles that appear from known authors are the same "marching mantra" that they have used a thousand times over in other books, articles, and presentations. We hope to bring a fresh perspective to this conversation.

If there is a single hope that we hold for this book, it is that the users of this material will find it increasingly easy to demonstrate the knowledge, confidence, and decision-making prowess that today's organizational leaders are looking for in their business partners.

Ethan S. Sanders
Alexandria, Virginia
August 2001

INTRODUCTION

Since the dawn of history, people have been obsessed with improving human performance. Leaders, statesmen, scientists, and scholars have vigorously pursued this goal and come up with a variety of methods and techniques. Like blind people around the elephant, people from different professions and disciplines convinced themselves that only they have the correct perception of the best method for improving human performance. They began spreading their method and preaching their message to everyone around them. As a part of this activity, proponents of one method vehemently attacked the infidels who espoused other methods.

During the early 1960s, a group of people interested in instruction began having second thoughts about the importance and infallibility of their discipline and articulated a thought that had been lurking beneath the human consciousness for a long time: What if there is no one single method for improving human performance? Instead of asking, "Which method is the best one?" they began asking questions like these:

- ◆ Which method is the best one in a specific context?
- ◆ Which method works with what types of performers?
- ◆ What combination of methods produces the most improvement in human performance (in a given context with a given group of people)?

This reflection and dialogue resulted in the development and dissemination of a comprehensive integrating model for improving human performance. People in the new multidisciplinary field of human performance improvement (HPI, also known as human performance technology) stopped making such claims as "Training is *the* solution to *all* performance problems." They did not even claim that "Training is the solution to *this* performance problem." Instead, they toned down their claim and said, "Training is a solution to some performance problems."

THE HPI MINDSET

The core of the HPI movement is the belief that human performance can be best improved through the use of a process that is *systematic, systemic,* and *results-based.*

The last of the three elements, a results-based process uses quantitative data that shows increases in areas such as profits, productivity, and customer satisfaction and decreases in areas such as cost, waste, and customer complaints.

A systemic process looks at the complex, dynamic, and comprehensive picture and focuses on interrelationships among components and changing patterns in these relationships. For example, a systemic mindset realizes that a salesperson's performance is affected not only by his or her behaviors but also by those of co-workers and team members; by the work of other departments in the organization including research, production, manufacturing, marketing, and after-sales services; and by outside factors such as the prime lending rate, societal changes, technological improvements, and the fluttering of butterfly wings in a rain forest.

A SINGLE PROCESS FOR MULTIPLE INTERVENTIONS

The steps in the HPI process and the interrelationships among them are shown in figure 1. This process incorporates the results-based nature (particularly during performance analysis and evaluation of results) and the systemic nature (particularly during business analysis) of the HPI mindset. The systematic nature of the process is obvious in the sequence and iteration of the steps.

Although most performance improvement models closely resemble this model, this version has a few unique features. One of the dangers of using a model like this is that it appears to be sequential and somewhat linear. In fact, only certain phases of the model actually happen in a specific order. In this model we have placed change management off to the side and

Figure 1. HPI model.

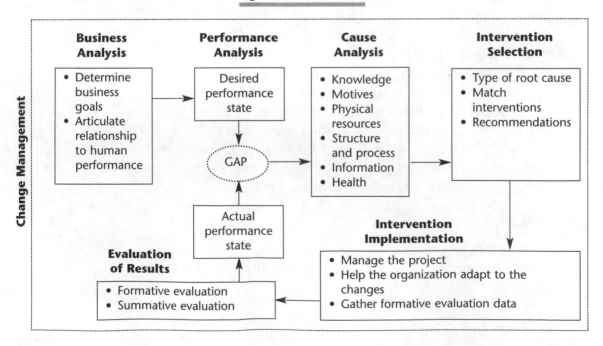

added a dotted line that circles the entire process, to demonstrate how change management occurs throughout the process (more on this later). We have also added a more carefully defined phase that precedes performance analysis, called business analysis. Although most performance models elude to business analysis (that is, they tell you to start by defining the organization's goal), they do not clearly label this as a distinct phase of the HPI process. Because of the importance of organizational goals to the entire HPI process, we feel this clearer distinction is warranted.

In general, the HPI process is only linear from business analysis through intervention implementation. Obviously, you cannot recommend a solution if you do not know what the problem is. Likewise, you cannot uncover the root cause if you do not know what the performance gap is. You cannot establish a performance gap without knowing the business goal, the desired level of performance, and the actual level of performance. Change management and evaluation, however, are really occurring throughout the life cycle of the HPI project.

At the heart of this model is the cause analysis. The cause analysis is what makes HPI systemic because it seeks to find the root causes of problems and definitively solve them. This is quite different from just treating the surface-level symptoms.

Here is a brief summary of what we (as performance consultants) do during the different steps in the HPI process:

- *Business analysis:* During business analysis, we find out the business goals from key decision makers. This ensures that all subsequent HPI activities will be aligned to achieving desirable business results.

- *Performance analysis:* We begin the performance analysis step by describing the desired levels of performance that are directly linked to the business goals (identified in the preceding step). We now collect data to identify actual levels of performance. The difference between the desired and the actual levels of performance reveals the performance gap.

- *Cause analysis:* During cause analysis, we identify the reasons for the gap between the desired and actual levels of performance. In this important step of the systematic HPI process, we probe beneath surface symptoms to discover the underlying root cause.

- *Intervention selection:* Once we have identified the root cause (or causes), we proceed to intervention selection. In the HPI terminology, an intervention is a combination of tools and techniques that is clearly and directly related to a performance gap.

- *Intervention implementation:* During intervention implementation, we work with a team of specialists to design and implement the selected intervention that removes or reduces the impact of the root cause.

- *Evaluation:* During evaluation, we return to the measurement of the actual performance and compare the data with the desired level of performance. If the gap still exists, we revise our intervention (or develop additional interventions) to further reduce the gap. When the gap is closed, we produce an evaluation report that summarizes the business results.

♦ *Change management:* The process of designing, developing, and implementing a systematic, systemic, results-based intervention always involves change. These changes must permeate the individual, team, and organizational levels. That is why change management is incorporated throughout the HPI process.

CLASSIFYING INTERVENTIONS

HPI uses a single, systematic process to produce a wide variety of interventions. Ever since Thomas Gilbert's (1996) original elaboration of the behavior engineering model, there have been several attempts at classifying performance interventions into logical categories. Most of these classification systems try to identify commonalities between the interventions based on characteristics of the interventions themselves. In this book, we use a classification system that is based on the type of root cause that the intervention is trying to address. For example, an intervention in the skills and knowledge category is trying to solve some sort of knowledge gap (for example, coaching). However, this same intervention could be used in other categories of root causes (for example, coaching could also be used to solve motivational problems). This flexible system of categorization is far more user-friendly and adaptable than other systems in the selection of an intervention for a client. Brief descriptions of six categories of this system follow (see also table 1).

Improving Knowledge and Skills

This category of interventions focuses on improving the essential knowledge and skills that are required for job performance. Notice that we have intentionally left out the word *training* to describe a specific intervention. In general, training describes a broad array of interventions used to improve a performer's knowledge and skills. We have chosen instead to give more specific descriptions of training interventions, such as accelerated learning and coaching. These interventions help the performer master a variety of technical and interpersonal skills along with the corresponding conceptual frameworks.

Here are some sample indicators of performer behaviors that suggest the use of interventions in this category:

♦ cannot identify essential behaviors that are necessary for effective job performance
♦ uses incorrect or inefficient actions on the job
♦ is unfamiliar with a new system, process, or tool that is being implemented
♦ lacks fluency with the use of the required skills and knowledge.

Improving Motives

This category of interventions focuses on improving performers' levels of interest, enthusiasm, and commitment. Motivation systems and other interventions in this category provide external incentives and intrinsic value to each performer's job activities.

Here are some sample indicators, in terms of what the performer does and what the performer receives, that suggest the use of interventions in this category:

- ◆ lacks feedback
- ◆ has competing priorities
- ◆ has conflicts between personal values and job requirements
- ◆ gets rewarded for incorrect behavior
- ◆ is punished for appropriate behavior
- ◆ lacks appreciation for accomplishments
- ◆ lacks adequate compensation, benefits, and other monetary incentives.

Improving Physical Resources

This category of interventions focuses on such physical resources as tools, equipment, furniture, hardware, and software, and such environmental resources as temperature, lighting, and ventilation. By improving the physical space that people work within, we create an environment that is conducive to sustained performance at high levels.

Here are some sample indicators of what is given to a performer that suggest the use of interventions in this category:

- ◆ inferior materials and supplies
- ◆ lack of appropriate tools and equipment
- ◆ broken and damaged tools, equipment, supplies, and materials
- ◆ tools and equipment that are not adjustable to an individual user's physiological characteristics and preferences
- ◆ inappropriate and unhealthy work area (that is, too cold, too hot, too moist, or too dry).

Improving Structure and Process

This category of interventions focuses on the structure and sequence of workflow processes. Conflict management, process improvement, and other interventions in this category provide smoother, more efficient, and more effective structures to the way work is completed.

Here are some sample indicators that suggest the use of interventions in this category:

- ◆ turf battles between managers
- ◆ lack of accountability
- ◆ unequal distribution of work
- ◆ superfluous, redundant, and incomplete work processes

- inefficient sequence of steps in the work processes
- mismatch of performer characteristics and job requirements
- inappropriate management strategies
- frequent conflicts among performers.

Improving Information

This category of interventions focuses on the effective distribution, management, and storage of information about different individuals, teams, and departments in an organization. Newsletters, knowledge management, and other interventions in this category are designed to improve information exchange within the organization.

Here are some sample indicators that suggest the use of interventions in this category:

- distribution of unnecessary, complex, incomplete, outdated, conflicting, or inaccurate information
- limited access to information
- lack of standards for electronic transfer of information
- problems in converting information from one system to another.

Improving Health

This category of interventions focuses on elements of the performer's physical and mental health that have an impact on job performance. Energy management, work-life balance, and other interventions in this category are designed to improve performers' physical and mental health, endurance, and energy level and to compensate for various disabilities.

Here are some sample indicators that suggest the use of interventions in this category:

- emotional illnesses such as depression and phobias
- attention deficit disorder (ADD)
- lengthy absences due to physical illness
- substance abuse problems
- injuries that prevent adequate performance
- visual or hearing impairment.

A CAVEAT

Our intention in designing this classification system for interventions is to provide a convenient structure for exchanging information, not to provide a scholarly taxonomy. Sound reasons could be given for placing some of the interventions in other categories. Although we placed *team building* as part of "Improving Motives," for example, someone else might legitimately place it in "Improving Structure and Process." The many ways in which one could interpret these interventions should not diminish the use of these categories.

TABLE 1. INTERVENTION CLASSIFICATION SYSTEM.

Root Cause Categories	Examples of Root Causes	Description of the Category	Examples of Interventions
Improving Knowledge	Does not know how to perform the task. Does not understand the essential behaviors that are necessary to be successful at the tasks. Has learned the wrong behaviors or skills to do the job. Has never had a chance to develop the skills in an appropriate context. Is confusing steps from one task with another task.	• Skill-related factors that are intrinsic to the performer. — Performance barriers caused by an inadequate amount of skills, inappropriate behaviors, inappropriate skills, or underdeveloped skills. — These skills can either be technical or interpersonal in nature.	• Accelerated learning • Action learning • Coaching • Electronic performance support systems (EPSSs) • Job aids • On-the-job training (OJT) • Training games • Self-directed learning
Improving Motives	Lacks feedback. Has competing priorities. Has conflicting values. Is rewarded for incorrect behavior. Is punished for appropriate behavior. Lacks appreciation for accomplishments. Lacks adequate compensation, benefits, or monetary rewards. Has inadequate structure.* Has inadequate skills. Has inadequate information. Has inadequate commitment. Has inadequate resources. Has poor mental or physical health.	• Motivational factors that are intrinsic to the performer but may be influenced by the work environment. — Performance barriers caused by a performer's perceived lack of urgency, importance, or value for the desired behaviors, performance, organization, or industry in which the performer works. — This misperception could be caused by an experience the employee had in the workplace (for instance, being punished for performing in the prescribed manner) or by a factor outside of the workplace (for example, the performer's personal values, religious beliefs, family obligations, or perceptions of family and friends).	• Rewards and recognition • Compensation systems • Playfulness • Motivation systems • Team building

(continued on page xiv)

*Notice that knowledge, information, structure, resources, and health are categories of root causes, and they are examples of root causes that create motivational performance barriers. This is because all these items can have the residual effect of lowering a performer's motivation to produce valuable outputs.

TABLE 1. INTERVENTION CLASSIFICATION SYSTEM. (continued)

Root Cause Categories	Examples of Root Causes	Description of the Category	Examples of Interventions
Improving Physical Resources	Receives inferior raw materials to work with. Receives incorrect materials to work with. Does not receive correct materials in a timely manner. Materials are too heavy to handle. Tools or equipment are missing or broken. Tools or equipment are not easily accessible. Tools or equipment are not well suited to the task. Tools or equipment are difficult to manipulate. New tools or equipment are difficult and too slow to procure. Work area is too cold, too hot, too dangerous, too small, too wet, too disorganized, etc. Is competition for scarce resources.	• Tangible resource factors that are extrinsic to the performer and can be changed regardless of who will be performing the task. — Performance barrier caused by an inappropriate amount, access to, or condition of tangible resources. — These resources can include tools, equipment, furniture, technological hardware and software, temperature, or lighting.	• Ergonomics and human factors • Automation and computerization • Physical resource management
Improving Structure and Process	Turf battles between managers. Lack of accountability for outcomes. Illogical reporting relationships. Unequal distribution of work. Redundant work processes. Incomplete work processes. Illogical sequencing of work processes. Misalignment of workers to the tasks that need to get done.	• Workflow factors that are extrinsic to the performer and can be changed regardless of who will be performing the task. — Performance barriers caused by illogical sequencing of tasks or an impractical allocation of work across individuals and work units. — How the work gets done, in what order, and who is officially supposed to do it.	• Conflict management • Culture reshaping • Process leadership • Performance appraisals • Staffing • Process redesign • Job interviews

Improving Information	Receives inferior, outdated, or inaccurate information.	• Factors that pertain to the ineffective exchange of data between people or between machines.	• Knowledge management
	Does not receive information in a timely manner.	— Performance barriers caused by data that is not transmitted effectively among two or more people, between a person and a machine, or within an information management system (that is, some type of electronic network).	• Networks for information
	Information is too complex or complicated to be useful.		• Balanced scorecard
	Does not receive complete information.		• Meetings and dialogue
	Information is difficult to access.		• Newsletters
	Receives irrelevant information.		• Public relations campaigns
	The information is in a physical format that is difficult to manipulate.		• Debriefing
	Difficult to procure better information.		
	Has lack of standards.		
	Has unrealistic standards.		
	Has inappropriate standards.		
	Has incorrect facts.		
	Lacks feedback.		
	Has overabundance of information.		
	Has unorganized or incorrectly organized information.		
	Has trouble converting data from one system to another (either computer system or procedural systems).		
	Has conflicting information.		

(continued on page xvi)

TABLE 1. INTERVENTION CLASSIFICATION SYSTEM. (continued)

Root Cause Categories	Examples of Root Causes	Description of the Category	Examples of Interventions
Improving Health	Cannot focus on his or her work due to clinical depression. Continually misses deadlines due to attention deficit disorder (ADD). Argues constantly with co-workers due to severe anxiety related to home-life issues. Has missed a lot of workdays due to physical illnesses. Has an erratic work schedule because he or she is caring for a sick child, spouse, or parent. Comes to work late due to a substance abuse problem. Cannot lift materials related to the job because of a weak back. Forgets to show up at meetings due to Alzheimer's disease. Cannot work in his or her new, top-floor office due to acrophobia (fear of heights). Cannot attend large company functions due to agoraphobia (fear of crowds).	• Factors related to an employee's physical or emotional well-being as they affect performance. — Performance barriers caused by the mental or physical deficiencies of a performer as they relate to job performance. Not included are deficiencies that are not relevant to the performer's job responsibilities (such as the physical limitations of a person whose work does not require those physical capabilities).	• Energy management • Work-life balance • Employee assistance program • Counseling • Win-win negotiating • Violence prevention

HOW TO USE THE INTERVENTION SELECTION MAPS

One of the unique features of this book is its classifications system. By classifying interventions according to the root causes they address, we feel we have made this information far more practical and easier to apply. However, there is more we can do here. We can help you to assess the interventions in terms of the three main variables that a performance consultant considers.

When selecting interventions, consider the following::

♦ *People:* Whom will these interventions affect, and what is their physical proximity to each other?

♦ *Money:* How much is the client willing to spend on these interventions in relation to the cost of the problem to the organization?

♦ *Time:* How quickly does the client need these interventions?

While these variables appear to be straightforward at first glance, they each have important factors that may not be obvious and must be taken into account.

♦ *People:* While it is true that you may need to consider the cultural differences that exist between groups and between individuals, it is often impractical to customize interventions to the point that they meet all of the preferences that exist between human beings. For purposes of the intervention maps, our decision-making variables concerning people are more basic. They fall into the categories *individual versus group* and *together versus spread out.*

• *Individual Versus Group*

First we need to know if the required intervention is intended to be implemented on a one-on-one basis, such as a mentoring program, or if this intervention is intended to be delivered to a group of performers simultaneously, such as an instructor-led training program. It is possible to have an individual intervention that gets delivered multiple times to multiple people. For example, you may find out that the cause for turnover in an organization is a lack of personal development plans. So the intervention is career counseling for each member of the organization. Even though we might consider "all employees of XYZ corporation" a group, the nature of career counseling requires it to be delivered to one person at a time. Therefore, we would consider career counseling to be an "individual intervention". Compare this with most types of team-building exercises that must be delivered in a group setting.

This distinction is important because it helps us select interventions that are better suited to the target population. It is not difficult to imagine how silly it would be to bring a group of people together to begin using a series of new job aids. The point of job aids is clearly to assist the performer at the point of performance, not in a contrived group setting that tries to reenact the performance environment.

- *Together Versus Spread Out*

  The other important consideration about performers is their physical proximity to each other. There is a major difference between delivering an intervention to a group that is located in a single facility and to a group that is spread throughout the world. For example, there could be disastrous results from a decision to improve performance through action learning for a group that is located on three different continents. Even when we are discussing individual interventions that will be delivered multiple times to multiple people, having these people separated geographically can affect which intervention you recommend to your clients.

  We have made the following distinction between populations that are together versus spread out:

  — Target populations are spread out if they are in three or more locations, or in two locations that are separated by three or more time zones, or both.
  — Target populations are together if they are in one or two locations and are within two time zones.

♦ *Money:* There is not a simple distinction between cheap and expensive interventions. Obviously, a detailed return-on-investment (ROI) analysis must be done to determine the true value that the intervention promises to give. Even after a proper ROI is done, however, there is not a standard that decides what is an acceptable ROI versus an unacceptable ROI. Some organizational stakeholders might think a two-to-one ratio of return is outstanding, while others are not willing to take a risk on anything that is less than a five-to-one ratio. Here again, our maps take a simplified approach. In general, we have placed interventions into the cheap category if we feel there is a reasonable chance that it would take six months or less from the time of the intervention to recoup its cost. We have placed in the expensive category those interventions that tend to be more expensive and from which it takes longer to reap the benefits Obviously, this is not a scientific method, but it should help you gauge which interventions are riskier and require more planning and caution.

♦ *Time:* Although it often seems that our clients want everything right away, in reality we can often determine a delivery schedule for each part of the intervention. Those interventions that appear in the need-it-fast column can normally be developed and implemented within a three-month time span. Those interventions that are in the have-time column normally take more than three months to design and deliver. Here again, we are basing this on general rules of thumb.

MULTIPLE VARIABLES

The intervention maps make it quite easy for you to select an intervention within the appropriate category, assuming you are only trying to satisfy two variables (such as time and money). Often, however, more than two variables will affect your intervention selection process. For example, your client may want an intervention delivered within three months to a dispersed population and insists that the cost of the intervention be recouped within four months. Because the intervention maps are two dimensional, they do not allow more than two variables at a time. In situations like this, locate interventions that fulfill two of the variables you require. Next, see if you find the same interventions when comparing across other variables. For example, if job aids are one of the possible solutions that appear for need it fast and spread out, and job aids also appears for cheap and individual, it would be possible to work with multiple variables. Remember, these intervention maps are a guidepost for you, they cannot possibly begin to calculate all of the factors involved in a successful selection of interventions.

REFERENCE

Gilbert, Thomas F. (1996). *Human Competence: Engineering Worthy Performance.* Washington, DC: International Society for Performance Improvement.

CHAPTER 1

TELL ME HOW: IMPROVING KNOWLEDGE AND SKILLS

1. Accelerated Learning *by Lou Russell*
2. Action Learning
   by Michael J. Marquardt
3. Coaching *by Andrew Kimball*
4. Electronic Performance Support Systems
   by Kim E. Ruyle
5. Job Aids *by Paul H. Elliott*
6. On-the-Job Training
   by Rick Sullivan
7. Training Games
   by Sivasailam Thiagarajan
8. Self-Directed Learning
   by George Piskurich

"There is only one good, knowledge, and one evil, ignorance."
—Socrates

KNOWLEDGE

	Individual	Group	Cheap	Expensive	Together	Spread Out	Need it Fast	Have Time
Individual			Accelerated Learning Coaching Job Aids OJT Self-Directed Learning	EPSS		Accelerated Learning Coaching EPSS Job Aids Self-Directed Learning	Accelerated Learning Coaching Job Aids Self-Directed Learning	EPSS
Group			Action Learning Games	Classroom Training E-learning	Action Learning Classroom Training Games	E-learning Games	Action Learning	Classroom Training E-learning
Cheap	Accelerated Learning Coaching Job Aids OJT Self-Directed Learning	Action Learning Games			Action Learning Games	Accelerated Learning Coaching Job Aids OJT Self-Directed Learning	Accelerated Learning Action Learning Coaching Job Aids Self-Directed Learning OJT	
Expensive	EPSS	Classroom Training E-learning			Classroom Training	E-learning EPSS		Classroom Training E-learning EPSS
Together		Action Learning Classroom Training Games	Action Learning Games	Classroom Training			Action Learning Games	Classroom Training
Spread Out	Accelerated Learning Coaching EPSS Job Aids Self-Directed Learning	E-learning Games	Accelerated Learning Coaching Job Aids OJT Self-Directed Learning	E-learning EPSS			Accelerated Learning Coaching Job Aids OJT Self-Directed Learning	E-learning EPSS
Need it Fast	Accelerated Learning Coaching Job Aids Self-Directed Learning	Action Learning	Accelerated Learning Action Learning Coaching Job Aids Self-Directed Learning OJT		Action Learning Games	Accelerated Learning Coaching Job Aids OJT Self-Directed Learning		
Have Time	EPSS	Classroom Training E-learning		Classroom Training E-learning EPSS	Classroom Training	E-learning EPSS		

Special Note: To make this classification more accurate, we have added the interventions "classroom training" and "e-learning," since these specific types of interventions have varying characteristics from each other. There are no sections on classroom training and e-learning since many of the interventions listed are just more specific descriptions of classroom training and e-learning.

1

ACCELERATED LEARNING

Lou Russell

WHAT IS ACCELERATED LEARNING?

In 1910 Brigadier General Billy Mitchell said that using airplanes to sink battleships was "damn nonsensical." In fact, he offered to stand on the bridge of any battleship and let anyone try. Any person who does not continue to learn is at risk of missing the wave of the future, as Mitchell did.

By simply realizing the underlying value of accelerated learning (AL)—that people intake differently, process differently, and need different environments to maximize their learning—individuals can make a dramatic improvement in their own abilities to learn more thoroughly and quickly. Additionally, training organizations and project leaders can improve and accelerate information transfer using these ideas. Attention to learning techniques can also turn meeting drudgery into fun—and speed learning in the process.

Different practitioners define AL differently. My definition is as follows:

> *Accelerated learning is rapidly developed content that is of benefit to the business and results in long-term retention by the learner. This is accomplished by honoring the different learning preferences of each individual learner.*

What is contained in this definition:

♦ emphasis on a business (or personal) goal, not on learning for the sake of learning, which is valuable, but is not something that needs to be done quickly
♦ emphasis on speed with retention, not to the detriment of retention, and therefore applicability to the business problem
♦ emphasis on the diversity of each person's learning style and an ever-present focus on the learner.

What is not contained in this definition:

♦ a set of rigorous standards or methods to achieve the results
♦ a practice (this is more a philosophy)
♦ a set of techniques or mediums (AL can be used in all forms of learning using many traditional and nontraditional techniques).

AL challenges everyone involved to address the question, How can we learn better?

AL is based on honoring certain things currently known about how people learn. These include:

♦ intake styles
♦ multiple intelligences
♦ whole brain
♦ the triune brain.

It also leverages many things being discovered about memory and retention, which is beyond the scope of this chapter but is covered in my book, *The Accelerated Learning Fieldbook* (Russell, 1999).

Intake Styles

In the field of neurolinguistic programming (NLP), studies on how individuals prefer to get new information have been conducted for years. They have found that preferences fall into three categories:

♦ *visual,* intake by seeing
♦ *auditory,* intake by hearing
♦ *kinesthetic,* intake by doing, touching.

People vary in their orientation toward these three styles. Some people learn primarily through one style, others mix and match styles. Intake styles are not the same as intelligence: Whether you prefer to learn by seeing, hearing, or doing has no bearing on how intelligent you are. It is just your preference for receiving new learning.

It is easy to identify your own preferences and guess someone else's from certain physical characteristics that track with these preferences. Visual learners prefer books or videos, tend to speak quickly and somewhat high pitched, look up when they are thinking, and say things like "I see what you mean." Sixty percent to 72 percent of the population prefers to learn this way, as figure 1-1 shows. Auditory learners prefer speeches, discussions, or tapes. They speak slowly and quietly, look straight ahead when they are thinking, and use phrases like "I can hear what you are saying." They make up 12 percent to 18 percent of the population. Kinesthetic learners prefer to move when they are learning. They speak quickly and with great changes in intonation and body language, look down when thinking, and use phrases like "I get it." Although 18 percent to 30 percent of the general population prefers to learn kinesthetically, I have found that there is a higher percentage of people who prefer both kinesthetic and auditory learning technical occupations than those numbers suggest. Also, training people tend to be kinesthetic learners.

If you are trying to communicate something new to someone (like a client), you tend to communicate in the way you would like to be communicated to, reflecting your own preferences. For example, if you are a visual learner, you will create beautiful graphics and fancy documents to

Figure 1-1. Intake styles.

	MODALITY	AVERAGE
	Visual	60–72%
	Auditory	12–18%
	Kinesthetic	18–30%

communicate. If your client is an auditory learner, he or she does not want the picture; that client wants words, short and brief. This mismatch creates a barrier to communication.

In certain situations, you may have to learn something fast. Perhaps your training department has arranged for video training in Windows Me to be held during lunch. You go to the video presentation and come out sleepy and with no idea what you just saw. Chances are you are not a visual learner. If you are a kinesthetic learner, your time might have been better spent playing around with Windows Me. If you are an auditory learner, you may have learned more listening to an audiotape. Faster learning comes from better choices of learning media.

The Multiple Intelligences

Whereas intake styles reflect how people prefer to receive information, the intelligences reflect how people prefer to process information. Howard Gardner, from Harvard University, has been challenging the basic beliefs about intelligence since the early 1980s. Gardner believes that intelligence is more multifaceted than has been thought and that traditional measurements, like IQ tests and SATs, do not accurately measure all its facets. He also says intelligence is not fixed. He defines intelligence as:

♦ a measurable aptitude
♦ an aptitude you use to create and solve problems
♦ an aptitude valued by the culture.

In *Frames of Mind,* Gardner (1985) describes his initial list of intelligences. In 1987, he added three additional intelligences to his list and said he expects the list to continue to grow. The intelligences are

♦ *interpersonal:* aptitude for working with others
♦ *logical/mathematical:* aptitude for math, logic, deduction
♦ *spatial/visual:* aptitude for picturing, seeing
♦ *musical:* aptitude for musical expression
♦ *linguistic/verbal:* aptitude for the written/spoken word
♦ *intrapersonal:* aptitude for working alone
♦ *bodily kinesthetic:* aptitude for being physical
♦ *emotional:* aptitude for identifying emotion

- *naturalist:* aptitude for being with nature
- *existential:* aptitude for understanding one's purpose.

How does this affect your learning? Gardner believes that most people are comfortable in three to four of these intelligences and avoid the others. For example, if you are not comfortable working with others, doing group case studies may interfere with your ability to process new material. Video-based instruction will not be good for people with lower spatial and visual aptitudes. People with strong bodily and kinesthetic aptitudes need to move around while they are learning.

If you find you are in a situation where you have to use an aptitude that you are not comfortable with, you may need to practice this aptitude or enhance it with others in which you feel competent. For example, if your job requires you to study large technical documents but you are not strong in visual and spatial, you may find that drawing on your strong bodily and kinesthetic aptitude by taking notes, taking frequent moving breaks, or highlighting will help you adjust. Knowing your own strengths and weaknesses can allow you to positively transform a learning situation.

The Whole Brain

There has been a great deal of research done on right- and left-brain behaviors. Your left brain's job is words, language, analysis, order, logic, numbers, and sequence. Your right brain's job is music, rhythm, imagination, patterns, mental models, appreciation, and synthesis. Most people think with both, but have a strong preference to think on one side or the other. A left-brain person will tend to be very organized—the clean-desk syndrome. A right-brain person will tend to be nonlinear—the messy-desk syndrome. Real power comes from combining the two; when the right and left brain are combined, long-term learning occurs.

If you prefer left-brain thinking, you will migrate toward left-brain topics—mathematics, programming, problem solving (partitioning of problems). If you prefer right-brain thinking, you will migrate toward right brain topics—patterns, modeling, synthesis of different disciplines. During a reengineering project, for example, it is clear that both sides are needed. A practitioner needs to think analytically and sequentially (left brain) but also needs to be able to synthesize conflicting views and imagine new approaches (right brain). Recognize your own preferences and practice stepping into the side of the brain you are least comfortable with.

The Triune Brain

The "triune" brain is composed of three functional areas: neocortex, limbic, and reptilian. The limbic system deals with the emotional aspects of learning. Think of your most vivid memories. Generally, they are "hooked" to a strong emotion, often negative. Emotions power learning. Negative emotions turn learning off; positive emotions turn it on. One of the best emotions for learning is fun. Whether planning a seminar or a meeting, the organizers should be asking, "How can we make learning fun?"

The reptilian brain is the front gate to the neocortex. If you are threatened, the reptilian brain will figuratively shut, blocking any new learning from getting in. This fight-or-flight syndrome means that it is nearly impossible to learn under pressure. The reptilian brain fights, and the neocortex takes flight. Thinking and learning occur in the neocortex so triggering a reptilian response is fatal to learning.

Think how much change has occurred since 1977 when Ken Olsen, head of Digital Equipment Corporation, said, "There is no reason for a person to have a computer in their home." However, *mandatory* learning, driven by the pace of business and technology change, is physiologically impossible. Learning can only be achieved when people are relaxed, open, and responsive. As Peter Senge (1990) says, "The harder you push, the harder the system pushes back."

In terms of yourself, what environment do you need to be productive in learning? Are there elements that can be changed that limit your reptilian response to learning? The best way to ensure that we are helping people to learn to learn and, therefore, learn to adapt to the world is by honoring the diverse needs of the learners who are using AL.

RELATED INTERVENTIONS

Accelerated learning has similarities to brain-based learning, whole-brain learning, and thematic instruction.

- ◆ *Brain-based learning:* Many people (generally people in the field of kindergarten through grade 12, or K-12, education) who were originally working in accelerated learning now refer to their work as brain-based learning.
- ◆ *Whole-brain learning:* Ned Herrmann (1996; and now his daughters) promotes learning around the four brain dominance quadrants that he defined in his research. I believe whole-brain learning is included in AL.
- ◆ *Thematic instruction:* Promoted by Susan Kovalik, this approach to teaching (K-12) designed materials around a theme. Instead of teaching math, reading, science, and social studies as separate, disconnected thought areas, thematic instruction combined all the disciplines around a topic, for example, the Civil War. Many of the thematic instruction people leverage Howard Gardner's work with multiple intelligence and the experimental schools he started called the Key Schools.

WHEN TO USE AL

Michael Treacy and Fred Wiersema (1995) noted in their book *The Discipline of Market Leaders* that, because of the constantly changing world of new technology and business, business people are aging like dogs, with one year equal to seven years. If you have experienced the sinking feeling that you cannot keep up but you must, that the world has changed, that you do not have enough time, that you will lose your job, then change your strategy. Instead of trying to learn harder, learn better.

AL is a philosophy that helps people build a structure that focuses on each individual's ability to learn more with less effort. It also supports the concept of personal mastery described by Peter Senge (1990) in *The Fifth Discipline*. Increased learning capacity lowers stress, reduces conflicts, and builds self-esteem. In contrast, ineffective learning increases stress, triggers blame, and challenges feelings of self-worth.

Figure 1-2 is a template for building your own learning profile. As you complete it, you will better understand how AL can help you in all aspects of your life. This profile includes

- learning beliefs
- intake styles
- multiple intelligences
- whole brain
- triune brain.

WHEN NOT TO USE ACCELERATED LEARNING

Like all other learning interventions, accelerated learning should only be applied in situations in which performers have a documented skill and knowledge gap. Accelerated learning programs will only worsen problems that are the result of a lack of proper motives, tools, or processes. It is also important to remember to focus on the outcome that you wish people to produce, not the new behaviors you are trying to teach. Performers must never get the impression that you are using accelerated learning merely to manipulate the way they do things. If, during the learning process, performers can demonstrate that they have a better way of producing the same accomplishment, be sure to recognize their approach. Always remember that accelerated learning is a highly personalized and intimate approach toward improving performance. Therefore, we must never impose our own preferences onto others.

EXAMPLES

- *Hog Heaven Problem:* I was asked to help a marketing manager build a three-day sales conference. Audience members were sales-people in the Far East (English as a second language) who were chicken experts. They sold chicken health products, but were now going to be selling hog health products. The manager had three days to teach them hog basics and how to sell the hog products. We had two days to build the program. Previously, he had lectured, and he already had thousands of overheads ready, but he agreed that did not work.

   We narrowed the behavior that he wanted to see: a basic understanding of hogs and the ability to sell two specific products for hog health—one for pneumonia and one for dysentery. Here are

Figure 1-2. Accelerated learning template.

1. Learning Ghosts: _____

My learning ghosts are: ___ _____

Work History _____

Classroom History _____

Time/Life Demands _____

I am not good at _____because _____

I am not good at _____because _____

I will exorcise my ghosts by _____

2. Intake Styles

Circle the things you do a lot from the lists below. By observing in which columns your preferences fall, you will have a quick look at your learning preferences.

form mind pictures	say syllables	write with finger
take notes	use mnemonics	write lists
use color codes	listen to tapes	pace/walk as you work
watch TV	watch TV	physically "do it"
watch movies	listen to music	breathe slowly
use charts, graphs	listen to speakers	role play
use maps	read aloud	exercise
demonstrate	make up poems	dance
draw/use drawings	talk to yourself	write
use mnemonics	have discussions	take notes

Your learning preference is:

Visual	Auditory	Kinesthetic

3. The Multiple Intelligences

For each aptitude, choose the three or four you feel you are strongest in. Also select the ones you presently use most often at work and in your personal life.

Interpersonal	Intrapersonal
Logical/mathematical	Bodily/kinesthetic
Spatial/visual	Emotional
Musical	Naturalist
Linguistic/verbal	Existential

(continued on page 12)

Figure 1-2. Accelerated learning template (continued).

4. The Whole Brain

Circle the words that you prefer (one per row):

I	II	III	IV
conscious	image	analysis	passive
formulas	subconscious	time	diffused
reductive	songs	details	whole
ego	inclusive	pieces	creativity
reason	impressions	numbers	holistic
cognitive	nonverbal	active	rhythm
logical	patterns	speech	emotion
sequential	affective	verbal	intuition
knowledge	geometry	thought	sounds

Total:

A.   Column I and III: Left-brain preference
B.   Column II and IV: Right-brain preference

The closer together these numbers are, the more flexible a learner you are.

5. The Learning Environment

Do you learn best in total, partial, or no quiet?

1. When others are talking, is it hard or easy for you to concentrate?
2. When the TV or radio is on, is it hard or easy for you to concentrate?
3. When the room is very, very quiet, is it hard or easy for you to concentrate?

Would you prefer learning in dim or bright lighting?

Would you prefer to learn in cool or warmth?

Physically, where do you prefer to work: at a table or less formally on the couch or floor? Do you prefer to sit in one place or move around?

1. Where do you go to work if you really have to concentrate?
2. Where do you go to work at home if you really have to concentrate?
3. Do you prefer to sit in one place when you work or move around?

Are you motivated by self, management, or family in terms of learning and development?

1. When you finish a large project, do you put it away or show it to others?
2. Do you talk about your work successes at home to your family?
3. Which one is most like you: I'm proud of the work I do? Nobody cares what anyone does at our work?

Is it difficult or easy for you to finish things that you start?

1. When you are working on a new project, do you sometimes leave it unfinished, or do you finish it no matter how long it takes?
2. Do you often forget things you've been asked to do?
3. Do you often set up a project to work on, but then work on something else?
4. Is it hard for you to finish projects?

Figure 1-2. Accelerated learning template (continued).

Do you need structure when you work or learn, or do you prefer to work freestyle?

1. When you get a new project, do you prefer that your manager tell you exactly what is required and how to do it, or do you prefer to figure some things out yourself?
2. When you are working on a project, do you prefer ongoing directions on what to do next, or do you prefer to be left alone?
3. Do you like to work on one or many things at a time?

In what situations do you work better, alone or with others?

1. Do you like to work on projects with others or by yourself?
2. When you have a very important project to get done, or something very critical to learn, do you prefer to work with others or by yourself?

---

some of the techniques we implemented with remarkable retention and success:

— *Intervention:* Teach salespeople to create pig balloon animals with pink balloons. Demonstrate how to do it. Give them the supplies, but do not give them a pump to blow up the balloons (these kinds of balloons are really hard to blow up). As they struggle, tell them, "That's how the pig with pneumonia and the farmer taking care of it feels." Now, give them a faulty pump with the competitor's name on it. It can blow up a little, but not much. Review the market differentiators. Now give them a snazzy pump with the product name: That's it!

— *Intervention:* A vet talked for too long on hog basics, and the salespeople were all given a huge binder of information. To keep it lively, we used Lecture BINGO, a Thiagi technique. Whenever the vet used a term, the participants could mark it on their BINGO card. When they had BINGO, they stood up and had to define their terms to win.

— *Intervention:* We used the "disappearing water powder," sold by Trainers Warehouse, to demonstrate the problems with dysentery. Let's not talk about this. . . .The result was better-than-usual sales, better retention of new product information, and enthusiastic salespeople (and trainers). Quote from senior executive to head of HR, "What the h_____ did you do to that trainer?!! Well, whatever it was, do it to the rest of them!"

♦ *Ponderous Process Problem:* When teaching a boring process, the following are a couple of tips we use:

— *Intervention:* List each process step on a strip of paper and put the strips in an envelope. Have teams compete to put the strips in the right order using the documentation. They learn to navigate the documentation and support information and teach themselves the process.

— *Intervention:* Play the game of clue. Break people into teams, devise clues, and have the teams discover from the clues what role, what milestone, what deliverable, which phase, and so forth. Again, give them the support materials and documentation to self-discover. For more fun, create color-coded hats or pennies to make the teams like the board game (Colonel Mustard, Miss Scarlet, and so forth).

AL is also appropriate for speaking, newsletters, trade show booths, and any other place you need to communicate effectively.

Design Guidelines

The best design criteria for AL is to

- Focus on the learner.
- Lecture as a last resort (fewer than 20 percent of the learning experience).
- Allow people to discover learning. Do not pour it into them.
- Create simulation activities that are close enough to the real world that learners will easily apply the information and retain it.
- Always keep learning safe. The reptilian brain prevents learning.
- Map flow to the multiple intelligences. For example, each activity in a session should map to all seven (if not 10) multiple intelligences. If you have just done a highly interpersonal learning experience, follow it with a highly intrapersonal experience. This validation ensures that people are able to learn with the least amount of energy expended, and so can learn and retain with ease. And their brains will not get full so fast.

Some techniques associated with AL are frequently misunderstood, implemented badly, and characterized incorrectly. A technique can be applied in a way that honors each learner's diversity and the needs of the business, or it can be applied in a way that disregards both. For example, many AL practitioners have researched how music can help people learn. By leveraging what has been researched, the appropriate music can be played at the appropriate time to increase learning. In contrast, the wrong music can be played just about any time, or music can be played at inappropriate times. In those cases, learning has not been accelerated.

Similarly, many traditional AL practitioners applied passive and active imagery (guided meditation) to their learning events. When done by a person with the appropriate skills, this type of imagery can be a powerful magnifier of learning. Other AL practitioners choose different techniques to accelerate learning. That does not mean that they are not accelerating learning; it just means they choose other techniques to accomplish the goals.

Finally, some AL practitioners have rigid methodologies and steps for implementation of AL. In my opinion, the very rigidity of these methods encourages developers to focus on the method and not the outcome. The core value of AL is its focus on the learner, and this focus dictates certain flexibility since people are far from predicable.

IMPLEMENTATION GUIDELINES

♦ Do not call it accelerated learning and do not use the word *fun*.

♦ Leverage the speed of learning and the retention to make a business case. No one will fund wacky, entertaining stuff in today's business climate.

♦ Be clear what behavioral changes are required by the business: How will you measure the success or failure of this learning? I call these learning objectives, but it is critical that all parties be constantly aware of the "why."

♦ Ease into it. Take people from where they are to where they can go. Everybody moves at a different pace. If one day you were lecturing to them nonstop, and the next day you are zooming around the room in a princess costume, burning incense, playing spooky music, and flying a kite, people are going to go reptilian. Change one thing at a time.

♦ You have the creative genius to really help people. Give yourself permission to do it.

REFERENCES AND RESOURCES

Books

Gardner, Howard. (1985). *Frames of Mind.* New York: Basic Books.

Gardner, Howard. (1993). *Multiple Intelligences: The Theory in Practice.* New York: Basic Books.

Herrmann, Ned. (1996). *The Whole Brain Business Book.* New York: McGraw-Hill.

Higgins, James W. (1994). *101 Creative Problem Solving Techniques.* Winter Park, FL: The Management Publishing Company.

James, Jennifer. (1997). *Thinking in the Future Tense.* New York: Simon & Schuster.

Russell, Lou. (1999). *The Accelerated Learning Fieldbook.* San Francisco: Jossey-Bass.

Senge, Peter. (1990). *The Fifth Discipline.* New York: Currency Doubleday.

Senge, Peter, Art Kleiner, Charlotte Roberts, Richard Ross, and Bryan Smith. (1994). *The Fifth Discipline Fieldbook.* New York: Doubleday.

Treacy, Michael, and Fred Wiersema. (1995). *The Discipline of Market Leaders.* Reading, MA: Addison-Wesley.

Weinberg, Gerald M. (1992). *Quality Software Management. Vol. 1: Systems Thinking.* New York: Dorset House.

Wycoff, Joyce. (1995). *Transformation Thinking.* New York: Berkeley Publishing Group.

Internet

DCI, 204 Andover Street, Andover, MA 01810. www.dci.com.

Imaginative Concepts, 1922 Buckington Drive, Chesterfield, MO 63017; phone: 314.207.6452; email: pahager@worldnet.att.net.

www.irl.org. Institute for Research on Learning, 66 Willow Place, Menlo Park, CA 94025; phone: 650.687.7900.

www.kepner-tregoe.com. Kepner Tregoe.

http//:learning.mit.edu. MIT Organizational Learning.

www.pegasuscom.com. Pegasus Communications, 1 Moody Street, Waltham, MA 02154; phone: 800.272.0945.

www.russellmartin.com. Russell Martin & Associates, 6326 Rucker Road, Suite E, Indianapolis, IN 46220; phone: 317.475.9311;.email: lou@russellmartin.com.

Associations

North American Simulation and Gaming Association (NASAGA). www.nasaga.org.

International Alliance for Learning. www.ialearn.org.

2

ACTION LEARNING

Michael J. Marquardt

WHAT IS ACTION LEARNING?

Action learning is both a dynamic process and a powerful program that involves a small group of people solving real problems. At the same time, it focuses on what they are learning and how their learning can benefit each member, the group itself, and the organization as a whole.

An action learning program derives its power and benefits from six interactive and interdependent components. These components must be interconnected and reinforced in order for action learning to be successful. The components are as follows:

1. *A problem (project, challenge, opportunity, issue, or task):* Action learning is built around a problem (be it a project, a challenge, an issue, or task), the resolution of which is of high importance to an individual, team, or organization. The problem should be significant, be within the responsibility of the team, and provide an opportunity for learning.

2. *An action learning group or team:* The core entity in action learning is the action learning group (also called a set or team). The group is composed of four to eight individuals who examine a problem that has no easily identifiable solution. Ideally, the makeup of the group is diverse so as to maximize various perspectives and to obtain fresh viewpoints. Depending on the type of action learning problem, groups can be composed of individuals from across functions or departments. In some situations, groups comprise individuals from other organizations or professions, such as the company's suppliers or customers.

3. *A process that emphasizes insightful questioning and reflective listening:* By focusing on the right questions rather than the right answers, action learning looks at what one does not know as well as on what one does know. Action learning tackles problems through a process of first asking questions to clarify the exact nature of the problem, then reflecting and identifying possible solutions, and only then taking action.

4. *A resolution of taking action:* There is no real learning unless action is taken, for one is never sure the idea or plan will be effective until it has been implemented. Therefore members of the action learning group must have the power to take action themselves or be assured that their recommendations will be implemented, barring any significant change in the environment or the group's obvious lack of essential information. Action enhances learning because it provides a basis and anchor for the critical dimension of reflection described earlier. Knowing that action will be taken increases the energy and commitment of the group to be serious and creative.

5. *A commitment to learning:* Solving an organizational problem provides immediate, short-term benefits to the company. The greater, longer-term, multiplier benefit, however, is the learning gained by the members and how the group's learnings can be applied on a systemswide basis throughout the organization. The learning that occurs in action learning has greater value strategically for the organization than the immediate tactical advantage of solving one problem.

6. *A learning coach or group facilitator:* Facilitation is important to help the group slow down its process in order to allow sufficient time to reflect on learning. The learning coach helps the group members reflect both on what they are learning and how they are solving problems. The learning coach also helps participants focus on what they are achieving, what they are finding difficult, and what processes they are employing as well as on the implications of these processes. The learning coach may be a working group member (possessing familiarity with the problem being discussed) or an external participant (not necessarily understanding the problem content or organizational context, but possessing action learning facilitation skills).

RELATED INTERVENTIONS

Action learning has similarities to case studies, leadership development, coaching, and team building.

WHEN TO USE ACTION LEARNING

Action learning can be used whenever an organization or individual has a challenge or problem that requires creative solutions that a group of people with a variety of fresh perspectives can provide. In addition to problem solving, organizations use action learning for building teams, developing leaders, and creating learning organizations.

The power of action learning is its ability to simultaneously solve complex problems or challenges and provide the following four benefits:

♦ *Team building:* Groups solve real problems and are accountable for implementation of strategies identified from cohesive, powerful teams as a result of their shared vision, strong communications, mutual respect and caring, and high expectations inherent in the action learning process.

- *Leadership development:* A rapidly growing number of organizations place leaders and potential leaders in action learning groups to work on real problems of the organization. Leaders get feedback from other leaders in an environment in which one's leadership attributes and skills are developed and strengthened during the reflection guided by the learning coach.
- *Organizational learning:* Action learning groups are minilearning organizations as they model all the attributes of a learning organization, such as linking learning to action and business objectives, everyone being responsible to help others to learn, creating and transferring knowledge, and recognition of the importance of learning for organizational success.
- *Career planning:* Through reflection and feedback, members develop professionally and personally while they become more aware of their values, interests, and capabilities.

WHEN NOT TO USE ACTION LEARNING

Action learning should not be used under the following circumstances:

- The problem or challenge is not urgent or important.
- The group is used only to provide recommendations for action, and they may or may not be applied.
- The focus is only on developing action strategies, not also on capturing the learning.

EXAMPLES

- *Poor Customer Service Problem:* A corporate customer of a global semiconductor company was so dissatisfied that it threatened to seek another supplier.
  — *Intervention*: An action learning team with four members from both companies met two times a month over a 90-day period. A number of key action initiatives were developed including new ways of delivering services, increasing lead-time updates, developing critical device lists, and establishing prealert reports. The customer was so pleased that it gave the semiconductor company its "world-class supplier" award.

- *Leadership Development Problem:* New leaders in a manufacturing company lacked the skills to work in teams and manage the company's rapidly expanding programs.
  — *Intervention:* The organization placed the new leaders in action learning teams for a period of 12 months and assigned them the responsibility of developing solutions and strategies for improving a number of projects around the world. In addition to developing highly successful action plans, the leaders developed a

variety of management skills as a result of regular reflections on their actions and how each of them demonstrated leadership competencies during the action learning sessions.

♦ *Performance Appraisal Systems Problem:* A global airline determined that its performance appraisal system was not effective.
— *Intervention:* Instead of contracting for outside expertise, the company appointed an action learning team to create a new performance appraisal program. Over a period of two months, the team sought ideas from within and benchmarked outside the company. The result was a performance appraisal system that was relevant and highly successful as well as the emergence within the company of a group of performance appraisal experts who were able to update and improve the system in succeeding years.

DESIGN GUIDELINES

Action learning may be one of the following two types:

♦ *Single problem, in-company program:* In this type of action learning program, all members of the team work on a single problem or challenge received from the organization. Participants may be chosen by management or may be volunteers.
♦ *Open-set or multiple-problem program:* Each group member brings his or her problem, project, or task to the table. The members support and assist each other for an agreed-upon period of time. Usually the members are from different organizations, although the group may also be made up of people from different departments of the same organization.

The following guidelines can help in designing an action learning intervention:

1. An organization-wide workshop is conducted to ensure that everyone understands both the importance of action learning to the organization and the principles and components of action learning.
2. Learning coaches are identified (internal or external to the organization) and provided training and practice opportunities.
3. A project or projects are identified for one or more action learning sets, projects that are important to the organization and for which there is not an already-identified strategy.
4. Teams are formed that consist of four to eight people from diverse backgrounds, so as to allow the problem to be examined from fresh perspectives.
5. The action learning teams meet on a periodic basis (daily, weekly, monthly) depending on the complexity of the problem and on the time frame by which action strategies must be implemented.
6. At the end of each session, the learning coach facilitates the group's reflection on how well it has solved the problem, how the participants

have worked as a team, what they have learned, what learnings can be applied to other parts of the organization and to their professional lives, what assumptions shaped their actions, and so forth.

IMPLEMENTATION GUIDELINES

♦ Emphasize the importance of questions and reflection. The natural response to problems is to immediately come up with solutions, which often leads to solving the wrong problem. Questions ensure a more comprehensive, systems approach to framing the problem as well as more open, creative solutions to the problem. Every problem should eventually lead to the alpha questions (what are we trying to accomplish, what are the obstacles, and how can we overcome these obstacles?) and the beta questions (who knows, who cares, and who can?).

♦ Take time to capture the learning. At appropriate times during the session, but particularly at the end, time needs to be set aside to focus on the learnings. Most groups want to continue working on the problem until they disperse, thus leaving little or no time for learning.

♦ Test the action strategies. One cannot be sure if the solutions will work until they are applied. Between sessions, action steps should be taken and the results reported at the next meeting.

REFERENCES AND RESOURCES

Publications

Marquardt, Michael. (1997, April). "Action Leaning," *Info-line.* Issue No. 9704. Alexandria, VA: ASTD.

Marquardt, Michael J. (1999). *Action Learning in Action: Transforming Problems and People for World-Class Organizational Learning.* Palo Alto, Calif.: Davies-Black. Provides an overview of the principles and best practices of action learning as well as the theoretical foundations of action learning.

International Journal of Action Learning. Available online; provides latest research and discussion on action learning practice.

Internet

www.action-learning.org. Features resources, degree and certificate opportunities, links to other action learning sites.

Professional Association

International Foundation for Action Learning. Conducts conferences around the world and publishes a quarterly newsletter on action learning activities.

3

COACHING

Andrew Kimball

WHAT IS COACHING?

Coaching is a process in which one person (the "coach") helps another person (the "performer") reinforce and develop the skills and practices necessary to rise from the performer's current performance state to the performer's desired performance state.

What distinguishes coaching from other performance interventions is the use of:

♦ feedback
♦ ideas
♦ facilitative questioning
♦ empathetic listening.

Successful coaching has the following features:

♦ *Information gathering:* identifying performers' felt and unfelt developmental needs through dialogue and direct observation.
♦ *Performance needs analysis:* categorizing and prioritizing the performers' needs to determine optimal
  — content: what performance feedback, ideas, and developmental action steps will yield the greatest return on coaching time and energy invested
  — process: how should the performance conversation be organized.

♦ *Performance conversations:* communicating the high-yield feedback, ideas, and action steps so that performers:
  — understand and commit to continuing the observed positive practices
  — understand and commit to implementing new proposed practices
  — understand and commit to implementing the developmental action plan that will help them develop the new proposed practices
  — value the performance conversation and leave wanting to come back for more.

◆ *Follow-up:* monitoring and communicating about performers' success at implementing their commitment to new practices and their success at completing items on their own developmental action plans.

RELATED INTERVENTIONS

The term *coaching* is often used to describe a variety of performance-related activities including teaching, counseling, and performance consulting.

While there is no one right way to distinguish coaching from these three other interventions, it may be useful to organize them according to the four performance elements that have an impact on performers' probability of achieving their desired results: knowledge, skills, attitudes and beliefs, and performance environment.

◆ *Teaching:* Primary objective of helping the performer understand and remember useful information or knowledge.
◆ *Coaching:* An intervention that has a primary objective of helping performers develop the skills, behaviors, and practices that move them toward their performance goals.
◆ *Counseling:* Primary objective of helping performers become aware of or develop more useful attitudes and beliefs.
◆ *Performance consulting:* Primary objective of developing a more useful, supportive performance environment.

Coaching also is often associated with mentoring, performance evaluation, performance management, and performance leadership.

WHEN TO USE COACHING

You should consider coaching anytime your goal is to help a performer reinforce or develop new, more effective behaviors or practices. Coaching is especially useful in conjunction with skill training. The purpose of skill training is usually to teach the principles of a new skill, give the performer a chance to practice, and receive feedback.

When the performer returns from training to work, his or her new skills often experience a training spike followed by a radioactive half-life deterioration. Coaching can help to sustain the training spike and minimize the half-life deterioration of the skills.

Practiced consistently, coaching can both minimize deterioration and extend and expand the skills to higher and higher levels of performance.

The coaching process is also scalable.

◆ You can coach someone through a structured process of planned observation, followed by a scheduled, formal performance conversation.
◆ You can also catch a performer practicing a new, effective behavior then deliver well-structured positive feedback in a two-minute performance conversation at a water cooler.

The skills and strategies of both of these interactions will be similar. The difference is the quantity of feedback and ideas discussed.

In general, you should consider using the skills and strategies of coaching whenever you are trying to persuade someone to try a new skill, practice, or behavior. The feedback and idea models (headline, specifics, value, dialogue question) can be used to respond to ideas during problem-solving meetings, project planning meetings, and strategic planning meetings.

The performer needs dialogue can be used effectively to resolve conflict, initiate a counseling intervention, or introduce a mentoring process.

The observation process can be used to gather objective, credible performance data for counseling, performance management, and instructional design.

The performer's needs dialogue combined with the performance needs analysis process can be used to analyze any performance-related individual, team, or organizational problem.

WHEN NOT TO USE COACHING

Do not use coaching if your intention is to tell a performer that his or her performance is below, at, or above the bar. This is the domain of the performance evaluation. If this is your goal, do the following:

- ◆ Tell the performer what the bar is.
- ◆ Tell the performer what his or her performance is.
- ◆ Ask the person, "How do you feel about that?"
  - — If the performer's answer is, "I would like to move to a higher level," you should start considering coaching to help the person along that path.
  - — If the performer's answer is anything else, you should shift to counseling strategies, such as empathetic listening or facilitative questioning.

Do not use coaching to establish behavioral boundaries, such as sexual harassment, threats of violence, unsafe factory behavior, or lying. All of these situations demand a direct conversation about how inappropriate, illegal, or dangerous such behaviors are and what the consequences of continuing might be.

Once you have had such a boundary conversation, you might consider asking the question, "How do you feel about that?" Once again, if the performer's answer is, "I would like to improve," you should start considering coaching to help the person along that path.

Consider the following common scenarios:

- ◆ What if the performer does not want to change his or performance state? Do you use coaching to try to convince the person to move to a higher level of performance? If your goal is to convince the performer to value higher performance (shift his or her attitudes and beliefs), you are operating in the domain of counseling. The counselor may use many of the same tools, skills, principles, and processes that the coach uses, but it is with the intention to shift attitudes and beliefs, not to develop skills.

♦ What if the coach and the performer differ on what the desired performance state should be? Same as the first question: If your goal is to convince the performer to value a different desired state, you are trying to shift attitudes and beliefs. This also is the domain of counseling.

♦ What if the performer is consistently underperforming or acting in a way that if continued could lead to dismissal? Again, if your intention is to help the performer develop skills and practices that will help him or her move toward a desired state, then coaching will be a useful intervention. If your intention is to warn the performer that a continued behavior may result in dismissal, you are in the domain of counseling and would use boundary communication tools such as negative feedback or warnings.

EXAMPLES

♦ *High-Tech Problem:* A rapidly growing high-tech organization was burdened with extraordinarily high turnover, poor manager-employee relationships, and minimal measurable internalization of its business skills training programs.

— *Intervention:* The organization instituted a strategic coaching initiative. Following an initial three-day coaching workshop, the CEO began a series of needs dialogue meetings with each of her direct reports. The senior vice presidents ran similar meetings with all of their managers. The managers had needs dialogues with their performers. All levels reported that these meetings were some of the most valuable they had ever had with their employees. Not only did they surface valuable needs that the "coaches" could help their "performers" fulfill, but the meetings also resulted in substantially better working relationships among all parties.

Following the needs dialogues, all levels of management began to practice performance observation, performance needs analysis, and performance conversation. Performers interviewed after six months reported that the feedback and ideas coming out of these meetings were useful and made the performers feel valued as employees, recognized for their achievements, and motivated to step up to the next level. Turnover rates dropped by 27 percent. Employee satisfaction measures increased by 22 percent. Productivity increased by 12 percent.

♦ *Software Sales Problem:* A veteran salesperson, used to selling a simple software product, was having difficulty selling a new, complex solution that involved innovative electronic design software and electronic design services. Once a top performer, he had failed to achieve his sales goals the last two quarters in a row.

— *Intervention:* The performer's sales manager spent an hour in a needs dialogue with the performer. She determined that the performer was eager to be a rainmaker again, and felt that the problem was his lack of understanding of the new design service solutions.

The sales manager rode on a call to observe the salesperson. She observed that the salesperson spent most of the meeting talking about the old software products and spent little time asking questions or developing an understanding of the client's needs. What questions he did ask were closed-ended and manipulative, such as "If I could show you a way, would you be willing to give us a PO today?"

After reviewing her notes, the sales manager praised the salesperson for his knowledge and effectiveness at explaining the old products. She then suggested that the salesperson try using facilitative questions to identify the client's key objectives and challenges, then offer to go back to the office and work with design services specialists to put together a presentation that was specifically focused on addressing these objectives and challenges. She explained this would help the salesperson not only to write more compelling proposals but also to learn more about the design services. She further suggested that she would be happy to do some role-playing with the salesperson later in the week to help him internalize the skill of asking open-ended questions. The salesperson lost that sale, but won the next three. He found the role-playing so valuable that he, the sales manager, and two other salespeople regularly got together to role-play as a way of preparing for critical sales calls. The salesperson made his sales objective for the next quarter, and the sales manager's team won Region of the Year at the next sales meeting.

DESIGN GUIDELINES

There are three basic schools of coaching: facilitative coaching, traditional coaching, and mastery path coaching.

♦ *Facilitative coaching:* It uses many of the practices and strategies of counseling and relies on three primary tools: facilitative questioning, empathetic listening, and SMART (for *S*pecific, *M*easurable, *A*ctionable, *R*ealistic, and *T*ime bound) action planning. This method is most effective with performers who recognize a developmental need and openly seek help.

♦ *Traditional coaching:* This method assumes that performers' perceptions of their own needs are one data point that may not reveal the full spectrum of their developmental needs. It relies on tools such as performance observation, performance needs analysis, performance conversation, and follow-up. Traditional coaching is particularly useful in situations in which it is important to manage behavior to comply with defined boundaries and highly structured process steps, such as for factory-floor machine tool operation, assembly line manufacturing, and financial control processes.

◆ *Mastery path coaching:* This method builds on aspects of both facilitative and traditional coaching. Mastery path coaching has five components: needs dialogue, performance observation, performance needs analysis, performance conversation, and follow-up.

Following are specific design guidelines for performers' needs dialogues and performance conversations:

◆ *Performers' needs dialogue:* Organize questioning strategies to identify the performers':
  — current feelings about their performance
  — developmental vision
  — values
  — performance objectives
  — greatest performance challenges
  — enhanced knowledge, skills, or attitudes required to address these performance challenges
  — ideas for how they might develop the knowledge, skills, or attitudes they think they need
  — ideas for how the coach can best coach and support their development.

◆ *Performance conversation:*
  — Short (10 to 15 minutes), frequent (weekly or monthly) performance conversations are more effective than long (30 to 60 minutes), infrequent (quarterly or annually).
  — The greater the relative expertise of the performer compared to the coach, the more the coach should focus on identifying areas of unconscious performer competence.
  — The number of developmental ideas offered in a performance conversation should be directly proportional to the level of trust the performer feels for the coach: If there is no trust, offer only positive feedback. If there is moderate trust, offer mostly positive feedback and only one developmental idea. If there is great trust, balance positive feedback and ideas.
  — Organize the performance conversation along the following framework:
    • *Framing:* Establish rapport, confirm objectives and agenda, establish a time contract.
    • *Needs summary:* Summarize understanding of the performer's high-level needs, based on the previous performer needs dialogue.
    • *Feedback and idea dialogue:* Offer positive feedback, positive ideas, and SMART action ideas in a way that encourages frequent response and dialogue.

- *Wrap up:* Confirm next steps and debrief the meeting before thanking the performer for his or her time.

IMPLEMENTATION GUIDELINES

- ◆ *Performer needs dialogue:*
  - — Keep the needs dialogue to an hour or less.
  - — Revisit the needs dialogue once a quarter or at least once every six months.
  - — Use double-clicking questions to help the performer reveal deeper, more meaningful needs (for example, "Tell me more. Can you be more specific? Give me an example of that.").
  - — Resist talking about yourself, your expectations of the performer, or your observations of the performer.

- ◆ *Performance observation:*
  - — Stay neutral; try not to participate in an interaction you are observing. Coaches' participation may reduce their neutrality and credibility in performers' eyes.
  - — Note as thoroughly as possible the performers' words, tonals, nonverbals, and actions as well as the reactions of others with whom the performer is interacting.
  - — Avoid analyzing the data during the observation process.

- ◆ *Performance needs analysis:* Identify feedback and ideas that meet two criteria:
  - — Resist the temptation to have a performance conversation based on third-hand information.
  - — Offer feedback and ideas only on behaviors you have observed directly. If someone else has observed a behavior that the person thinks needs reinforcement or improvement, ask that person to coach the performer.

- ◆ *Performance conversation:*
  - — Take time to organize your content and process. Resist the temptation to jump right to the performance conversation after observation.
  - — Structure feedback to include:
    - *Headline:* Summarize the key behavioral principles of your feedback, such as "I liked how you asked open-ended questions on that last sales call."
    - *Specific behavioral example:* Provide actual quotes or concrete observations, such as "Specifically, I liked such questions as, 'What are your objectives?' and 'What are your most critical challenges?'"
    - *Value to the performer:* Frame the value using references to the performer's needs dialogue, such as "As I recall from our conversation earlier, writing compelling proposals was a skill you felt was important to develop. I feel your open-ended

questions helped the client to reveal his most critical needs to you. The more needs you uncover, the more compelling you will be able to make your proposal."

- *Dialogue question:* Ask an open-ended question to draw the performer into the dialogue. This increases the performer's comprehension and retention of the feedback or idea, such as "How do you organize your questioning strategy? What types of open-ended questions do you find identify the most critical client needs?"

— Structure ideas to include:

- *Frame the value to the performer:* Frame the value of your idea and invite the performer's permission to offer it, such as "As I recall from our conversation earlier, writing compelling proposals was a skill you felt was important to develop. I have an idea for how you might improve that skill. Would you like to hear it? Obviously, the more client needs you uncover, the more compellingly you will be able to frame your recommendations in your proposal."
- *Headline:* Summarize the key behavioral principle, such as "One way to get the client talking about his most critical needs is to ask more open-ended questions."
- *Specific behavioral example:* Use actual quotes or concrete observations, such as "For example, you might try such questions as, 'What are your objectives?' and 'What are your most critical challenges?'"
- *Dialogue question:* Draw out the performer's response, such as "What do you think? How do feel about that idea?"
- Resolve objections by using double-clicking questions to clarify the need underlying the objection, followed by empathetic listening to confirm understanding of the need.

◆ *Follow-up:*

— Find opportunities to catch the performer implementing the ideas.
— Debrief SMART action plans by celebrating and praising successful completion of action items, while treating lack of completion as challenges that the performer and coach need to figure out how to resolve. Resolve challenges by facilitating a minicreative problem-solving dialogue.

REFERENCES AND RESOURCES

Publication

Performance Improvement. Journal of the International Society of Performance Improvement (ISPI).

Association

ISPI, 1400 Spring Street, Suite 260, Silver Spring, MD 20910; phone: 301.587.8570; email: www.ispi.org.

4

ELECTRONIC PERFORMANCE SUPPORT SYSTEMS

Kim E. Ruyle

WHAT IS AN EPSS?

An electronic performance support system (EPSS) is a software program that provides just-in-time, on-demand information, guidance, examples, and step-by-step dialogue boxes to improve job performance without the need for training or coaching by other people.

An EPSS is, in other words, a comprehensive computer-based job aid. EPSS applications often include several of the following:

- database of job-related information, organized to facilitate rapid access and optimize clarity
- calculators and wizards that simplify and automate procedures
- decision-support modules that provide intelligent assistance with problem solving
- embedded tutorials and simulations that provide instruction in work-related concepts and procedures.

Just as a hand tool leverages physical capabilities, an EPSS leverages cognitive capabilities. An EPSS can provide adaptive support for a full range of cognitive tasks. In effect, it makes performers smarter!

A well-designed EPSS is more than an electronic page turner or multimedia document. It incorporates the decision support of expert systems, the information accessibility of electronic text retrieval systems, the individualized instructional capabilities of CBT and Web-based training (WBT), and perhaps advanced communication features.

RELATED INTERVENTIONS

An EPSS is a particular type of job aid based on software. EPSS applications are sometimes called integrated performance support or online performance support. Abridged, miniversions of EPSS applications are referred to as online help or embedded help systems. A related intervention promoted by the Department of Defense is called an interactive electronic technical manual (IETM). Other related applications include expert systems, knowledge management tools, agents, and wizards.

An EPSS, or any job aid for that matter, addresses the same performance needs as training, the primary related intervention. In fact, when performers lack the knowledge or skill required to perform the job at hand, there are only two possible interventions: training and job aids. Of course, performance improvement opportunities are not generally either-or situations; training and job aids are often employed together as complementary interventions.

EPSS applications are interesting in that they are hybrid job aid solutions. Generally, instructional intent is latent or nonexistent; the emphasis is on performance rather than learning. When a performer accesses an embedded tutorial or instructional simulation, however, the EPSS stops being a job aid and becomes a training intervention.

When to Use EPSS

All of the following should be true before you decide to use an EPSS application:

- There is a performance problem caused by a knowledge or skills deficiency.
- Tasks related to the performance problem are relatively difficult to perform.
- The tasks are performed infrequently.
- The tasks do not have to be performed in emergency situations.
- There are serious implications if the tasks are performed inadequately.
- The performance environment accommodates the EPSS hardware.

EPSS applications are especially useful when the performance is cognitive rather than psychomotor. Also, when the supported tasks involve software, EPSS applications are a natural fit.

Whenever possible, use an EPSS (or other job aid) instead of training to address knowledge or skills deficiencies. There are four problems with training:

- Training is expensive.
- Training is hard to schedule.
- Training is temporary. Learners do not retain knowledge or skills unless they have opportunities to practice.
- Training is transient. It moves with performers when they leave the job.

A job aid is a permanent company asset that does not require scheduling. Almost always, it costs less to address knowledge and skills problems with a job aid than with training. When all costs are considered, this is true of most EPSS applications.

WHEN TO NOT USE EPSS

Do not use an EPSS just to have a technology-based solution. Use a conventional job aid (paper based) if it can do the job more simply or cost-effectively.

EXAMPLES

♦ *Motorcycle Service Problem:* A business has high turnover of its motorcycle service technicians. Most have a short tenure on the job. Typically technicians are male, ages 18 to about 45. They have relatively low levels of formal education. Some have high school and some vocational training. Their jobs are troubleshooting and repairing modern, high-end motorcycles. These machines are complex and have as many or more component parts than an automobile. The technicians lack enough understanding of equipment theory, especially related to electronic controls and electrical systems, to be able to competently troubleshoot problems. There is high turnover, so training is a very expensive solution.

— *Intervention:* A comprehensive EPSS application is employed in computers on roll carts in the service bay. The application has easy-to-find, simplified procedures for maintenance and repair. High-quality graphics support tasks. A symptom-driven expert system provides intelligent diagnostic support. Animated electrical schematics allow performers to follow electrical circuits and pop-up component locators and links to test and repair procedures. Technician effectiveness is increased dramatically. Instead of hit-or-miss parts replacement, technicians troubleshoot effectively and employ appropriate test procedures. Work is performed faster and more accurately. Warranty costs drop dramatically. End customers rate the quality of service much higher.

♦ *Insurance Underwriting Problem:* At a firm, insurance underwriters range in age from 23 to 65. All have a high school education, but some have attended college. The staff are career-oriented professionals. Traditionally, new underwriters received several months of classroom instruction to learn underwriting rules that are documented in massive manuals. They apply a complex set of rules to determine whether to underwrite a new applicant and, if so, to calculate appropriate rates. The rules are many and complex. Documentation is ridiculously cumbersome. Traditionally, training has been a big yawner—weeks of classroom review of rules (pages from the manuals displayed with an overhead projector)—and ineffective. There is far too much information to remember and insufficient opportunity to practice. Once on the job, novice underwriters perform poorly, sometimes for years until they gradually form a mental model that helps them find and apply information and business rules quickly and correctly.

— *Intervention:* An EPSS application is developed to serve as a decision support tool for underwriters. The EPSS and novice underwriter interact, querying each other, and the EPSS uses the information to apply appropriate rules and make recommendations. An explanation feature is available so performers can see the rationale for recommendations made by the EPSS. Underwriter training is reduced from more than two months to two weeks. Using the EPSS, novice underwriters are much more efficient and qualitatively perform at a level approaching that of experts, even on the first day at their desk.

♦ *Semiconductor Manufacturing Problem:* Clean-room fabrication equipment operators range in age from 21 to 55. They receive extensive on-the-job training in operating semiconductor fabrication equipment in a clean-room environment. Mistakes are terribly expensive. For instance, one batch of wafers going through a "wet bench" process may represent several million dollars of computer chips. An interruption in the process can scrap the entire batch. Operators must carefully monitor the equipment and process and make adjustments as required to ensure product quality. Operators understand the manufacturing process but are not experts in the processing equipment. They only have about 15 minutes to save the batch if there is an interruption, and it takes longer than that for an equipment technician to suit up (they wear "bunny" suits in the clean room) and get decontaminated. Certain classes of problems are therefore not resolvable in the required time frame.

— *Intervention:* A comprehensive EPSS is designed and installed on the machine control PC. The application runs in a browser and has real-time communication with control points on the machine. The machine itself is actually given an internet protocol (IP) address that allows service engineers at the equipment manufacturer to access the machine over an intranet to see real-time points on the machine and perform remote diagnostics. The EPSS can provide guidance to operators to perform tests and make adjustments, even repairs. Huge cost savings are realized because scrap and downtime is reduced.

♦ *Utility Company Dispatch Center Problem:* Dispatchers who work in regional call centers are about 35 years old and have a high school education. Fewer than 60 dispatchers staff 14 centers. Most have spent a long time on the job—at least six or more than 20 years— and turnover is very low. Their jobs are to answer calls to utilities' help lines, then make recommendations or take action to solve problems. A question about a consumer's bill might result in a recommendation to call the business office during regular business hours. A customer reporting a strong gas smell would be told to immediately leave the premises without touching any electrical switches and to wait for the arrival of a dispatched technician. Management perceives that an EPSS, especially an expert system module, could make better recommendations than a human.

— *Intervention:* An EPSS application is developed and implemented in the regional call centers. The application has natural language-processing capability and allows dispatchers to type in consumers' questions. Recommendations are then provided to the dispatcher to be passed along to the consumer; links to other resources and information can also be provided. The EPSS is never used. This EPSS application was a poor choice by nearly all criteria:

- There was not a significant performance problem.
- Dispatchers knew their jobs, and 99 percent of the time, the job was simply routine. The only time they had a problem dealing with calls was during an emergency, such as an ice storm or downed power lines.
- There was no reason to consult the EPSS, so it is not surprising it went unused. When dispatchers were having problems with job tasks, the conditions were extreme and unpredictable so the EPSS was not able to provide assistance.

Perhaps the application would have been successful if it had been implemented as a first level of customer service on a Website for consumers.

DESIGN GUIDELINES

You have done the front-end analysis and identified a good EPSS application. But you are not sure users will receive the application. Something about the target population (maybe it is their age or education level or lack of technological sophistication) makes you doubt that they will actually use the application. It is easy to forecast how well an application will be accepted by end users. If you can answer yes to two questions, you can be sure users will embrace the application:

- ◆ Does the application solve a meaningful problem for end users?
- ◆ Does the application have a good interface?

More specifically, a well-designed EPSS application will demonstrate the following:

- ◆ An organizational metaphor is selected to relate to end users. The metaphor provides a good model of how the application works.
- ◆ Multiple paths to information are provided. Information pathways are sensible and not overwhelming. Information is organized by both subject matter content and task.

- There is a graphical map of the application. Figurative signposts are provided throughout the application to aid navigation. Shortcuts are provided for experts.
- Users can vary the amount of system control, especially for decision making. Varying levels of detail are available. Remedial information and instruction are readily accessible for novices.
- A clear model of the performance environment is provided for the user.
- Restart and exit functions are always available. Context sensitive help is always available.
- Graphics are used extensively. Performance support works well when designed in pictures, like a wordless comic book. Graphics are developed first, then text is written to succinctly support the graphics.
- Graphics are simple. Generally, a line art illustration is better than a photo. Any unneeded information is noise that the user must filter. Video is used only when necessary.
- Key words are used as a doorway to levels of embedded performance support. Abstract thought is impossible without a written language. We think with words; vocabulary is extremely important.
- Information is provided in the language of the performers. Jargon is OK if linked to explanatory information for novices.

IMPLEMENTATION GUIDELINES

Nothing gets better without change. Properly implemented, EPSS technology will change the way an organization does business. Training development and delivery will change. Technical documentation will change. Customer service and service management methods will change. Some functions might even go away completely. The uncertainty about impending changes often creates resistance and sets up hurdles to EPSS implementation. The technology and associated change must be managed to avoid obstacles and achieve expected outcomes.

The greatest challenges of managing EPSS implementation are generally organizational, not technical in nature. To address these challenges, it is wise to convene a performance technology steering committee early, when an organization is initially considering EPSS technology. The steering committee will facilitate the adoption of the technology and ensure it is implemented effectively by developing far-reaching management strategies that address all performance improvement interventions, not just EPSS.

To begin, a performance support strategy for the organization needs to take shape. This strategy will encompass all the methods the organization uses to support performers—both employees and external customers, if appropriate. In most organizations there are many methods used for performance support before EPSS tools are even considered. Here are a few:

- informal, peer support and coaching
- informal, unstructured training and formal, structured training

- documentation, such as paper reference manuals and service bulletins
- other paper-based job aids, such as posted schedules and job instruction sheets
- online documentation
- help desks
- consultants and experts, both internal and external.

Generally, it is possible to identify particular situations for each performance support method in which it is the most appropriate approach. Most organizations, though, do not create a comprehensive plan that identifies the role of particular interventions. Each performance support method tends to be added to the stable of interventions in reaction to the failure of current methods.

The steering committee should develop and articulate a performance support strategy, a focused proactive assault on performance problems instead of a haphazard and reactive response. The strategy will characterize all the performance support methods the organization uses and describe the extent to which each method is employed. Then it will define circumstantial boundaries between methods and develop criteria for evaluating the effectiveness of the various methods. Finally, it will implement a plan for continuously improving performance support interventions.

A well-designed performance support strategy enables organizations to consistently:

- solve problems correctly the first time
- solve problems as close to the source as possible
- minimize time required to solve problems
- minimize the number of people involved in problem resolution
- minimize the number of steps in problem resolution
- minimize the total cost of problem resolution
- enhance customers' regard for the organization through problem resolution
- enhance the quality of performers' work life.

In the creation of an implementation strategy, the following tasks must be done:

- Devise a performance support strategy for the organization.
- Articulate a business rationale for adoption of EPSS technology.
- Identify and approve EPSS applications.
- Procure resources.
- Resolve build-versus-buy decisions.
- Address ownership issues and the resulting impact on functional areas in the organization.
- Devise a business model for EPSS implementation.
- Create a distribution plan.
- Create a maintenance plan.

The steering committee will develop a communication strategy to convey

♦ business purpose of EPSS
♦ benefits to users and the organization
♦ positive results as they occur.

The steering committee will develop a marketing strategy to inform, educate, and motivate

♦ management
♦ implementers
♦ users
♦ developers
♦ others in the organization affected by the implementation.

The steering committee will develop an incentive strategy to

♦ revise performance standards and expectations if necessary
♦ bring the organization's reinforcement system into alignment
♦ anticipate and respond to hindrances using the EPSS.

The steering committee will develop a workplace design strategy to
♦ design and layout work processes to match new methods and requirements
♦ anticipate and respond to changes in space and equipment needs.

The steering committee will develop an evaluation and effectiveness strategy to

♦ identify and build links to business goals
♦ determine what is important to measure
♦ collect and analyze data
♦ initiate and manage improvements.

REFERENCES AND RESOURCES

Publications

Gery, G. (1991). *Electronic Performance Support Systems*. Boston: Weingarten Publications.

Brown, L. (1996). *Designing and Developing Electronic Performance Support Systems*. Boston: Digital Press.

Stevens, George, and Emily Stevens. (1995). *Designing Electronic Performance Support Tools*. Englewood Cliffs, NJ: Educational Technology Publications.

Internet

http://www.epss.com/.
http://www.epssinfosite.com/.
http://www.pcd-innovations.com/index.htm.
http://lpsl.coe.uga.edu/default.html.

5

JOB AIDS

Paul H. Elliott

WHAT ARE JOB AIDS?

A job aid is a storage place for information that performers use while performing a task. A job aid provides a signal—audio or visual—to the performer about when to carry out the task and steps, reducing the amount of recall necessary and minimizing error. In everyday life, people use job aids when they are at the local ATM or self-serve gas pump, for example. At work, job aids may appear as simple, linear instructions on how to assemble equipment, as complex algorithms to analyze systems, and as software "wizards."

RELATED INTERVENTIONS

Electronic performance support systems (EPSSs) include an electronic form of job aids. All of the information design principles that apply to job aids also apply to EPSSs.

WHEN TO USE JOB AIDS

Job aids are not limited to a particular type of task. Job aids have been developed for linear tasks such as equipment assembly and filling out forms, but they have also been developed for complex tasks such as medical diagnosis, business negotiation, and the analysis of complex systems. The amount of information available in a job aid is not limited; a job aid may be one page or many volumes.

The following job performance tasks are ideal candidates for job aids:

- ◆ *A task performed with relatively low frequency:* A task performed once a month or less is considered infrequent.
- ◆ *A highly complex task:* A task with numerous steps is more complex than a task with few steps. A task might be qualitatively complex if fine discrimination of stimuli is involved, if it requires recognition of different stimuli belonging to the same class, or if it is a series of binary discriminations such as when inspecting or troubleshooting equipment.

- *A task with a high consequence of error:* Some tasks have criteria that would result in a high consequence of error if they were not met. These criteria may be high financial loss or loss of life, for example. Preflight checklists would fall into this category.
- *A task with high probability of change in the future:* The way in which certain tasks are performed are likely to change because of changes in technology, policy, or equipment. In such cases, other variables being equal, it is often not worth devoting time and other resources to the costly, time-consuming process of storing information in memory. For example, why would you bother trying to teach someone how to proficiently operate a machine in your factory when you know that a whole new line of machines is coming out in the next month and the new machines will operate entirely differently. It would make a lot more sense to just give the person a job aid so he or she can get by until the new machines arrive.

Job aids may also be provided for performance consultants—the designers and implementers of other performance interventions. Joe Harless's peak performance system is an entirely job-aided system for analyzing human performance, designing multiple interventions (skills, knowledge, selection, performance management, and the like), implementing, and evaluating the impact of those interventions in terms of measurable business results.

WHEN NOT TO USE JOB AIDS

Certain tasks are inappropriate for job aids, such as those that have severe time requirements. The response time of a pilot during flight must be immediate, for example, and could not be guided by a job aid. Another inhibiting factor might be the performance environment. A scuba diver could find it difficult to manage a booklet in dark, wet conditions, and a surgeon would face the problem of how to render a job aid sterile. Social barriers might be another inhibiting factor in the use of job aids. If bosses, peers, and customers give more credit to recalling information from memory, the job performer might not use a job aid no matter how appropriate it is for the task at hand.

EXAMPLES

- *Bank Problem:* A local bank is finding it difficult to keep up with the number of transactions that its tellers need to perform. Each transaction that a teller performs costs the bank an estimated $2.75. Also, customers are demanding that the bank be open more hours, including weekends.
  - *Intervention:* The bank installs ATMs at numerous locations around town. To diminish the number of customer inquiries, the bank installs a robust job aid on how to use the ATM. Bank

customers now pay $1 for each visit to the ATM, and noncustomers pay $1.50.

◆ *Airline Problem:* A large airline is having trouble making sure that all supplies are aboard the planes before takeoff. Each flight has different supply requirements, and the crew members change frequently as well.

— *Intervention:* The airline designs a preflight checklist for the flight crews.

◆ *School Bus Problem:* The local school bus company has had a dramatic increase in breakdowns. Through a cause analysis it determined that it could reduce the number of breakdowns by 30 percent if the buses receive regular, preventive maintenance. Also, it can lower the severity of mechanical problems by 50 percent if it catches defects at an earlier stage.

— *Intervention:* A job aid that lists the preventive maintenance procedures is created for the bus drivers. A second job aid helps them interpret the warning signals (such as the oil pressure reading gauge) that the buses' instrument systems provide. The school bus drivers are asked to perform simple tasks such as checking the oil and coolant before leaving the school bus depot each morning. A short training program is created to take them through the steps of the job aid the first time, and an incentive program is tied to the number of mechanical defects they discover and report in a month.

◆ *Software Company Problem:* A software company is overwhelmed with customer calls on a new product. People cannot seem to figure out how to load it and get started using it.

— *Intervention:* The company includes in its next release a software wizard that takes customers through the steps in the install process and a procedural help program that teaches the customer the basic functions of the program.

◆ *Turnover Problem:* The maintenance department of a large corporation has experienced terrible turnover in its building support positions. The booming economy has made it impossible to hang on to competent employees for a very long time. The employees are all complaining that the heating and cooling system has become incredibly unreliable. Some offices are too hot while others are too cold. Someone needs to keep this system adjusted properly.

— *Intervention:* A job aid is created that helps a new employee learn the proper start-up procedures for this complex system, and a second job aid tells the employee how to diagnose inconsistencies in the building's temperatures.

- *Toy Company Problem:* A toy company needs to create a set of directions for its customers who tend to be three to six years old and have not yet developed reading skills.
  - — *Interventions:* The directions for assembling toys are created using only pictures. These directions represent a totally visual job aid using line drawings.

- *Multifaceted Problem:* A famous (and highly paid) job aid designer has managed to convince an airline, a doctor's office, and a local hotel to allow him to design job aids for the following tasks: For the airlines, he will design job aids for recovery of loss of engine power for commercial aircraft; for the doctor's office, he will design a job aid for taking a patient's blood pressure; and for the local hotel, he will design a job aid for doormen that shows them the proper way to open and close doors for customers.
  - — *Intervention:* All three of these job aids fail miserably for the following reasons: The one for pilots would be too slow to follow during an actual emergency (speed factor); the one for the doctor's office would make patients too nervous (psychosocial barrier); and the one for the doormen is for too simple a task. If the doormen are failing to open doors properly, there must be some other reasons besides that they don't know how!

DESIGN GUIDELINES

Job aids should be classified by the type of behavior they support rather than the delivery medium they use. Types of job aids include

- cookbooks: linear, nonbranching procedures without calculations or data capture
- worksheets: linear procedures with calculations or data capture
- decision tables: if-then; if-and-then
- algorithms to address complex branching: troubleshooting, diagnosis
- combination: the most frequent type because complex behavior is the most common type of behavior encounter; combination job aids contain features of two or more of the other types.

The following tasks outline how to develop job aids:

- *Task 1: Collect data.* The analyst discovers the regulations, speed, physical conditions, social conditions, frequency, consequences, complexity, and change probability governing the performance of the task.
- *Task 2: Select information storage alternative.* Choose among job aid only, long-term memory storage only (that is, training), job aid plus supporting instruction, or instruction plus prompting job aid.

◆ *Task 3: Determine if barriers to job aids can be overcome.* Even though a barrier to a job aid is present, sometimes it can be minimized or outweighed by the potential benefits.

◆ *Task 4: Determine if training support for job aids is needed.* It is rare that job aids can stand on their own without being introduced in some formal way. Simply preparing a job aid and sending it out has not met with as much success as introducing the job aid in briefings or, more typically, by building training seminars and courses around when and how to use the aid. Although this method is more expensive, the chance of improving the probability of use is usually worth it.

◆ *Task 5: Select format for job aids.* Common examples of job aid formats include cookbooks or step-by-step directions, worksheets, decision tables, algorithms, and checklists. Many job aids have a combination of formats.

◆ *Task 6: Develop job aids.* The development of job aids is an act of engineering as opposed to a creative one. Job aids are built according to specifications, and they are guided by theories of how humans process information. Each format has specific writing and layout rules, but there are some general rules that apply to all job aids:

— Use specific terms that are less open to interpretation such as *daily, turn until resistance is felt,* and *before the end of the shift.* Do not use ambiguous terms like *often, a few turns,* and *several.*

— Use active terms like *push, touch, press,* and *solder,* not passive terms like *understand, create, satisfy,* and *communicate.*

— Write in short sentences using short words. Job aids should be user-friendly.

— Organize steps into 15-second increments, providing enough time to read the step and then do it before the short-term memory declines significantly.

— Put the stimulus first and directions for the action after. For example, "when you see a red light, apply the brakes" is better than "apply the brakes when you see a red light."

— Use line drawings rather than photographs. Photographs often show too much detail and may obscure the relevant parts of the environment the job performer needs to attend to. Also, photographs are more expensive to reproduce.

— Put drawings on the left and directions for taking action on the right. This layout imitates the job performance situation: I see something, and then I do something. (This would reverse in a culture where language is read right to left.)

— Avoid humor. Typically, something is funny once. The job performer uses the job aid more than once. Humor could also detract or distract from the task at hand.

◆ *Task 7: Edit job aids.* A new job aid should undergo three types of edits before testing.
  — Content edit: Is the job aid technically correct? Is it complete? Does it omit extraneous information? Does it put the job performer under stimulus control?
  — Structure edit: Is the format appropriate for the characteristics of the task? Does it tell when before what? Are the steps in small enough increments to minimize the need for retention? Is the information needed in one place? Have drawings been made from the job performer's perspective? Has critical information been highlighted? Are the steps numbered?
  — Language edit: Is the text written in the active voice? Do action statements begin with verbs? Are clear behavioral terms used? Are statements positive? Are pronoun references clear? Are sentences short? Are modifiers close to what is modified? Of course, a different set of rules would apply for languages other than English.

◆ *Task 8: Test the job aid.* Next the job aid should be tested to determine if the job performer produces the desired accomplishment as a result of using the job aid. To find this out, the job aid must be put through a series of tryout-revision cycles. Tryouts (developmental tests) are carried out one-on-one with employees for whom the job aid is designed and are conducted in the actual environment, if practical, where the job aid will be used.

IMPLEMENTATION GUIDELINES

◆ Test the job aids on the target audience or a less experienced group. Some people have had great success with job aids aimed at various working populations by testing them on schoolchildren.

◆ Do not assume that job aids won't require training support when they are introduced. Determine the degree of training required, if any, during pilot testing.

◆ Provide a method for keeping the job aids current and ensuring their use. Design accountability into the system.

REFERENCES AND RESOURCES

Publications

Booher, H.R. (1978, July). *Job Performance Aids: Research and Technology State of the Art (Technical Report No. 78-26).* San Diego, CA: Navy Personnel Research Center.

Elliott, P.H. (1999). "Job Aids." In *The Handbook of Human Performance Technology.* San Francisco: Jossey-Bass Pfeiffer.

Gilbert, T. (1996). *Human competence: Engineering worthy performance.* New York: McGraw-Hill. (Originally published 1978.)

Harless, J.H. (1978). *Job Aid for Selection and Construction of Job Aids.* Annapolis, MD: Human Performance Technologies.

Harless, J.H. (1990). *The Peak Performance System.* Annapolis, MD: Human Performance Technologies.

Harmon, P. (1984). "Extending Working Memory With Job Aids." *Performance & Instruction Journal, 23*(6), 5–6.

Lineberry, C.S. (1977). "When to Develop Aids for On-the-Job Use and When to Provide Instruction." *Improving Human Performance Quarterly, 6,* 87–92.

Mager, R.F., and P. Pipe. (1970). *Analyzing Performance Problems. Or "You Really Oughta Wanna."* Belmont, CA: Fearon/Lear Siegler.

6

ON-THE-JOB TRAINING

Rick Sullivan

WHAT IS ON-THE-JOB TRAINING?

On-the-job training (OJT) is an intervention for improving an employee's work performance. An experienced practitioner at the work site conducts OJT one-on-one with the learner as the learner performs assigned work tasks.

OJT programs can be designed and delivered using two basic approaches:

♦ structured, or formal, OJT experiences built on an organized process

♦ unstructured, or informal, OJT experiences, involving little or no planning, which pair a worker to be trained with an experienced worker.

Structured OJT is the preferred approach for achieving desired skill levels, accurate training content, and standardized methods of performing job skills. Key features of structured OJT include

♦ clear training objectives based on an identified need to improve job performance

♦ structured OJT materials including information presented in printed directions, or through computer-assisted learning, or through performance checklists

♦ OJT trainers or job coaches who are experienced practitioners and have been prepared for their role in facilitating the learning process

♦ guides for both the learner and the trainer, which include the training schedule, responsibilities of the learner and trainer, evaluation information, and step-by-step instructions for implementing the training

♦ job aids to support the learning process and for use on the job following training

♦ evaluation tools including knowledge assessments and performance checklists.

RELATED INTERVENTIONS

The objective of training is to improve the performance of employees by increasing their knowledge and skills. The focus of well-designed OJT programs is on the specific knowledge and skills required to improve performance, thus making OJT one of the most effective training interventions.

Other names for structured OJT include planned OJT, work-based training and, in some areas of health care, site-based training (referring to the health-care delivery site). Some features of structured OJT are also in self-directed learning, self-paced learning, individualized learning, and distance learning.

Structured OJT may include elements of self-directed learning and coaching, especially in the development of job skills. Job aids, training games, and simulations are often in the design of OJT, and many electronic performance support systems for equipment are part of a structured OJT program.

WHEN TO USE OJT

Use structured OJT when the root cause of the performance problem is that the performer lacks the knowledge and skills to do the job. Structured OJT is especially useful in the following situations:

- Employees need to be trained immediately without waiting for a scheduled course (just-in-time, or JIT, training).
- There is high staff turnover, or large numbers of employees require training.
- Training must be customized to meet local needs and standards.
- Skill practice is difficult to obtain away from the job site (for example, it is difficult to accurately simulate job site equipment and processes).
- There is a need to focus training on specific employees and a desire to avoid the inappropriate selection of training participants, which often happens when a number of employees travel to a central site for training.
- Structured OJT is in place and part of an existing system, and has become more sustainable than courses requiring the employee to leave the work site for training.
- Increasing numbers of employees have completed a structured OJT course, so that OJT becomes more cost-effective than traditional group-based training requiring the employee to travel away from the job site.

Structured OJT can also strengthen other interventions in other performance improvement areas. It can improve

- *Motivation:* For many workers, the opportunity to acquire new knowledge and skills to improve performance or to prepare for a new job can be very motivating.

♦ *Structure and processes:* The redesign of work processes may be an ideal application of structured OJT.

♦ *Information:* The self-study aspects of structured OJT work well when used as part of an employee orientation program.

WHEN NOT TO USE OJT

Like any other training intervention, structured OJT should be used only when appropriate. OJT may be inappropriate or ineffective for the following reasons:

♦ For certain topics, a great deal of interaction is required with other learners and a trainer (for example, courses that focus on communication skills).

♦ Problems occur when learners have limited reading abilities because most OJT courses require reading of print or computer-based materials.

♦ There is a misconception that any supervisor or worker can serve as an OJT trainer or job coach without some training and preparation.

♦ Structured OJT may not be cost-effective in situations where there is limited turnover of employees.

♦ Without proper instructional design, structured OJT may become unstructured. The employee receiving OJT may just watch another worker, and therefore fail to acquire all the required knowledge and skills.

EXAMPLES

♦ *Customer Service Problem:* A large insurance company has received an increasing number of complaints about poor customer service. A performance needs analysis determined that the cause is a poorly implemented training program for customer service associates. It had been assumed that it would be sufficient to provide new associates with a packet of information about how to do their job and ask their supervisors to work with them. Results of the analysis indicated that this was not the case.

— *Intervention:* Structured OJT is the appropriate intervention to increase the associates' knowledge and skills. The design of the OJT course includes a set of modules based on the associates' required knowledge and skills, including case studies, role plays, exercises, and several videotapes. The associates' supervisors are trained as job coaches and are oriented to the learning package. There is a structured training schedule so that the associates and job coaches know when specific activities are to occur (for example, skill practice and feedback sessions and observations with customers). Follow-up assessments indicate that the associates' performance has improved and that there is a reduction in the number of customer complaints.

♦ *New Time-Keeping System Problem:* A large company is installing a new time-keeping system. The system will allow employees to use the organizational intranet to access the program from anywhere in the world so that they can charge their time to the appropriate projects. The challenge in training all of the staff is that they are in many locations and work all shifts.

— *Intervention:* After completing an analysis of the time-keeping software, including the online help and information features, a decision is made to develop a tutorial to help employees learn to use the system. The online tutorial contains a series of lessons on the various features of the system. The employee has opportunities to practice creating various reports, accessing the system from a remote location and requesting online assistance. After an employee completes the modules, his or her supervisor receives a message and then follows up to ensure that the employee has no questions. By the target date, most employees had completed the tutorial and had successfully started using the new system. Those experiencing difficulties were given access to technical support personnel for coaching.

♦ *Assembly Line Upgrade Problem:* A large manufacturing facility has three assembly lines. Sections of each line were recently upgraded with newer versions of several pieces of equipment. Because the functions of the newer pieces of equipment were similar to those of the older ones, management assumed there was no need for formal training. Several weeks after the lines were back in operation, however, quality assurance reports indicated problems. A performance needs analysis indicated that the operators were not performing to standard in those sections of the line with the new equipment. The root cause was determined to be operators' lack of the necessary knowledge and skills to operate the equipment correctly.

— *Intervention:* Using the manuals from the equipment manufacturer, a self-study packet is designed as part of a structured OJT course. Operators are able to step away from the line for two hours of self-study. Following completion of the self-study packet, each operator takes a brief test covering the essential information. Once back on the line, an OJT trainer works with each operator to demonstrate key skills and then observe and coach as the operator practices. The OJT trainer signs off when the operator demonstrates mastery of the key skills. Once all of the operators completed training, quality assurance reports indicate that product quality has more than returned to normal. It has improved.

DESIGN GUIDELINES

The key to successful OJT is to design a program that will increase the knowledge and skills of workers and result in improved performance.

Below are several of the more common factors to consider in designing a structured OJT intervention:

♦ The content focus may be on increasing knowledge, developing skills, improving attitudes, or on a combination of all three.

♦ The information may be presented through a variety of media, such as print documents that incorporate graphics and photographs, video, interactive multimedia on a CD-ROM, a corporate intranet, or via the Internet.

♦ The sequence of learning may be totally individualized or may require periodic interactions with a trainer or supervisor.

♦ The learning activities may be totally self-contained or may require the learner to attend group sessions, interview a colleague, or observe a subject matter expert performing a skill.

Following are some tips for designing structured OJT:

♦ Make sure that structured OJT is the right intervention to improve performance.

♦ Analyze the instructional content. A thorough analysis of the essential knowledge, skills, and attitudes is required to ensure that the materials and training will be effective.

♦ Design the OJT strategy. How will OJT work? What is the sequence of learning activities? Should the learner interact with a trainer, supervisor, or others? Will there be knowledge assessments? Skill assessments? Will there be other learners to interact with? Does completion of this course result in any type of qualification or certification? Must the learner be at a specific location to learn? Are there prerequisites? Answering these and other questions will help to shape the OJT strategy.

♦ Develop the OJT materials. Materials may include print, electronic, audio or video media; job aids; real objects and equipment; simulations; and games. Consider the designing materials for the learner and for an OJT trainer or supervisor. The designer is limited only by creativity and budget.

IMPLEMENTATION GUIDELINES

♦ Train the OJT trainer or job coach. Effective OJT programs include trained trainers or job coaches. This is the person providing support, giving demonstrations, observing, providing feedback, answering questions, and assessing competence. Investing time in training these individuals is key to the success of an OJT program.

♦ Conduct a pilot test. Before implementing structured OJT on a wide basis, it is a good idea to conduct a pilot test. This test affords the designers an opportunity to test the strategy and materials in one or two locations before expanding the program to other sites.

♦ Revise the OJT strategy and materials. As a result of the field test, there will likely be adjustments to the strategy and supporting materials.

◆ Implement your OJT strategy. Expand the implementation of the structured OJT program to prepared sites (for example, where a trainer or coach is available, the learner is prepared, and equipment and supplies are available).

REFERENCES AND RESOURCES

Publications

Jacobs, R.L., and M.J. Jones. (1995). *Structured On-the-Job Training.* San Francisco: Berrett-Koehler.

Technical Training and, before its renaming in 1997, *Technical Skills & Training.* ASTD journals.

Internet

http://pages.prodigy.net/pblair/ttthome.htm. This site has suggestions on designing, developing, implementing, and maintaining technical job-task training programs to improve human performance in the workplace. Be sure to scroll down to the section focusing on structured OJT.

Association

ASTD.

7

TRAINING GAMES

Sivasailam Thiagarajan

WHAT ARE TRAINING GAMES?

Training games have the following four features:

- *conflict:* competition between teams or tension between a goal and limited resources
- *control:* rules for taking turns, making moves, and scoring points
- *closure:* special rules that determine how the game comes to an end and who wins
- *contrivance:* qualities that make people say, "It's only a game."

Fun and playfulness are desirable features of training games. These aspects generate high levels of motivation and voluntary participation in training games.

The focus on training highlights these additional features of training games:

- Achievement of the training objectives is related to winning the game.
- Aspects of play that are correlated with effective learning (such as interaction, teamwork, active participation, frequent feedback, and learning through experience) are emphasized in a training game.

RELATED INTERVENTIONS

Other names for training games include instructional games, activity-based training, experiential learning, and learning activities. These games are similar to on-the-job (OJT) training because they both incorporate hands-on, experiential approaches. However, OJT is not a contrived situation.

WHEN TO USE TRAINING GAMES

Use training games if the performer lacks skills and knowledge and does not know what to do, how to do it, or when to do it.

Training games are particularly useful when:

♦ Participants require repeated practice and immediate feedback to become fluent in applying the skill.
♦ It is important to apply the skill to a variety of on-the-job situations.
♦ The training content includes significant amounts of dry, factual information.
♦ The training content includes subtle patterns and relationships that become more memorable when "discovered" by participants.
♦ Participants require interpersonal skills and teamwork competencies.
♦ Trainees are younger participants who have been brought up on electronic games.

You may also use gamelike activities to strengthen different types of HPI interventions. Here are some examples:

♦ *Improving motivation:* Outdoor adventure games motivate teams to reach peak-performance levels.
♦ *Improving communication:* Improvisational games help players communicate spontaneously and clearly.
♦ *Improving physical resources:* Computer games familiarize employees with new hardware systems.
♦ *Improving health:* Team games that involve physical activity improve participants' cardiovascular fitness.

WHEN NOT TO USE TRAINING GAMES

Do not use training games in a contrived attempt to lighten up the learning task. Position the training game as a hands-on learning exercise rather than as a fun activity. Be particularly careful with participants from other cultures that value respectful learning from an authoritative figure. Do not use activities that highlight mutual learning to disguise your lack of knowledge. Take time to brief and debrief the participants and give objective feedback on individual performance.

EXAMPLES

♦ *Cultural Conflict Problem:* A multinational corporation is plagued by interpersonal conflicts among employees from different cultures. Performance analysis suggests a lack of knowledge of cultural assumptions and a lack of skills in identifying and accommodating different values.
  — *Intervention:* The training intervention is structured around a game called BARNGA. Groups of participants at each table learn to play a card game. After a few rounds, the players turn in their instruction sheets and play the game seriously and silently. After three minutes of play, the facilitator sends the winning partners at each table to the next table for a tourna-

ment round. Some players notice that their opponents are cheating, but the no-talk rule prevents them from protesting. Only later do players realize that the group at each table learned to play the game under slightly different rules. During the debriefing discussion, the facilitator relates what happened in the game with what happens in cross-cultural communications and teaches a procedure for identifying and checking hidden assumptions.

♦ *Hazardous Learning Problem:* Employees at a trucking company incur heavy fines for violating regulations related to the transportation of hazardous materials. These violations also delay the delivery of merchandise. Performance analysis reveals a lack of knowledge of these governmental regulations.

— *Intervention:* A daylong training session involves a series of quiz games. Participants are organized into teams and asked to cooperatively study the first section of a manual that explains governmental rules and regulations. After a suitable pause, participants are assigned to different contest tables where they compete with members of other teams to earn poker chips in a quiz game that reviews the section they studied. The training activity alternates between cooperative learning sessions (with other members of one's own team) through subsequent sections of the regulations manual and competitive play of different quiz games (with members of other teams). After each contest game, the poker chips won by members of each team are combined. At the end of the day, the team with the most poker chips wins the game.

DESIGN GUIDELINES

Training games may be of the following types:

♦ *Review games* are used for recalling and practicing skills and knowledge introduced through lecture presentations or reading assignments.

♦ *Framegames* are generic templates that permit easy removal of the current content and loading of new content.

♦ *Simulation games* use procedures and objects that reflect their real-world counterparts. In *metaphorical simulation games*, the relationship between the game and reality is abstract. *Board games* and *card games* refer to the main materials used in the play of the game. *Computer games* present the game information and play interfaces through software programs or the Internet. They are particularly useful in conducting complex simulations or rapid drill practice activities.

Some tips for designing training games include the following:

♦ **Make it relevant.** Make sure the game aspects do not overpower the training content and objectives. Participants react negatively to games that appear to be unrelated to skills and knowledge required on the job.

♦ **Select the most appropriate format.** Since there are so many different types of games, be careful that your selection meets your needs. Take into consideration the preferences and characteristics of participants, competency level of facilitators, the requirements of the training objective, and the type of learning content.

♦ **Play-test your game from the early stages of its design.** Get representative players involved as early in the development of the game as possible. Encourage these players to become your co-designers. Let them identify weak areas in your game design and suggest suitable modifications.

♦ **Use the framegame approach.** Identify game structures that work effectively with different types of learning content (such as factual information, concepts, principles, and procedures). Rather than design a game from scratch, load new content into the structure of these proven games.

IMPLEMENTATION GUIDELINES

♦ **Let the games begin.** Keep your initial instructions short and get into the training game as quickly as possible. In the beginning, present the most important rules in an outline form. Introduce and explain additional rules just before they are needed.

♦ **Maintain the flow.** If players are absorbed in the game, do not interfere. True facilitation requires keeping your activities invisible. Maintain an optimum balance along such dimensions as cooperation and competition, seriousness and playfulness, rigidity and flexibility, and outcome and process. Do this balancing act unobtrusively so your facilitation is invisible to participants.

♦ **Prevent disruptive behaviors.** Before starting the game, work with participants to establish suitable ground rules. Then, trust the process and the players. Make it easy for participants to monitor and manage their own behavior.

♦ **Take time to debrief.** Much of the learning in games (especially in simulation games) comes not from the experience but from reflecting on the experience and sharing the insights from it. Make sure that you have set aside enough time to process the experience. Depending on the complexity, intensity, and ambiguity of the experience, you may need more time for the debrief than for the play of the game.

REFERENCES AND RESOURCES

Publications

Darraugh, Barbara. (Ed.). (June 1991). "More Great Games," *Info-line,* Issue No. 259106. Alexandria, VA: ASTD.

Pfeiffer, J. William (Ed.). (1995). *Experiential Learning Activities Library Collection.* San Francisco: Jossey-Bass Pfeiffer. Probably the most expensive book ($745), but the seven volumes contain the best collection of different types of training games. The emphasis is on the soft-skills area.

Sugar, Steve. (November 2000). "More Great Games" (rev. ed.). *Info-line,* Issue No. 259106. Alexandria, VA: ASTD.

Thiagi GameLetter. Published 10 times a year by Jossey-Bass/Pfeiffer. Each issue contains a featured ready-to-play training game, a tool kit section with examples of a specific type of game, and tips for facilitators.

Internet

www.games2train.com. Features interesting examples of drill-practice games in a variety of corporate training topics.

Association

North American Simulation and Gaming Association (NASAGA). Conducts an annual conference that features many hands-on demonstrations of training games.

8

SELF-DIRECTED LEARNING

George Piskurich

WHAT IS SELF-DIRECTED LEARNING?

Self-directed learning (SDL) is a general term that usually refers to self-paced training programs that use a wide variety of delivery media. These delivery media can range from print products to Web-based systems. SDL can also refer to less formalized types of learning such as learning in teams, knowledge management systems, and self-development programs.

Self-directed learners do not develop by chance. It is a process that begins with their recognition of their own ability to guide their own learning, evolves into self-directed behaviors, and culminates in their eager participation in self-directed leaning programs.

RELATED INTERVENTIONS

Knowledge management systems, aspects of learning organizations, continuous learning, individualized or prescriptive development, and asynchronous Web-based training are all related closely to SDL.

The instructional design of learner-controlled instruction (LCI) is also closely related to SDL, and the two terms are often used interchangeably. LCI usually includes learner choice mechanisms for learning methodology and evaluation, whereas an SDL instructional design most often does not.

WHEN TO USE SDL

In its instructional design aspect, SDL is most useful when:

- ◆ The learner audience is large or dispersed, or both.
- ◆ The subject matter is mostly cognitive in nature.
- ◆ There are many individual needs among the learners.
- ◆ The resources for classroom-based training are not available.
- ◆ Just-in-time training is required.
- ◆ The time to do a proper design is available.

In its behavioral or psychological aspect, SDL is one of the foundation concepts for any intervention that is individualized to the point that each participant is responsible for some or all of the decision making. The employees' and managers' self-directedness must be analyzed and, if necessary, augmented if the intervention is to succeed.

The level of self-directedness in the learner, and thus the ability to apply self-directed behaviors, is a key factor in interventions such as creating a personal development plan, determining what newly learned knowledge should be placed onto the organization's knowledge management system, or taking full advantage of the company's e-learning facility.

These self-directed behaviors include the following: self-confidence; inner-directedness; achievement motivation; reflectiveness; and effective skills in goal setting, decision making, observing, listening, and reading.

WHEN NOT TO USE SDL

Do not use SDL with people who are not prepared for it. Their level of self-directedness is low, and simply putting them into a self-directed situation is not going to change this. This is one of the reasons why self-instructional media such as CD-ROMs and Web-based training have failed. It is also why personal development programs and knowledge management systems are not fulfilling their potential.

Do not use SDL unless there is a self-directed designed program in place. Self-directed designs require a much greater emphasis on objectives and criterion-referenced evaluation than classroom designs. This in turn means a stronger up-front analysis and greater degree of specificity in content. The usual facilitator guide and participant guide are not normally a sufficient amount of detail for the average SDL program. Since the instructor has been removed from the learning process, the instructional designer must do a better job of anticipating questions about the content and the delivery mechanism (for example, the technology and the job aid).

EXAMPLES

♦ *Instructional Design Problem:* A large multinational corporation had to train over 100,000 employees with a variety of needs on a just-in-time basis and do it cost-effectively.

— *Intervention:* Using its worldwide computer information network the organization established an infrastructure for self-directed programming that allowed employees access to server resident programs and gave them the ability to order CD-ROM packages. The organization uses specialized software to allow for quick and easy instructional design of programs that are unique to the company. Training costs have decreased by over 20 percent since the adoption of the self-directed approach.

♦ *Psychological Process Problem:* A real estate marketing and relocation firm is planning for a move to both Web-based training and a learning organization format.

— *Intervention:* The company created a program that introduces SDL and the concept of self-direction to its employees by giving them a chance to practice it as part of their personal development system. The managers were trained to be facilitators of the process, allowing them to both experience it and become responsible for acting as the gatekeepers of SDL. The orientation to self-direction and the chance to practice SDL in an area that was of personal concern to each individual paved the way for a smooth transition to the Web training environment and later to a Lotus Notes facilitated knowledge management system.

DESIGN GUIDELINES

All of the normal principles of classroom instructional design apply to SDL programs. Following are some other important steps:

- ◆ Undertake a complete job analysis that includes specific information on the tasks that must be performed.
- ◆ Prepare participant-centered learning objectives. They must specifically describe what participants will be able to do once they have completed the program.
- ◆ Be sure the content matches the objectives perfectly and is as specific as possible. This step ensures that SDL programs are shorter than classroom-based programs.
- ◆ Build plenty of activities into the curriculum to keep the participants' interest.
- ◆ Plan a strong review process. Criterion referenced evaluation ensures that participants learned what you wanted to teach. An evaluation process that includes objective-content-evaluation match, beta testing, and piloting will make sure that there are no design mistakes. Instructors in classroom teaching can often smooth over design mistakes, but that option is not available in SDL.

IMPLEMENTATION GUIDELINES

There are some basics of implementation that are common to all approaches regardless of the delivery process.

- ◆ Prepare the participants for SDL by following the guidelines about the behavior and psychological aspects.
- ◆ Prepare the organization for SDL through communication, especially with managers.
- ◆ Be sure your delivery system works. This is the main reason for your pilot.
- ◆ Plan for early and often evaluation of the learning, the effectiveness of the program, and the ability of your trainees to access and use the program.
- ◆ Plan for updates at regular and even irregular intervals as content or needs change.
- ◆ Communicate the effectiveness and efficiency of the program to those who should know.

In its behavior and psychological aspects, implementation of self-direction is just as important. To enhance self-directedness and bring out necessary self-directed behaviors, it is important to start slowly, load the dice for success, and provide a human-based support system.

- Don't throw your participants into SDL. Introduce it to them. Give them time and a mechanism to see how it differs from what they are used to and how it will be advantageous to them.
- Build their confidence by challenging them with a simple but personally important self-directed process at which they cannot reasonably fail.
- Give them knowledgeable people to talk to about self-direction. This support structure is critical and often overlooked. Remember that they are used to instructors who tell them what to learn and do. Wean them slowly from this viewpoint to one of "I can do it myself."
- Involve their managers. The managers will be the facilitators and in many cases gatekeepers of self-directed processes. Involve them early, make them proponents of the process, and be sure they are given the training to prepare them to handle their responsibilities.
- Use a system of feedback and evaluation such as a learning contract or a learning diary.
- Find out the level of self-directedness in your target audience by using an instrument such as the SDL readiness scale before you begin, and use that data as a springboard for your program.

References and Resources

Hiemstra, Roger, and Burton Sisco. (1990). *Individualizing Instruction*. San Francisco: Jossey-Bass.

Piskurich, George. (1993). *Self-Directed Learning: A Practical Guide to Design, Development, and Implementation*. San Francisco: Jossey-Bass.

Tobin, Daniel. (2000). *All Learning Is Self-Directed*. Alexandria VA: ASTD.

The Proceedings of the International Self-Directed Learning Symposium. Volumes 1-14 under separate titles. Norman, OK: University of Oklahoma Press.

Internet

www.sdlglobal.com. Website for the International Self-Directed Learning Symposium.

CHAPTER 2

TELL ME WHY: IMPROVING MOTIVES

9. Reward and Recognition
    by Linda Beck Halliburton

10. Compensation Systems
    *by Ethan S. Sanders
    and Jacqueline B. Visnius*

11. Playfulness
    by Sivasailam Thiagarajan

12. Motivation Systems
    by Matthew S. Richter

13. Team Building
    by Sivasailam Thiagarajan

---

*"Persons attempting to find a motive in this narrative
will be prosecuted; persons attempting to find a moral in it
will be banished; persons attempting to find a plot in it will be shot."*

—Mark Twain [Samuel Langhorne Clemens],
Adventures of Huckleberry Finn

MOTIVES

	Individual	Group	Cheap	Expensive	Together	Spread Out	Need it Fast	Have Time
Individual	Reward/Recognition Compensation Systems Playfulness Motivation Systems	Team Building	Reward/Recognition Playfulness	Compensation Systems		Reward/Recognition Playfulness	Reward/Recognition Playfulness	
Group	Team Building		Team Building		Team Building	Compensation Systems Motivation Systems	Compensation Systems Team Building	Motivation Systems
Cheap	Reward/Recognition Playfulness	Team Building	Motivation Systems Team Building		Team Building	Reward/Recognition Playfulness Motivation Systems	Reward/Recognition Playfulness Team Building	Motivation Systems
Expensive	Compensation Systems			Compensation Systems Motivation Systems	Compensation Systems	Compensation Systems	Compensation Systems	Motivation Systems
Together		Team Building	Team Building	Compensation Systems			Team Building	
Spread Out	Reward/Recognition Playfulness	Compensation Systems Motivation Systems	Reward/Recognition Playfulness Motivation Systems	Compensation Systems			Reward/Recognition Compensation Systems Playfulness	Motivation Systems
Need it Fast	Reward/Recognition Playfulness	Compensation Systems Team Building	Reward/Recognition Playfulness Team Building	Compensation Systems	Team Building	Reward/Recognition Compensation Systems Playfulness		
Have Time		Motivation Systems	Motivation Systems	Motivation Systems		Motivation Systems		

9

REWARDS AND RECOGNITION

·

Linda Beck Halliburton

WHAT IS IT?

Reward and recognition are part of an organization's overall management strategy to involve employees in the organization and to recognize and reward their achievements. As extrinsic motivation, reward and recognition are designed to work synergistically with intrinsic motivation to make people feel special and energized, thereby increasing their satisfaction and performance.

Recognition is the act of highlighting performers' accomplishments by presenting them with objects or activities (rewards) that the performers value and to have an important person deliver that recognition personally as an immediate reward for measurable achievements related to organizational goals. Typical recognitions include employee-of-the-month awards, trophies, plaques, announcements in the company newsletter, lunch with the president of the company, certificates, personal notes from the CEO, gift certificates, and photographs displayed on a company bulletin board.

In many recent surveys, employees have said their primary motivator in the workplace is appreciation for a job well done. Rewards and recognition serve as extrinsic tools and systems that work together with intrinsic motivation to encourage employees to perform at higher levels. A large part of this is acknowledging that motivators are highly individual: One size does not fit all. Through recognition and rewards of their achievements, the individuals on the receiving end as well as their peers are motivated to perform at higher levels. This motivation leads to improved employee satisfaction, improved productivity, improved customer satisfaction, and higher profits.

RELATED INTERVENTIONS

Recognition is a nonmonetary part of management's total compensation system. In today's work climate, employees give high value to well-designed work-and-life programs. These performance-based recognitions are relatively low cost and can take the form of flex time, paid time off, tuition assistance, health and wellness programs, and the like.

Recognition is also related to incentives. Recognition highlights employees who perform and meet objectives, whereas incentives induce achievement of those objectives. Incentives act more as the carrot to perform a specific task than as a recognition, which is designed to set an example for future accomplishment.

WHEN TO USE REWARDS AND RECOGNITION

This intervention can be most appropriate when employees feel their accomplishments are not adequately appreciated. Employees who feel underappreciated may not make a commitment to the organization. Recognition and rewards are particularly useful when employees lack feedback or do not feel that they are a part of the department or organization.

Before giving rewards and recognition to improve performance, supervisors should determine that the recipient has the requisite knowledge, resources, structure and processes, information, and health to perform the job. Motivation to perform is what is lacking.

WHEN NOT TO USE REWARDS AND RECOGNITION

A key premise behind rewards and recognition is that people tend to repeat that which gets rewarded. It is careful not to reward the wrong performance. Be careful to structure your rewards so that the performance you want is what is actually rewarded. Special care should be given in a team environment. If teamwork is desired, but individual performance is rewarded, the end results will not be achieved.

EXAMPLES

- *Public University Problem:* A department within a public university wanted to recognize the efforts of individual employees as record success and growth were achieved over an extended period.
  - *Intervention:* A representative group of employees was created to develop a multipronged approach. The approach adopted considered a variety of kinds of recognition. Departmental employees, others within the university, or students could nominate a person for special recognition. The recognition consisted of a special plaque, a traveling crown, half a day off with pay, and a special announcement in the newsletter and within the building.

- *Manufacturing Corporation Problem:* A division of a major manufacturing corporation was experiencing excessive lost-time injuries. This had an obvious impact on the profitability of the division.
  - *Intervention:* A plan was developed to reduce injuries and reward all employees when certain milestones were reached. These milestones were celebrated with special T-shirts and special dinners prepared and served by supervisors, managers, and vice presidents during an extended meal break on each shift.

The result was a significant reduction in lost-time injuries and a dramatic increase in profitability.

♦ *Small Business Problem:* A small business wanted to reward its employees for the success that was achieved as a result of group effort. In the past, a cash bonus had been issued to employees at a year-end celebration. The cash was soon spent and the reward forgotten.
— *Intervention:* Each employee received a wrapped holiday gift. The cash bonus was tucked in the front pocket of an attractive shirt bearing the company's logo. Anticipation built as each employee opened his or her gift. Everyone went home with a story to tell their families. And whenever employees wear the shirt, they are reminded of the reward that recognized their accomplishment.

♦ *Drug Store Problem:* A national drug store chain wanted to encourage its employees to go the extra mile in serving customers.
— *Intervention:* It developed a prestigious award that it gave to only a few employees during the year for extraordinary service. Some months no one received the award. Recipients were given special recognition at the end of the year, when all recipients and their families were invited to a dinner hosted by the leaders of the organization. By being selective in who received the award, the chain encouraged extraordinary performance, such as a pharmacist delivering prescriptions by boat during a flood. Clearly, this was going the extra mile.

♦ *Team Building and Team Strife Problem:* A company wanted to foster a sense of teamwork as it moved toward achieving the coveted Malcolm Baldrige National Quality Award. It also wanted to analyze processes to see where there were problems and bottlenecks.
— *Intervention:* The company instituted a sophisticated recognition and reward system that encouraged employees to recognize one another's accomplishments. They recognized specific achievements by completing forms for "ataboys" that they sent to a co-worker and that person's boss. Employees accumulated points each time they got one of these "ataboys" and when they had enough, they used them to order gifts from a catalog. At the same time that the recognition system was taking place, however, the company analysis of problems and bottlenecks resulted in much finger-pointing and blame-laying. Rather than the interdepartmental team-building that the company had hoped for, departmental solidarity was intensified.

DESIGN GUIDELINES

Recognition and rewards may be informal or highly formal or somewhere in between. The cost tends to be inexpensive in that the investment can be recouped in six months. No matter the cost or system, people basically want to be noticed for what they do and to know that someone cares. Following are some types of recognitions and rewards:

- *Informal recognition:* Informal recognition tends to be the most powerful and the least expensive form. It is an instant, personal recognition from a manager and can take place at any time. Examples of informal recognition include the following: a handshake accompanied by the statement of job well done, a personal note to acknowledge an accomplishment, public recognition of an employee for good performance, or a special meeting to celebrate success.

- *Trophy:* The addition of some kind of trophy or other tangible item to signify the accomplishment helps to make it more memorable. The trophy may be lunch with the boss, a coveted parking space, a pin or badge, a balloon bouquet, or a gift certificate. These noncash trophies tend to be more memorable than cash, which is quickly spent and forgotten as a reward. Each time the employee sees or thinks about the trophy, he or she is reminded of the performance that triggered it and thereby motivated to repeat the performance.

- *Formal rewards:* More formal rewards recognizing the balance between work and personal life are becoming popular. These include paid time off to pursue volunteer or charitable activities, tuition assistance, loaned executives, donating banked sick time to other workers, and the like.

- *Multilevel systems:* Multilevel or point systems can be very effective long-term recognition strategies. Employees earn points for certain behaviors. By accumulating a certain number of points, they are entitled to their choice of rewards. At the lower level, it might be choosing a shirt from a rewards catalog or saving up points for a television. At the higher level, a family vacation to an exotic port might be an option. These systems have the characteristic of letting employees choose what is most important to them, thereby creating an individualized approach to rewarding performance.

- *Creative recognitions:* Most of us are familiar with recognition and rewards such as plaques and employee of the month. Other more creative forms could include using the employee in commercials or ads (Wal-Mart does this), a gift the whole family can enjoy, paid time off to use the company's products, or letting employees choose which holidays to take. The possibilities are endless. By involving your employees in creating your recognition and reward systems, you are sure to generate other ideas.

These guidelines will help you as you design reward and recognition interventions:

- Determine your objectives. What behavior do you want to reward? Does this behavior help you meet your objectives?

♦ Involve your employees. Because one size does not fit all, it is crucial to involve your employees in designing an effective reward and recognition intervention. Find out what is important to them and build your intervention around that.

♦ Develop a meaningful way to present your rewards and recognition. Remember that timing and involvement of senior management are critical.

♦ Revisit your reward program on a regular basis. Doing this helps you avoid rewarding the wrong behavior and accomplishments. It also keeps you in touch with what is important to your employees. Be careful not to change your program too often; you do not want employees to perceive it as the program of the month.

IMPLEMENTATION GUIDELINES

The best-designed plan can lose its impact if not properly implemented. By following these guidelines, you will be positioning your reward and recognition interventions for success.

♦ It must mean something to the recipient.

♦ It must be administered fairly.

♦ It must be in proper relationship to the level of accomplishment and contribution.

♦ It must be presented in a timely manner, as close as possible to the event that triggered the recognition.

♦ It must be presented with warmth and sincerity and with senior management's involvement.

♦ It must mean something to co-workers and peers, and they should share and enjoy its presentation.

♦ Where practical, it should be shared with family, friends, and the community.

REFERENCES AND RESOURCES

Publication

Nelson, Bob. (1994). *1001 Ways to Reward Employees*. New York: Workman. This easy-to-use book has lots of ideas for rewards, from the simple and inexpensive to more complex and costly systems.

Internet

www.hr.com. This Website does not require membership for access to its many articles related to motivation, rewards, and recognition. Also a great source for other resources related to the HR field.

Association

Incentive Marketing Association. http://www.incentivemarketing.org.

10

COMPENSATION SYSTEMS

Ethan S. Sanders and Jacqueline B. Visnius

WHAT ARE COMPENSATION SYSTEMS?

Compensation is defined as extrinsic rewards, pay practices, and reward systems that organizations offer employees in exchange for their commitment, performance, and certain desired behaviors. Compensation plans are often structured as the total package of tangible returns (financial, services, benefits) that an organization provides to its members. How the total compensation package is designed and administered is referred to as the *compensation system*.

Compensation systems are used to influence employee motivation and satisfaction, which play a strong role in encouraging employees to perform. The type of reward structure that an organization chooses can take many forms, including salary, bonuses, stock options, profit-sharing plans, benefits, and promotions. While many compensation systems can be complex in design, the purpose must be straightforward and clear to all organization members. Employees must clearly understand the system and see tangible results of their work efforts.

Organizations must take a strategic view of their compensation plans. Rather than just throwing money at the problem or increasing benefits in a reactionary way, many organizations are taking a systems view of compensation and regarding it as a key element of their overall business strategy. Plans are often ineffective and achieve unsatisfactory results if they were designed with little thought or commitment or were based on traditional practices that were designed primarily to attract and retain employees. These compensation structures, often based on entitlement, reinforce unsatisfactory performance while ignoring desired performance.

Compensation plans must:

◆ support the mission and culture of the organization
◆ communicate to employees what is important and why
◆ ensure the ongoing success and viability of the organization.

RELATED INTERVENTIONS

Compensation systems are similar to rewards and recognition, incentive systems, and motivation systems, which are also designed to encourage the performance of organization members.

Often, compensation systems are linked to individual performance (for example, pay-for-performance plans), and performance appraisal interventions are used to measure individual performance. The use of performance appraisals in the design and implementation of compensation systems is widely used, yet there is some debate about the type of impact, positive or negative, that the process has on motivation.

WHEN TO USE COMPENSATION SYSTEMS

Compensation systems are most often used in return for an employee's labor. The effectiveness of a compensation system, however, often depends on how well the plan is designed to align individual performance with overall organization performance. Compensation plans can be used to reframe a company's paradigm from one that centers around entitlement to one that focuses on performance. To do this, employees must have a clear sense of what they are contributing to the organization and how that contribution is being recognized in terms of compensation and rewards. Compensation systems are an integral part of an organization that wishes to employ individuals who are interested in knowing how they add value to an organization. This is often translated into how they are compensated and rewarded by the organization.

Effective and well-designed compensation systems can be successful in improving performance and helping organizations achieve a competitive edge. In addition, a mutually rewarding compensation system that achieves the successful integration of employee performance with the organization's strategic goals can have a powerful effect on overall business success.

It is also possible to use compensation systems to do the following:

- establish linkage between company goals and individual performance goals
- encourage employees to develop skills and knowledge
- reinforce the overall strategic direction of the organization
- provide tangible feedback on individual performance
- establish effective communication channels for organizational success.

When Not to Use Compensation Systems

The use of compensation systems in reactive ways very rarely produces the desired effects of performance improvement and increased satisfaction. Often, increasing pay or incentives without linking them to business goals or desired performance will have the opposite effect by resulting in lackluster performance and low productivity.

In tight labor markets, many organizations beef up their compensation plans to attract and retain talent, and bidding wars ensue. This type of approach is unlikely to improve performance or positively affect the bottom line. It may, in fact, be quite costly to implement. Organizations must view compensation as a key element of an overall business strategy and not one that can be changed at whim to produce the desired, albeit short-term, results.

EXAMPLES

♦ *Low Morale Problem:* Steve Russell, director of human resources, has been concerned about low morale and high turnover for some time. After completing a lengthy performance analysis project, Russell and his team determined that compensation was a factor in the high turnover rates. Employees were leaving the company for a competitor that paid them $5,000 more per year.

— *Intervention:* Russell's initial reaction was to propose raising salaries to match the competitor's rates, but he knew from experience that a reactive response would only be a stopgap measure. With the support of the company, he decided to do a full-scale compensation study that would align compensation with the organization's goals. He also decided that in order to make his new compensation plan a success, he would have to get employees involved. After 18 months, he reported a turnover rate of less than 4 percent. The company's new compensation system is competitive and has been critical in attracting and retaining staff. Russell looks to his retention ratios as key indicators of the compensation system's success.

♦ *New Compensation System Problem:* Barker Industries has been in existence since 1960. It is a family-owned business that has strong ties to the community and has been a steady employer for nearly 30 years. In recent years, the company has experienced satisfactory financial success, nothing to brag about. As a long-established firm, Barker is slow to change and bases compensation on traditional pay practices, base pay plus annual bonus. The company has always felt that its pay policies were fair and equitable and that no change was needed. When the founder and patriarch of the company stepped down, the company decided it was time to look into some new and innovative ways to compensate employees. The ideal was a new system that would have more of an effect on quality and performance. The ultimate goal was to regain excellence and to achieve outstanding financial success.

— *Intervention:* Barker Industries began a yearlong process that involved a strategic focus on employee involvement, teamwork, performance and productivity, customer satisfaction, and excellent results. The compensation system was aligned with this new focus and became the company's key communication vehicle for rewarding success.

♦ *Poor Sales Problem:* Seafirst Investments was reeling from poor sales and was beginning to feel the burden of a very costly compensation and benefits program that was seriously affecting the company's cash flow. The company was in serious need of improving its financial picture, or it would surely face a dismal future.

— *Intervention:* The company completely scrapped its existing compensation program in two months time and began to implement a pay-for-performance program. After one year, the company was forced to sell off assets in order to increase cash flow, and the company closed its doors 15 months later. While Seafirst had good intentions, the new compensation system was a total failure. Employees were taken totally off guard when it was implemented because there had been a total lack of communication. The company explained that the change in compensation had to be done, but the new system had no tie-in to the company's goals or objectives. It was a short-term solution for a long-term problem, and it contributed to the organization's demise.

DESIGN GUIDELINES

Compensation systems may take one of the following forms:

♦ *Total Pay:* A balanced pay plan that addresses the four elements of pay: based pay, variable pay (cash and stock), rewards and recognition, and benefits.

♦ *Total rewards:* A complete compensation package consisting of total pay, employee growth, positive workplace, and future organizational success.

♦ *Gain sharing, goal sharing:* Similar to profit-sharing, which follows, however, here employee compensation is tied to the achievement of very specific goals (goal sharing). Gain sharing is an element of goal sharing in that if goals are achieved, the group shares part of the resulting gains.

♦ *Broadbanding:* A pay innovation that compresses pay structure with many pay grades into a structure with fewer pay ranges called bands.

♦ *Profit-sharing plans:* Compensation whereby employees share a percentage of company profits.

♦ *Pay for performance, skill-based pay, team-based pay:* Compensation plans that are based on a linkage to overall job performance, skills, or team performance

These guidelines can help you design a compensation system:

- Develop a compensation strategy. Outline the goals of the organization and establish a link between those goals and the design of the compensation system.
- Determine the role (minor or major) that the compensation system will play in the organization.
- Assess external and internal pay practices to identify how to design a system that is competitive in the marketplace.
- Establish a purpose for the compensation system. Determine individual and business goals for the plan structure (for example, motivating performance, rewarding team performance, and reinforcing company culture).
- Involve all levels of the organization in the design and development of the compensation strategy.
- Consider employee interests and perspectives in the design of the compensation system.
- Establish a compensation system that rewards behaviors and outcomes, that motivates employees, and that is consistent with the organization's goals and objectives.
- Evaluate the compensation system on an annual basis to ensure the plan is still focused on organization strategy.
- Measure results by revisiting objectives to determine if they are being met.

IMPLEMENTATION GUIDELINES

- Make decisions regarding compensation systems that are in line with the organization's compensation philosophy. In other words, if an organization considers implementing a skill-based plan, then emphasize training and skill development in the compensation philosophy.
- Create an effective communication vehicle to disseminate the compensation structure to the entire organization. A clear, consistent, and continual communication policy will help to increase the effectiveness of the system.
- Involve employees in developing, implementing, and evaluating compensation systems. Allowing organization members to play a role in implementing a compensation system is empowering and may contribute to the overall success of the plan. Organizations must balance the appropriate level of involvement, while structuring a plan that will meet both the employees' needs and the organizational goals.

REFERENCES AND RESOURCES

Publications
Compensation and Benefits Review.
Garvey, Charlotte. (April 2000). "Goalsharing Scores." *HR Magazine*, 99–106.

Lawler, III, E.E. (2001). *Rewarding Excellence*. San Francisco: Jossey-Bass.

Mirza, Patrick. (December 2000). "Mission Possible: Compensation Strategy Cooled Long, Hot Summers." *HR Magazine*, 50–52.

Schuster, J.R., and P.K. Zingheim. (1992). *The New Pay: Linking Employee and Organizational Performance*. San Francisco: Jossey-Bass.

Solomon, Charlene M. (February 1998). "Using Cash Drives Strategic Change." *Workforce*, 78–79.

Williams, Valerie L., and J.E. Sunderland. (May 1999). "New Pay Programs Boost Retention." *Workforce*, 36–40.

Wiseman, Robert M. (January 2001). "Rewarding Excellence." *The Academy of Management Review*, 135–138.

Zingheim, Patricia K., and Jay R. Schuster. (July-August 2000). "Total Rewards: Pushing the Pedal to the Metal." *The Journal of Business Strategy*, 15–17.

Internet

www.worldatwork.org (Website of Professional Organization for Compensation Benefits and Total Rewards).

Association

World at Work. This is the professional organization for compensation benefits and total reward (formerly American Compensation Association).

11

PLAYFULNESS

Sivasailam Thiagarajan

WHAT IS PLAYFULNESS?

Playfulness is an attitude that finds (or creates) amusement and enjoyment in all situations. On the basis of the principles of play therapy, research on recreation, and studies on flow state, playfulness emphasizes that a performer's job is too important to be taken seriously. This intervention, associated with fun, optimism, and a sense of humor, helps people not to sweat over the small details and suggests that everything is a small detail anyhow. Implemented with individuals and teams, playfulness supports other performance improvement interventions and improves performers' morale, mental health, and creative problem-solving abilities.

RELATED INTERVENTIONS

- ♦ *Ceremonies:* Ceremonies celebrate progress toward the achievement of different milestones to help energize performers, savor their achievement, and recommit themselves to the task. Spontaneous ceremonies share many features of playfulness.
- ♦ *Intrinsic motivation systems:* These systems increase performers' commitment and perseverance. Playfulness can help motivation systems to increase the interest level of work and to decrease the impact of negative mood.
- ♦ *Training games:* These games improve performers' skills and knowledge. They represent a special application of the principles of playfulness.

WHEN TO USE PLAYFULNESS

The following symptoms and root causes suggest the use of this intervention:

- ♦ when increased absenteeism, tardiness, low energy levels, accidents, lack of work-life balance, substance abuse, and physical and mental sickness suggest that employee morale is down
- ♦ when the job situation is filled with boredom, frustration, paranoia, tension, and other stress-producing factors

◆ when the organization has received (or anticipates receiving) a series of bad news
◆ when performers take standard policies and procedures too seriously by mindlessly applying them to all situations without thinking about flexible and innovative modifications
◆ when the number, frequency, and intensity of interpersonal conflicts suggest dysfunctional patterns of interaction.

Playfulness is also useful in doing the following:

◆ *Improving teamwork:* Playful activities provide effective team-building exercises.
◆ *Improving motivation:* A playful environment and culture increase performers' motivation level.
◆ *Improving training:* Interactive strategies reduce learners' anxiety and boredom and increase retention and application.
◆ *Improving communication:* Playful messages attract and maintain audience attention and drive home important points.

When Not to Use Playfulness

◆ Do not use playfulness when an organization treats play as the antonym of work and productivity. It is important to identify such biases and modify them before implementing playfulness as an intervention.
◆ One person's play could be another person's pain. It is important to ensure that performers are laughing with others, not laughing at others. Playfulness should be implemented in a sensitive and inclusive fashion.
◆ Do not use playfulness when it means some people are winners and others losers. Some types of play focus on winning and losing and encourage high levels of competition. In the spirit of cooperative new games, playfulness should be structured to ensure that everybody wins.

Examples

◆ *Fishing for Fun Problem:* An employee survey at the neuro-renal floor of the Missouri Baptist Medical Center identified low self-ratings in such areas as team participation, satisfaction, support, communication, and positive team attitude. The root causes probably included the typical chaos and stress in a hospital setting.
— *Intervention:* The group implemented a videotape series called FISH (created by ChartHouse Learning of Burnsville, Minnesota), which documented the transformation of the Pike Place Fish Market in Seattle. The basic intervention encouraged the key principles of play, mutual energizing, focus on the present task, and choosing to look for the best. The nursing staff implemented these principles with great enthusiasm,

distributing a plastic fish to others who have made their day. This plastic fish became a proud badge worn by patients, doctors, and staff members. Scores in the same survey collected eight months later indicated significant improvement in all areas. Another impressive business-related result of playfulness is a dramatic reduction in employee turnover.

♦ *Flying for Fun Problem:* The airline industry is a highly competitive sector in which small players are immediately gobbled up by the big guys. Southwest Airlines had to win several court battles even before its first flight in the middle of 1971. Large carriers consistently attacked this upstart airline in various ways, including blocking it out of the Travel Reservation Network, which made it difficult for passengers to purchase tickets.

— *Intervention:* Southwest Airlines has a well-earned reputation for being a fun place to work and a fun airline to fly. Employees are hired for their spontaneity and sense of humor through behavior-based interviews. Sometimes the interviewers wear pajamas to observe the candidate's spontaneous reactions. Everyone in Southwest is empowered and encouraged to play. The walls in their Dallas headquarters are plastered with photographs of employees having fun. Even the announcements during takeoff and landing are presented in a playful tone that encourages passengers to pay more attention. Playfulness has given the airlines a competitive advantage and the ability to think outside the box. For example, Southwest was the first to implement the concept of ticketless travel, which other airlines have since adopted. The U.S. Department of Transportation has rated Southwest as the leader in a variety of categories including online performance, baggage handling, and fewest customer complaints. It has received awards from business magazines as the best low-fair airline, best airline overall, and the best company to work for.

DESIGN GUIDELINES

In designing the intervention, it is worth considering that playfulness may vary along the following dimensions:

♦ *Individual and group:* Some playful activities are enjoyed by individuals (as in playing a solitaire game or solving a puzzle), whereas other activities require the presence of other people (as in playing basketball or throwing a birthday party).

♦ *Structured and spontaneous:* While spontaneity is often a key element of play, it is possible to set aside certain time periods and to provide minimal structure to playful activities.

♦ *Active and passive:* Some types of play require active physical participation, whereas other types involve amusing oneself passively by identifying the element of humor in different situations.

◆ *Ends and means:* Pure forms of play do not have any goals other than enjoying the present moment. However, playful strategies can be applied to other performance-improvement interventions to achieve training and team-building goals.

Here are some guidelines to follow as you design this intervention:

◆ Publicize the benefits of playfulness. Through posters and presentations, exhort performers to take their job seriously and themselves lightly. Spread these important benefits of humor, fun, and play:
— Laughter contributes to your physical and emotional health.
— Humor reduces work-related stress and tension.
— A playful spirit improves and increases interactions among team members.
— Humor is a powerful tool for defusing personal conflicts.
— Playfulness enables performers to think outside the box and come up with creative solutions to problems and innovative approaches for exploiting opportunities.

◆ Create a playful environment. The physical space, furniture, and various other factors can bring out the spirit of playfulness among employees. For example, the meeting room can be designed as an executive sandbox to encourage physical play. Balls and basketball boards can be placed at different locations. Bulletin boards can be adorned with humorous posters, cartoons, and jokes. The organization can display a humorous logo and a light-hearted slogan.

◆ Create playful events. Substitute parties for weekly meetings. Celebrate every small victory, personal milestone, and ethnic holiday. Hold frequent picnics and ball games. Make the new employee orientation into a playful welcome.

◆ Do not overdesign. When you think about it, systematic and careful design of an intervention works against the essential spontaneity of having fun. You cannot dictate spontaneity (as in this absurd statement: "At exactly 10 a.m., all employees will do something spontaneous."). Designing for fun requires a lean approach that encourages performers to give their own finishing touches to the environment and events.

IMPLEMENTATION GUIDELINES

◆ Empower and encourage. Human beings—*homo ludens* ("one who plays")—have a natural inclination toward playfulness. However, adults usually have this inclination extinguished from their repertoire through social pressure and systematic punishment. An important element in implementing playfulness is to authorize zany behaviors and get out of the way of the performers. Given a suitable physical and cultural environment, people will have no difficulty discovering creative ways to keep themselves amused.

- Model playful behaviors. Playfulness is contagious, and nothing dampens it as rapidly as the grim and grave behavior of the leaders. No job should be so high status that people cannot poke fun at it. To encourage the spirit of play in every area of the organization, make sure that top managers demonstrate their ability to see humor in even the most painful situation. Focus on bringing out the playful spirit among middle managers because they are the ones who inhibit themselves into behaving with dignity.

- Involve everyone. Pay special attention to cultural and personality differences. Avoid forcing people to have fun through approaches that seem to say, "We have methods for having you laugh." Involve introverts and traditionally serious groups in the early stages of the intervention design to ensure that people have a choice in how they will have fun. Encourage people to use humor as a tool and not as a weapon. Go beyond the organization and invite family members and customers to join you in your playful venture.

- Encourage teamwork. You can leverage the spirit of fun by encouraging teams to play together. Since most organizational work is currently conducted in teams, you can encourage members of these teams to have fun by coming up with a name for the team, a mascot, a secret handshake, a slogan, and other such frivolous things. You can also encourage teams to compete in ball games and game shows. You can reward teams by giving all members tickets to sports events and movies.

REFERENCES AND RESOURCES

Publication
Weinstein, Matt. (1996). *Managing to Have Fun*. New York: Simon and Schuster. Excellent collection of practical tips and corporate examples.

Internet
www.DeepFun.com. Explores the wisdom of games with the guru of playfulness, Bernie DeKoven.

Association
The Association for the Study of Play. A multidisciplinary organization whose purpose is to promote the study of play, to support and cooperate with other organizations having similar purposes, and to organize meetings and publications that facilitate the sharing and dissemination of information related to the study of play (http://www.csuchico.edu/phed/tasp/index.html).

12

MOTIVATION SYSTEMS

Matthew S. Richter

WHAT IS MOTIVATION?

Motivation is the driving energy that catalyzes behavior. Ultimately, our goal as managers is to create an intrinsically motivating environment. This environment occurs when an employee is able to excel using motivators found in the work environment. Essentially, when the motivators are present, employees have a choice about whether or not to be motivated.

Many prescriptive models have been developed as methods for increasing productivity and efficiency in the workplace. The big questions are which model works and how do we operationalize it. The challenge is that most motivators are externally regulating. It is easy to understand how money and other materialistic items can be controlling, but value systems, cultural constructs, and organizational dynamics also have the potential to be controlling. When a motivator is controlling, its benefits and its effect are short term and will remove the focus from the desired behavior. An explanation that further details some of the potentially damaging effects of extrinsic motivation will appear later.

The idea of internal and external motivation is, on the surface, easy to grasp. If I do a better job because my employer offers me a bonus, I have been *externally* motivated. If I do a better job because it makes me proud of myself, I have been *internally* motivated. However, the more complicated difference, and perhaps more useful, is between intrinsic and extrinsic motivation.

When one is motivated, either internally or externally, one is motivated in one of two ways:

- ◆ *Intrinsically:* Intrinsic motivation occurs when one is passionate about a task and performs it for the sheer pleasure of it.
- ◆ *Extrinsically:* Extrinsic motivation occurs when one performs a task because some force, either external to the individual (money, rewards, punishment) or internal to the person (a value or a belief that has an impact on an individual's sense of self-worth) drives that individual to perform (see table 2-1).

TABLE 2-1. THE MOTIVATION MATRIX.

	Intrinsic	Extrinsic
External	Not applicable	Money Bonuses Punishment or praise (contingent on performance)
Internal	When one has a passion for performing a task When one performs a task for the sheer pleasure of it When one freely chooses to perform a task	Belief and value systems Guilt Ego gratification Punishment or praise (attached to one's self-esteem)

Self-determination (from the work of Edward L. Deci and Richard M. Ryan [1985, for example]) is a model of motivation that incorporates some of the best attributes of other theories and then adds the one component many models miss—an explanation for more intrinsic impetuses for behavior. It is a system that prescribes methods for increasing intrinsic motivation and decreasing the impact of extrinsic motivation. Self-determination theory has three important components that must be present for an individual to be motivated:

♦ *Competence:* Competence is the need to perceive oneself as successful at goal-directed activities and goal attainment. A sense of competence must be present for a person to be intrinsically or extrinsically motivated. This can be achieved by providing the employee with the skills, knowledge, and resources to accomplish a task. It is also achieved by balancing, in partnership with the employee, what is on his or her plate so the employee is not overwhelmed with too much to do.

♦ *Autonomy/control:* Autonomy is the perception that self-determination or a sense of internal self-control is within one's capability. A sense of autonomy must be present for intrinsic motivation to occur. Control is the reverse of autonomy. In other words, if someone feels competent, but controlled, that will lead to extrinsic motivation. Control occurs when the employee senses that he or she does not have a choice in the matter. This undermines any sense of passion or pleasure that may arise from performing the task. Often managers fear being autonomy supportive. However, they must realize that supporting autonomy does not imply a permissive, no hold's barred excuse for anything goes. Rather, given the objectives and goals of the team, the questions are what choices are present in how a task can be done and how tasks can be prioritized. Any choice is contextualized within the reality of the work environment and the boundaries necessary for team, division, and company success.

♦ *Relatedness:* Relatedness is the feeling that one is emotionally tied to significant others in his or her life. By involving employees in discussions about policy and decisions, managers increase the sense of relatedness they have toward the team and the organization.

RELATED INTERVENTIONS

There are a variety of motivational models. Deci and Ryan stipulate that motivation is really on a continuum and that as managers we strive to create environments that are more autonomy supportive, more involved, and more structured around increased competence. But given the economic and cultural imperatives of work, they believe that intrinsic motivation is hard to find, let alone experience.

Kenneth Thomas (2000), however, argues that through the use of what he calls intrinsic rewards, managers can influence individuals to be more intrinsically motivated. Thomas labels the following as four rewards that improve intrinsic motivation:

♦ *a sense of choice:* the perception that one can perform a task the way one sees fit
♦ *a sense of competence:* the perception that one performs a task well
♦ *a sense of meaningfulness:* the perception that what one does has purpose
♦ *a sense of progress:* the perception that one is positively moving toward accomplishing a task.

Finally, stimulus-response models (for example, Skinner's), achievement models (for example, Seligman's), self-actualization (for example, Bandura's), and other motivation systems (all of which have inherently useful and benevolent components) avoid discussions about the individual's universal needs to be autonomous and competent.

WHEN TO USE MOTIVATION

It is essential to create a motivating environment in all management situations. However, it is important to identify when motivation, or a lack thereof, is the root cause of a performance challenge.

Some key indicators that a motivation system intervention is needed are

♦ When an employee does not believe she is capable of completing a task, either stemming from an inability to perform the task or an incapacity to perform the task. She might complain, "I don't know how to do that . . ." or "The company does not give me the resources to do that . . ." or "I feel overwhelmed . . . ."
♦ When an employee does not believe he has a choice in performing the task. He might complain, "I don't have a say in how this should be done . . ." or "I have no choice. I have to do this . . . ."
♦ When an employee does not feel like she belongs to the organization or the team. She might complain, "I don't belong here . . ." or "No one likes me . . ." or "I just don't fit in . . . ."

♦ When an employee sees no end in sight and believes that nothing he does matters. He might complain, "What's the point? Nothing I say or do matters to management . . ." or "No one ever listens to me. Why do I even bother?"

♦ When an employee does not receive any kind of feedback about her performance. She might complain, "I haven't received a performance evaluation since starting this job . . ." or "I don't know what my manager thinks . . . ."

♦ When an employee is more concerned about compensation and pay. He might complain, "What do we get for doing that?" or "I only do what they pay me to do and nothing more . . ." or "If you want me to do that, what do I get for it?"

Motivation has uses outside the workplace, too, including the following:

♦ *Raising children:* Children, like employees, develop best when they have choices, perceive their own competence, and feel loved by their parents and friends.

♦ *Spousal relationships:* Understanding why we do what we do in relationships can only strengthen the interactions.

♦ *Self-development:* Knowing the basis for our own motivation enables us to be more proactive in what we do, know more about how we succeed, and determine how we can grow and develop ourselves.

WHEN NOT TO USE MOTIVATION

♦ Avoid using only intrinsic motivation interventions as a short-term solution for immediately improving performance. It takes time to create a motivating environment, and most managers make the mistake of getting frustrated if an intervention does not work quickly.

♦ While over the long term, creating an intrinsically motivating environment has great value, extrinsic motivation, as a short-term behavioral modifier, can be effective. That said, be aware of the consequences. Money, reward structures, and bonuses do influence behavior, but they focus behavior on getting the external reward, not on improving the task at hand. Once the external reinforcer goes away, performance will dip again because the individual is not really motivated to perform. In a technologically rapid world, sometimes it is necessary to push behavioral modification through quickly. However, acknowledge to the employee that that is what is being done, and strive to create, in parallel, an intrinsically motivating workplace.

EXAMPLES

♦ *An Outbound Call Center Problem:* Performance metrics are down (number of dials is below the metric, number of sales is down, talk time has decreased, and quality of orders taken has eroded). Sales have decreased by 6 percent, and employee satisfaction is at an all-time low. Upon analysis, it has been discovered that the new supervisor has implemented several new policies. The first policy is that team members now have scheduled breaks and, in order to keep the phone metrics up, cannot leave their seats unless they have permission. Lunches have been tiered, and employees are assigned a lunch slot on the basis of the work schedule. And commission structures have been redesigned.

— *Intervention:* The supervisor pulled the team together and explained the reasons behind the new policies. Management felt that phone coverage was spotty, and sales were being missed during peak calling times. This intervention called for engagement and autonomy support. Once the mandate for coverage was explained, the supervisor then could ask team members to come up with a solution that met the given parameters. The solution this team developed was a weekly sign-up sheet for scheduled lunches and breaks. As for leaving their desks, team members agreed to be accountable for each other and only get up for bathroom breaks as needed. The solution this team found for this performance challenge is just one of many possible solutions.

♦ *Awaiting the Waiters Problem:* Waiters at a high-end restaurant in San Francisco have been continuously late for the lunch shift. Upon analysis, it was discovered that there were two reasons for the tardiness: (1) For two of the waiters, the bus schedule was incompatible with their work schedule; (2) three of the waiters are actors and have late performances the night before three days a week. All of these waiters felt that being on time was simply beyond their control, thus rendering them incompetent at showing up for work at the appropriate time. One set is harried by mass transit, and the other set is physically exhausted. Remember, without competence, neither intrinsic nor extrinsic motivation exists. To compound that problem, the second group of waiters is made up of actors who work solely to put food on the table and pay the rent.

— *Intervention:* Again, an engagement process is prescribed. Illustrate for the waiters the challenge the manager faces. Challenge them to adjust their schedules to meet their work needs as a team. Possibilities might include one or more of the following: staggering work schedules, carpools, and an incentive plan to establish some reinforcers. Remember that extrinsic motivation is beneficial for immediate and short-term results. Also establish a measurement system that supports waiter accountability for timeliness. For example, if late, a waiter covers cleanup for the other waiters that were on time. Note that this is a perfect illustration of Deci and Ryan's argument that intrinsic is incredibly difficult to encounter in the workplace. Here is an example of a group of employees that essentially work only for extrinsic reasons and, therefore, the managers must try to move them on the continuum toward intrinsic behavior, knowing they will never actually get there.

DESIGN GUIDELINES

♦ Engage. Employee involvement is one of the criteria for an intrinsically motivating environment. From the initial stages of designing a work environment that incorporates choice, competence, and relatedness, engage the team in developing the best process for that group.

♦ Know your team. Since your team is made up of many different individuals with many different intrinsic motivators, get to know what their passions in life are, at work and beyond. Knowing them, and letting them know you, is one of the best ways to increase a sense of belonging.

♦ Know your objectives and team goals. It is imperative to know the "facts" of what must be accomplished. You have a job to do, and your team has to achieve it. These objectives make up your boundaries and establish the rules for what and when tasks must be completed.

♦ Make sure you have resources and guides. Organizational and functional barriers to performance are some of the main inhibitors to intrinsic and extrinsic motivation. Make sure that you have the resources available to your team and the appropriate time allowances for completing what must be done.

IMPLEMENTATION GUIDELINES

♦ Make known the facts of life. Inform team members up front what is expected of the team and what boundaries, constraints, rules, goals, and measures are inherent to their work environment.

♦ Provide choices. Given the facts of life, engage team members in determining how to move forward, how to achieve what is expected, and how to establish their own measurement system to promote their own accountability. This process should also include a coaching process to help individuals be more self-determined within the boundaries of the organization and the team.

♦ Establish avenues for skill enhancement. Team members must perceive their own competence. Provide training, coaching, mentoring, and peer support when employees need it. Be proactive and ensure that employees are comfortable asking for help when they need it.

♦ Constantly engage the team. Inform the team about meetings you attend. Let them in on the secrets that may seem unimportant to you, but can be construed as hidden information. Share. Share. Share. When decisions need to be made, engage the team in that process. It might be as simple as informing them about a decision you had to make and questioning them on how they should implement it. Or it might include the whole team developing a solution to the problem. Either way, the name of the game is to involve.

♦ Evaluate. Obviously you will have objectives from up above that determine how you and the team will be measured. These measures need to be communicated as facts of life and then both the team and individuals need to be evaluated regularly and often. The focus of these evaluations should be on performance, not compensation and rewards. Remove any link between these evaluations to compensation and focus on individual development and growth.

REFERENCES AND RESOURCES

Publications

Deci, Edward, with Richard Flaste. (1996). *Why We Do What We Do*. New York: Penguin. This is the bible on motivation theory and my all-time favorite.

Deci, E.L., and R.M. Ryan. (1985). *Intrinsic Motivation and Self-Determination in Human Behavior*. New York: Plenum.

Thomas, Kenneth W. (2000). *Intrinsic Motivation at Work*. San Francisco: Berrett-Kochler. This is the book that puts the theory into motion.

13

TEAM BUILDING

Sivasailam Thiagarajan

WHAT IS TEAM BUILDING?

Sivasailam Thiagarajan and Glenn Parker (1999) define a team as "a group of people with a high degree of interdependence geared toward the achievement of a goal or the completion of a task." They explain team building in these terms:

> *The process of team building involves analyzing the strengths and improvement opportunities in a team, building on the current strengths, reducing the ineffective practices, and preparing a plan for ongoing team effectiveness. The team, guided by a facilitator, takes responsibility for the development of the plan and its implementation. A team-building session attended only by members of a specific team (referred to as an intact team) whose members regularly work together to achieve a goal or to accomplish a task. (Thiagarajan and Parker, 1999, p. 1)*

RELATED INTERVENTIONS

♦ Conflict management is an intervention that enables two or more team members (or subgroups in a team) to settle disputes through collaborative win-win outcomes. Especially useful in a diverse team, this intervention involves identifying incompatible concerns of different people and—through direct negotiation—finding a solution that satisfies both sets of concerns.

♦ Coaching is an intervention in which a coach improves the performance of a team by interactive questioning, collaborative goal setting, systematic observation, constructive feedback, and positive guidance. The facilitator in a team-building activity acts as the coach.

♦ Feedback is an intervention in which an individual purposefully provides timely information about a performance and its impact in order to improve individual, team, and organizational accomplishment. Effective feedback should be a critical component of all ongoing team-building activities.

♦ Dialogues and meetings are interventions that facilitate shared thinking, reflecting, problem solving, and decision making. Dialogues are open-minded divergent inquiries characterized by respecting different points of view, suspending judgment, listening without resistance, and speaking one's truth. Meetings are structured, convergent activities characterized by discussions that lead to effective decision making and problem solving.

♦ Culture change can be perceived as a large-scale team-building activity. This intervention is designed to bring about large-scale change in organizations by involving large numbers of people at different levels. Culture change involves planning or setting a direction for the organization and structuring or redefining working relationships among organization members.

WHEN TO USE TEAM BUILDING

If you were to search the Internet with *team building* as the key term, you would likely end up with hundreds of thousands of items describing everything from whitewater rafting to improvisational theater. Following are some uses you might discover for team building to improve the effectiveness of an intact team:

♦ When an organization undergoes profound changes in its mission.

♦ When communication problems hamper organizational productivity. These problems arise especially from the avoidance of unpleasant truth.

♦ When conflicts are ignored, avoided, or handled in a win-lose fashion.

♦ When frequent turf battles disrupt collaborative work practices.

♦ When new teams are established or when self-help groups emerge.

♦ When an organization shifts from a traditional hierarchy to a team-based structure.

♦ When there is an increase in the diversity among employees in an organization. Types of diversity that can benefit from a team-building intervention include culture, race, national origin, age, professional background, and functions.

♦ When there is duplication or absence of roles and functions assigned to different employees.

You might discover the following types of activities that are related to team building but not focused on improving the effectiveness of an intact team:

♦ Corporate adventure activities such as traversing a rope bridge between two tall structures increase the levels of interdependence, trust, and team cohesion. However, they appear to have very little transfer value to the behavior of intact teams in work-related settings.

♦ Games and simulations may help surface hidden issues in a team and enable effective understanding of group dynamics. However, unless the data they generate is clearly related to the team's goal, they may reduce the credibility of the team-building session.

♦ Training of groups of participants in knowledge and skills related to various aspects of teamwork (such as leadership, accountability, roles and functions, communication, and goal setting) usually results in generally positive outcomes. However, team-training sessions are not the same as team-building sessions.

WHEN NOT TO USE TEAM BUILDING

♦ Do not use when there is no outside facilitator to kick off the initial team-building effort. It is difficult (if not impossible) for the leader of the team (or one of its members) to conduct an effective team-building session.

♦ Do not use team-building sessions as group therapy or sensitivity training. Most teams have critical and urgent tasks to perform. Team members resent being subjected to touchy-feely activities by an outside facilitator.

♦ Do not use team building to push a personal agenda. The relationship between the facilitator and the team leader has to be a sensitive one. It is important for the team leader to understand that the facilitator's job is not to push his or her own agenda. It is equally important for the facilitator not to surprise the team leader by suggesting drastic interventions during a public meeting.

♦ Do not promise too much. The facilitator has to walk a fine line between creating unreasonable expectations about the impact of team building and presenting self-fulfilling prophecies of a pessimistic nature.

♦ Team-building sessions should not be positioned as single-shot events. They should be followed up by action planning and implementation.

EXAMPLES

♦ *Start-Up Problem:* A team was established by a traditional retail store to create an online store to pursue potential profits from e-commerce. Some members of this team were enthusiastic young techies with dot-com expertise, whereas others were skeptical old-timers with a lot of knowledge about the store's products and services. Several conflicts arose from the very first meeting, and they kept escalating during subsequent meetings. The team was about ready to self-destruct itself when Sue, a performance consultant, was brought on the scene. Her analysis confirmed that the root cause was diversity among team members' perceptions, values, priorities, and beliefs.

— *Intervention:* Sue interviewed different members of the team and administered various survey instruments related to commitment, values, acceptance, involvement, support, and satisfaction. She analyzed the information and prepared bullet-point slides to summarize her findings related to varying perceptions of the team's vision and mission, goals and objectives, and norms and values. After sharing a summary of these findings with the team leader and warning him to be prepared for confrontations, Sue conducted a team-building session. She presented her findings and answered questions related to the data, discouraging team members from suggesting immediate solutions. She then proposed a problem-solving approach to define different problems, brainstorm suitable solutions, and create action plans. Initial application of this procedure was marked by dysfunctional behaviors such as sniping, withdrawing, denying, polarizing, dominating, and attacking. Sue stopped the activity from time to time and asked team members to critique their own behaviors and to come up with suggestions for functioning more effectively. The team proceeded to identify different problem areas and to work out suitable solutions. The meeting ended with plans for increased and improved discussions during future meetings.

♦ *Survivors Problem:* Several members of a customer-relations department in a service organization lost their jobs when the department was downsized. The remaining employees were required to work more efficiently to handle the same workload with fewer team members. Most team members were anxious about their own job security and paranoid about who was going to be let go next. Mark, an OD consultant, was hired to handle this performance problem.

— *Intervention:* Mark administered a survey instrument on all team members and found that the trust level was alarming low. During the team-building session, he presented this feedback and, with the team's approval, conducted a few simulation games to highlight factors that influence trust levels and consequences of distrust among team members. He immediately conducted an extensive debriefing to relate the insights from the games to their workplace behavior. Mark then worked with the team to help them identify their negative mindsets and actions and to increase interpersonal trust. The team decided to follow up with monthly meetings (without an external facilitator) to openly share their progress and perceptions. Six months later, Mark administered the same survey instrument and discovered a significant increase in the trust level among team members.

DESIGN GUIDELINES

♦ Go through the stages. Teams have their own natural development pattern that should be taken into account in designing the team-building activities. All teams go through the stages of forming (with a focus on understanding the goal), storming (marked by conflicts among team members), norming (with a focus on ground rules), and performing (with a focus on achieving the goal). Team members' thought patterns and behavior patterns are strongly influenced by the stage they are in. During the forming stage, conduct team-building activities related to commitment to the goal and acceptance of each other. During the storming stage, shift the activities toward clarifying the goal and developing a sense of belonging. During the norming stage, focus on involvement in accomplishing the goal and support for each other. In the performing stage, focus team-building activities around achieving the goal and developing pride in team membership.

♦ Work with the team leader. You have a special relationship with the team leader who probably hired you in the first place. However, during your initial planning meetings, clarify that your task is to respond to the team's needs that you independently identify through interviews and surveys. Emphasize that while you welcome the team leader's perceptions and suggestions, you will merely treat them as one set of data. Before conducting the team-building session, share a summary of the data and warn the team leader about potential confrontations.

♦ Perform a balancing act. Team members have the classic conflict between achieving the goal and building relationships. When you are designing a team-building session, pay special attention to balancing the dual requirements of task and relationship goals.

♦ Do facilitate, don't control. Your success as a performance consultant is related to the speed with which the team can function effectively without you. During the design of the team-building session, be sure to minimize activities on your part and to maximize accountable and responsible behaviors on team members' part.

IMPLEMENTATION GUIDELINES

Following are some tips for conducting team-building sessions:

♦ Begin with performance analysis. Individual interviews and administration of survey instruments help you not only to collect data but also to establish a tone for the entire team-building activity. During interviews, model behaviors that demonstrate objectivity and maintain confidentiality. For example, never divulge information collected from previous interviews during the current interview even if only to validate the person's perceptions. This may bias the interview and raise doubts about the confidentiality of information.

♦ Present objective feedback. Analyze information collected from initial interviews and surveys. Prepare suitable displays (posters or slides) to summarize the data. Set aside ample time early in the team-building activity to present and clarify your data summary.

♦ Alternate between problem solving and awareness. Present a systematic approach for performance problem solving and facilitate team members through identifying their needs, focusing on root causes, brainstorming alternatives, developing suitable interventions, and implementing an action plan. Repeat this procedure with each need arising from the initial data. From time to time (preferably after solving each performance problem), debrief team members to reflect on their earlier behavior, gain useful insights about group dynamics, and come up with appropriate strategies for the next round of performance problem solving.

♦ Plan for follow-up action. During the team-building session, emphasize the fact that understanding and awareness are necessary but not sufficient for improving the team's performance. Explain that team building is not a one-shot event but a continuous process of developing the team's performance level.

♦ Encourage team members to develop an action plan and to schedule future activities for its implementation. Offer your facilitation services but remind team members that their ultimate goal should be to function without your help.

In modern corporations and nonprofit organizations, the major emphasis is on employee participation. Most performance-improvement interventions require teamwork for their initial implementation and continuing effectiveness. Hence, team-building activities should become an initial part of implementation activities of all types of interventions.

REFERENCES AND RESOURCES

Publications

Thiagarajan, Sivasailam, and Glenn Parker. (1999). *Teamwork and Teamplay: Games and Activities for Building and Training Teams*. San Francisco: Jossey-Bass/Pfeiffer.

Torres, Cresencio, and Deborah M. Fairbanks. (1996). *Teambuilding: The ASTD Trainer's Sourcebook* (ASTD Trainer's Sourcebook Series). New York: McGraw-Hill.

Internet

www.teambuildinginc.com. Although maintained by a commercial organization, this Website contains valuable resources and articles on team building, with a focus on employee involvement.

Association

International Association of Facilitators. The mission of this organization is to promote, support, and advance the art and practice of professional facilitation through methods exchange, professional growth, practical research, collegial networking, and support services. IAF conducts an annual conference and publishes *Group Facilitation: A Research and Applications Journal.* (Web site: www.iaf-world.org; phone: 612.891.3541.)

CHAPTER 3

GIVE ME TOOLS: IMPROVING PHYSICAL RESOURCES

14. Ergonomics and Human Factors
    *by Ethan S. Sanders and
    Jacqueline B. Visnius*

15. Automation and Computerization
    by Ralph Sanders

16. Physical Resource Management
    by Ralph Sanders

"Give us the tools, and we will finish the job."

—Sir Winston Churchill,
radio broadcast [February 9, 1941]

	Have Time	Need it Fast	Spread Out	Together	Expensive	Cheap	Group	Individual
Individual		Ergonomics/ Human Factors	Ergonomics/ Human Factors		Ergonomics/ Human Factors			
Group	Automation/ Computerization Resource Management		Automation/ Computerization Resource Management		Automation/ Computerization Resource Management			
Cheap							Automation/ Computerization Resource Management	
Expensive	Automation/ Computerization Resource Management	Ergonomics/ Human Factors	Ergonomics/ Human Factors Automation/ Computerization Resource Management		Ergonomics/ Human Factors Automation/ Computerization Resource Management		Automation/ Computerization Resource Management	
Together		Ergonomics/ Human Factors			Ergonomics/ Human Factors			Ergonomics/ Human Factors
Spread Out	Automation/ Computerization Resource Management	Ergonomics/ Human Factors		Ergonomics/ Human Factors	Ergonomics/ Human Factors			Ergonomics/ Human Factors
Need it Fast			Automation/ Computerization Resource Management		Automation/ Computerization Resource Management		Automation/ Computerization Resource Management	
Have Time			Automation/ Computerization Resource Management				Automation/ Computerization Resource Management	

PHYSICAL RESOURCES

14

ERGONOMICS AND HUMAN FACTORS

Ethan S. Sanders and Jacqueline B. Visnius

WHAT ARE ERGONOMICS AND HUMAN FACTORS?

Ergonomics and human factors involve the systematic and controlled study of the human body at work for the purpose of determining ways to fit work to people and products to users. The process involves a variety of activities including designing workspaces, products, and systems to facilitate human movement and musculoskeletal function.

Ergonomics programs address basic work principles and individual capacities enabling employees, supervisors, and management to carry out their work in a safe and efficient manner. Ergonomics and human factors engineering are concerned with workplace layout, equipment controls, instrument design, furniture and furnishings, and environmental conditions, such as lighting and noise, and how these elements can be adapted to the physical, mental, perceptual, sensory, and esthetic attributes, capacities, and preferences of people.

Awareness and identification of current problems are the first steps in designing an effective ergonomics program. Once established and working proactively, ergonomic improvements may result in higher productivity and higher product quality. The core principles of ergonomics programs are similar to those of other workplace safety interventions in that the ultimate goal is to anticipate and prevent problems from occurring in the workplace.

RELATED INTERVENTIONS

The focus of ergonomics and human factors is on providing an environment and working conditions that enable workers to perform at their full potential. Other examples of interventions intended to improve human performance and comfort through physical environment are resource management, facility and tool design, and facilities management. Each of these interventions deals with the people-machine-environment interface and the impact on worker health, productivity, and performance.

When to Use Ergonomics

Ergonomics should be introduced when performance problems result from musculoskeletal injury, stress, or strain that is tied to improperly designed tools and workplaces (for example, inflexible furniture that prevents proper posture), inappropriate work practices and habits (for example, improper patient-lifting techniques), and the like. The following examples highlight work activities that would benefit from ergonomic interventions:

♦ work that requires lifting or moving heavy loads
♦ excessive manual material handling
♦ repetitive motion activities
♦ intense work for prolonged periods of time
♦ repeated forceful activities that cause excessive fatigue
♦ other uncomfortable and potentially hazardous tasks.

In addition, there are warning signs to look out for that may indicate a mismatch between individuals and their physical work environment. Some of these signs may include

♦ increased episodes of tardiness and absenteeism
♦ low performance or productivity
♦ increase in on-the-job injuries
♦ increased worker compensations claims
♦ low motivation and low morale.

When Not to Use Ergonomics

Consideration must be given to situations where workplace injuries or unhealthful situations warrant immediate medical or professional attention. To avoid the possibility of a more serious incident or litigation, it is important to recognize the limitations of ergonomics. With a heightened awareness of stressors and injury-provoking activities, there is the potential for the overuse of ergonomics interventions. One must often look beyond choosing one intervention and provide a solution set that combines two or more cost-effective interventions to get to the root cause. Other limitations of this intervention include

♦ If an injury is the result of slips, falls, trips, motor vehicle accidents, or similar accidents, then an ergonomics intervention is not necessarily warranted. The specific situation should be studied to determine if the injury is work related.
♦ If the environment is especially hazardous or unsafe, the whole issue of workplace and occupational safety must be examined to determine if the appropriate level of protection against illness, injury, or death is in place.
♦ Ergonomics and human factors engineering programs must be implemented with the employee's interest and benefit in mind. If the program is implemented to cut costs and improve productivity

with little regard for employee benefit, the program may not gain the full support needed for success.

EXAMPLES

- *Oil Company Problem:* A technology subsidiary of a major oil company has recently undergone a significant downsizing. The effect has been an increased amount of work accomplished with fewer workers. With most of their tasks computerized, the employees are spending an average of 6.5 hours per day at their computer workstations. Recent worker compensation records verify that an increasing number of injuries were related to carpal tunnel disorder (CTD). In addition, 75 percent of all injury claims were CTD-related injuries.

  — *Intervention:* An ergonomic consultant was brought in to provide expertise in ergonomic program design and implementation. The ergonomic program was implemented, and the following ergonomic solutions were put into place: lower work surfaces; change of location and placement of computer terminals; and acquisition of articulating keyboard trays, mouse rests, glare screens, document holders, task lights, and lumbar back supports.

    These changes resulted in a decrease of CTD claims to zero. There were no new CTD claims after implementation, all former cases have been resolved; and workers' compensation costs have decreased by 77 percent.

- *Health-Care Facility Problem:* A midsized health-care facility has recently been acquired by a competitor and is now under new management. One of the issues that is to be emphasized and carried out by the new management is an emphasis on employee health. An alarming number of lost workdays and upper extremity musculoskeletal disorders were found during the due diligence process of the acquisition. Management vowed to find out what was causing these problems.

  — *Intervention:* An ergonomic lifting safety program was implemented after the root cause of the performance deficiencies was found to be improper lifting techniques of patients with restricted mobility. Training on proper lifting was implemented and lifting-assist devices were installed to reduce ergonomic stresses and improve patient security and well-being. The lost workday rate fell from 10.2 percent to 2.6 percent after 18 months. Upper extremity musculoskeletal disorders fell from 8.2 percent to less than 1 percent.

- *Automotive Trim Manufacturer Problem:* An automotive trim manufacturer has been deluged with employee complaints about decreased range of limb motion, loss of grip strength, and pain and stiffness in the hands. The rate of ergonomic injuries has risen to an unacceptable rate and has resulted in marked decreases in productivity and absenteeism. Of 10,000 employees, 1,000 ergonomic-related injuries have been reported. It is time to take action to determine what is causing these injuries.

— *Intervention:* The manufacturer decided to implement a corporate ergonomics program. The facility sent an engineer and one safety and health employee to a three-day training class. All employees were then given one hour of training in how to work safely in their given jobs. Design engineers were also trained in how to design jobs with good ergonomics built in. Some of the changes that occurred included the use of tilt tables, user-friendly tools, proper lifting techniques, and new-hire ergonomics orientation as well as the optimization of the location of parts bins. Musculoskeletal injuries were cut by 72 percent.

DESIGN GUIDELINES

Two types of ergonomic controls are used to effectuate changes in the workplace. The first is engineering controls whereby physical changes are made to a job, such as changing or redesigning workstations, tools, facilities, equipment, materials, or processes.

The second type is work practice controls. These are changes in the way an employee performs the physical work activities. Work practice controls include the use of neutral positions to perform tasks (such as lifting close to the body), the use of two-person lift teams, and observance of micro breaks.

Ergonomics are applied in many environments from offices to airport tarmacs. The design of an ergonomic program has much to do with the specific mismatch between worker and environment in any given area. A program may be, for example, office ergonomics, laboratory ergonomics, manufacturing ergonomics, manual material ergonomics, or patient handling and lifting ergonomics.

Typical guidelines for designing an ergonomics program would include

♦ Increase awareness of how to recognize potential musculoskeletal problems, such as frequent reports of aches and pains, or job tasks that require repetitive motion or forceful exertion.

♦ Gather data to identify jobs or work conditions that are most problematic, using sources such as injury or illness logs, medical records, and job analyses.

♦ Identify effective controls for tasks that pose a risk of musculoskeletal injury and evaluate these approaches once they have been instituted to see if they reduce or eliminate the problem.

♦ Establish a method for ongoing evaluation of the ergonomics efforts. As the work environment changes from turnover, new employees, new equipment, and the like, the program may need revision in order to address apparent or potential problems.

IMPLEMENTATION GUIDELINES

♦ Rearrange workspaces, furnishings, and equipment in order to position items in the safest, most efficient arrangement.

♦ Promote employee involvement either individually or in task forces.

♦ Establish health-care management to emphasize the importance of early detection and treatment of musculoskeletal disorders for preventing impairment and disability.

♦ Minimize risk factors for musculoskeletal disorders when planning new work processes and operations.

♦ Provide ergonomics training for employees (such as office ergonomics, laboratory ergonomics, ergonomics training for managers, manual materials handling, patient handling, and lifting training).

Employee involvement in the efforts to improve workplace conditions have many potential benefits:

♦ improved problem identification and problem-solving skills and capabilities

♦ enhanced worker motivation and job satisfaction

♦ increased acceptance of organizational change

♦ increased knowledge of the work and organization.

REFERENCES AND RESOURCES

Publications

BNA Occupational Safety and Health Reporter.

Kroemer, K.H., H.B. Kroemer, and K.E. Kroemer-Elbert. (2000). *Ergonomics.* Englewood Cliffs, NJ: Prentice-Hall.

Cohen, Alexander L., Christopher C. Gjessing, Lawrence J. Fine, Bruce P. Bernard, and James D. McGlothlin. "Elements of Ergonomics Programs." Cincinnati, OH: NIOSH. Available www.cdc.gov/niosh/ehome2.html.

Internet

www.cot.org. Center for Office Technology.

www.ergoweb.com.

www.osha.gov. Occupational Safety and Health Administration.

www.safety.duke.edu. Duke University.

15

AUTOMATION AND COMPUTERIZATION

Ralph Sanders

WHAT ARE AUTOMATION AND COMPUTERIZATION?

Automation and computerization are interventions that augment or replace human performance to obtain improved, reliable, and consistent outputs. Automation involves the use of mechanical, electrical, and robotic devices to perform large-scale or microscopic tasks that require strength and precision. It has the following major features:

♦ Automation chiefly relates to fully integrated manufacturing and other production processes.
♦ The system is based on the idea that knowledge falls into discernible arrangements that one can reduce to a routine by using probability distribution and feedback mechanisms.
♦ Those who apply this intervention practice programming rather than work. They decide by making judgments within a scope of patterns that the process can accommodate.

Computerization involves the use of hardware and software (including expert systems) to process significant amounts of data in a rapid, reliable, and objective fashion; computerization offers a major way to achieve automation. Computerization has the following major features:

♦ Computerization relates to the processing of information and data; once programmed it operates without human intervention.
♦ Computer systems process information and data with speed, reliability, and ease; above all they assist managers in decision making.
♦ Computer systems depend upon outside instructions to guide their activity, often in the form of programs (also called software).
♦ The computer process acquires, compiles, organizes, selects, correlates, stores, retrieves, and disseminates information and data accurately and at high speeds.

RELATED INTERVENTIONS

Because *computerization* and *automation* are rather broad terms, there really are not any interventions that are related to them on the same level. Within automation, there can be a host of interventions necessary to automate a system. These include ordering the automated machinery, installing the machinery, redesigning the work processes that coincide with the newly automated machinery, and training workers to monitor and maintain the new machinery. Within computerization, interventions may include diagnosing which systems are not operating efficiently, shopping for more appropriate systems, ordering new hardware and software, reconfiguring the existing system to accept the new system, and training employees in the best use of the new features of the system.

WHEN TO USE AUTOMATION AND COMPUTERIZATION

These interventions can be used to solve a wide array of large-scale and complex problems related to manufacturing or other production processes that often call for shorter processing times.

Automation and computerization are used in science, engineering, the arts, and management. In manufacturing, computerized automated processes have uses in machining, chemicals, metals, assembly, electronics, computer-aided designs, and computer-aided manufacturing. Nonmanufacturing uses include communications, transportation, services, biological engineering, and such consumer products as microwave ovens.

WHEN NOT TO USE AUTOMATION AND COMPUTERIZATION

Automation and computerization experience many of the same problems that plague all technological systems. Among these are

- These interventions are inappropriate in cases of highly qualitative problems, not susceptible to quantitative analysis.
- From time to time, these interventions have physical breakdowns, such as production lines run amok or computer tapes become tangled, so that they become counterproductive.
- Typical abuses include feeding the processes the wrong data, instructions, and software (garbage in—garbage out).
- Operators have difficulty finding the exact data needed from the flood of data that inundates them.

EXAMPLES

- *Missing Books Problem:* A city library system was facing some major problems. Each year approximately 8 percent of its books disappeared without a trace. It was difficult to tell where the theft was occurring. File cards were kept on each book that was checked out, and the information on them was to be entered into a central computer. However, the librarians often did not enter the necessary information into the computer or in entering data made errors in the spelling of people's names, in abbreviations, or the like. Also due to recent budget cuts, there simply were not enough librarians to help people find the books they needed, check them out, and monitor that no one left with a book that was not checked out. It was a well-known fact that stealing books from these libraries was as easy as putting them into a book bag or slipping them under a shirt. In one publicized instance, a library user who was irritated by all the missing books, made a citizen's arrest on a 91-year-old lady who had slipped a book into her purse and walked out the door with it.

— *Intervention:* The city hired a consultant to study the problem. After a careful review of the situation and discussions with library personnel in other parts of the country, the consultant recommended implementation of a new bar-coding and security system for all branches of the library. This new system placed a bar code in each book to track its current status. It also instituted bar-coded library cards that contained all the necessary information on each library user, including the person's email address. When a book was shown as overdue, the system would automatically send the borrower email reminders every two days until the book was returned. Bar-code tags in the books had alarm sensors to trigger an alarm at the front door when a book that had not been desensitized by the bar-code reader passed through the security scanners. Within one year of installing the new system, the disappearance rate of books dropped to below 1 percent. The system paid for itself by diminishing the book replacement budget, and the library was able to install computers with search engines to help people locate books. This system reduced the need for additional librarians to help people navigate the cumbersome card catalogs.

◆ *Customer Service Problem:* An international moving company was facing skyrocketing costs in its customer service department. It seemed that every time its gross revenue increased by 10 percent, the head count in customer service doubled. All of the customer service representatives (CSRs) seemed to be furiously working away. They spent most of their time on the phone with the people who were moving and with relocation officers from the company that was paying for the move.

— *Intervention:* A time-motion study revealed the type of information that the CSRs were exchanging over the phone: 70 percent were just reconfirming such details as who was moving, the originating and final destination, and dates of the move. A new electronic registration was installed, and terminals were given to all the major clients who placed at least 50 moves per month with the company. Now the clients could enter their own moves into the system without making a call (and some of this information was able to be automatically downloaded from the human resource data files), the CSR could check and verify the information, and an email could be sent to the employee being moved to verify the details and get any missing information. After a six-month pilot test, the moving company was able to freeze hiring in the customer service department for three years, despite the fact that its revenue grew 41 percent in that same time period.

DESIGN GUIDELINES

The following guidelines offer an effective method of designing the training content and objectives of these interventions:

- Before undertaking an upgrade in technology, be sure to carefully consider what the organization's needs are, what the real costs of the system are, how clearly the instructions for using the new system are documented, and how the new system will be evaluated as well as all of the logistics involved in installing the new system and making it operational.
- Identify the criteria for determining which type of system will meet the needs of both the organization and the users of the technology.
- Consider a full range of design choices and be sure to consider the skills and knowledge employees will need to operate this system.
- Using the criteria for determining a system, determine the complex set of decisions and definitions that the designer must consider when creating the system.
- Test a prototype of the system in numerous types of situations to be sure that it meets all of your criteria.

IMPLEMENTATION GUIDELINES

The degree to which individuals and organizations feel the impact of interventions depends on the complexity, intensity, and ambiguity of their experience over time. Groups periodically should discuss the functioning and status of these interventions and from time to time undertake written assessments. Managers should pay careful attention to whether these interventions have achieved their objectives, and in certain instances they might find it wise to establish a management-by-objectives approach. They should make certain to give these review activities enough time to gain proper insights into the situation.

REFERENCES AND RESOURCES

Publications

Brightman, Richard W. (1971). *Information Systems for Modern Managers.* New York: Macmillan.

Evans, Edward G. *Developing Library and Information Center Collections* (3d edition). Englewood. CO: Librarians Unlimited.

16

PHYSICAL RESOURCE MANAGEMENT

Ralph Sanders

WHAT IS PHYSICAL RESOURCE MANAGEMENT?

Physical resource management refers to interventions that control and direct tangible assets such as equipment, raw materials, facilities, and end products. These interventions involve planning, programming, budgeting, scheduling, and controlling assets. Many of these resources are in limited supply and in great demand. Specifically, the performance consultant helps organizations do the following:

♦ determine what resources to procure and when to produce them
♦ identify potential sources
♦ select the best source
♦ integrate new resources with existing ones
♦ optimize the use of these resources
♦ eliminate unwanted resources and waste products.

In short, resources are those assets that help managers get the job done. Physical resource management has the following major features:

♦ Management seeks to transform basic resources found in nature (raw materials) into useful resources that either take the form of finished goods (such as automobiles and business offices) or are developed into services that support the use of these resources.
♦ Managers generally apply resources as assets in their production processes and in leading and directing organizations.
♦ The ultimate aim of resource management by the private sector is to reduce costs, to maximize profits, and to achieve customer satisfaction; the public sector seeks to reduce costs and to maximize the satisfaction of a nation's citizens with government goods and services.

The public often believes that large firms suffer from highly centralized management that is unable to manage such giant operations. An erroneous idea exists that giant Japanese companies like Nissan, Fugitsu, and

Canon direct their resources from above through high-level authoritarian offices. In reality, "parent" organizations retain a few, highly competent resource management offices, preferring to subcontract much of this function. The same holds true for General Motors, which outsources many manufacturing functions in order to make the best use of its resources.

RELATED INTERVENTIONS

The following interventions all have an element of physical resource management:

♦ capital management
♦ purchasing management
♦ logistical management
♦ financial planning.

WHEN TO USE PHYSICAL RESOURCE MANAGEMENT

Some general indications that organizations need to focus more attention on resource management include:

♦ The organization is consistently paying more for raw materials than its competitors.
♦ There is an unacceptable amount of waste being produced during the manufacturing processes.
♦ The actual costs of resources consistently exceeds projected costs.
♦ There is an uneven distribution of resources between departments.
♦ Necessary resources often end up in the wrong place at the wrong time.
♦ There are shortages of critical resources.
♦ There are large standing inventories of resources that do not get used in a timely manner.
♦ Resources are difficult to access and requisition.
♦ The cost of acquiring resources fluctuates greatly between areas of the company or geographic regions.
♦ There is a high degree of conflict over resources between departments.
♦ There are underused, redundant resources in departments that are in close proximity to each other.

Although physical resource management has its primary uses in industry and government, it also relates to a variety of other institutions. Managing in the world of art and music also can call on some sort of resource allocation management. Setting up and conducting art exhibits and concerts require the application of considerable resources. For example, as some motion pictures now demand many millions of dollars to produce and exhibit, some sort of systematic allocation of resources becomes a necessity. As basic science projects become applied science ventures, resource management requirements will challenge them.

When Not to Use Physical Resource Management

- Do not use physical resource management until you have used sound quantitative analytical techniques for comparing viable alternatives (that is, cost-effectiveness analysis).
- Do not use without first taking into account the financial aspects of the life of the resources being applied.
- Do not use unless the review of the resource allocation plan occurs at a high enough management level.
- Resource managers sometimes do not direct integrated operations, but a series of separate, unconnected steps.
- Organizations often experience difficulty in developing useful objectives and valid comparative measures of performance.
- Conflict between an organization's departments often generates resistance to create solutions for resource sharing.
- Firms plagued with ineffective decision-making processes, including flawed common sense, inadequate cost-effectiveness techniques, and other inappropriate quantitative analysis are rarely able to manage their physical resources.

Examples

- *Department of Defense Problem:* In the 1950s, the U.S. Department of Defense suffered from gross cost overruns and late deliveries in procuring its weapons systems because the department did not use vigorous logic in managing its resources.
  - *Intervention:* In the early 1960s, Secretary of Defense Robert S. McNamara installed his seminal planning, programming, and budgeting (PPB) system, designed to allow him to exercise greater control in managing the enormous resources used by his department. PPB provided a more rational decision-making approach and eventually proved revolutionary for resource managers in both government and private firms throughout the United States.

- *Jumping Java Problem:* Jumping Java had been a very successful chain of retail coffee shops until about two years ago. Recently loyal customers have begun frequenting local mom-and-pop coffee shops that were springing up in most U.S. cities and towns. Jumping Java's executives began to worry that they could not compete with the cozy, friendly feeling of the local establishment.
  - *Intervention:* Jumping Java's CEO—"Crazy Joe," as he was known in Jumping Java's logistics department—had an idea. He randomly chose 10 stores around the country and had them completely renovated. Rather than going to the company's normal decor vendors, he flew to each city and frequented yard sales, art shows, and in a few cases the local Salvation Army thrift store. He only bought things that were exceptionally

comfortable and that he would want in his own house. He also offered to hang local artists' pictures on the wall and to sell their works right there in the coffee shop. He invited local musicians to a weekly open-mike night at which they would compete for a one-month supply of free Jumping Java coffee. Joe went to the used bookstore in each town and purchased all of the great works of literature he could find and put them on bookshelves and end tables around the coffee shop. In five of the stores (all in cooler climates) he installed fireplaces in one corner and big armchairs in front of them. Joe talked with a lot of the neighbors who lived around these coffee shops and tried to find a cause that they might rally behind. He then set up a charity fund that would funnel 3 percent of all profits from each location to that local charity. Finally, Joe contracted with one coffee bean vendor to provide all of the beans for these 10 stores. As the company had grown, it had begun to rely on a wider and wider network of bean providers, which made the quality inconsistent from store to store. Within nine months of the stores' reopening, sales had surpassed even the most optimistic projections. The company has now renovated 60 percent of its stores using this same model.

Design Guidelines

The following guidelines offer an effective approach to solving resource allocation problems:

- Identify the problems associated with managing resources.
- Set goals and objectives relating to the use of resources.
- Devise a strategy or means for achieving these goals.
- Determine priorities to guide you in allocating material and financial resources; these often appear in the form of programs.
- Determine a set of criteria by which to assess the progress toward achieving goals.
- Designate the individuals or organizations responsible for developing resource policies and supporting programs and projects.

Create a detailed implementation plan that shows managers how to access and use specific resources.

Implementation Guidelines

The degree of impact that physical resource management has on an organization's performance depends on the quantity, the quality, the types, the importance, and the financial implications of resources. Managers should document and distribute this information about resources so that decision makers and other interested persons can continue to make informed choices.

Managers should pay close attention to whether allocated resources achieve their objectives. They also should identify the mistakes and flaws in instances where they fail to do so. There should be period reviews to determine if resources meet the goals set for them. Managers should perform these reviews before flaws in allocation cause serious problems.

REFERENCES AND RESOURCES

Publications

Drucker, Peter. (1985). *Innovation and Entrepreneurship: Practice and Principles.* New York: Harper & Row.

Peters, Thomas J., and Robert H Waterman, Jr. (1981). *In Search of Excellence: Lessons From America's Best-Run Companies.* New York: Time Warner.

CHAPTER 4

TELL ME WHO DOES WHAT AND WHEN: IMPROVING STRUCTURE AND PROCESS

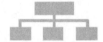

17. Conflict Management
     by Sivasailam Thiagarajan

18. Culture Reshaping
     by Tom Devane

19. Process Leadership
     by Andrew Kimball

20. Performance Appraisal
     *by Stewart Hickman
     and Jacqueline B. Visnius*

21. Staffing
     by Margo Prator

22. Process Redesign
     by Tom Devane

23. Job Interviews
     *by Matthew S. Richter
     and Andrew Kimball*

*"The management of a balance of power is a permanent undertaking,
not an exertion that has a foreseeable end."*
—Henry Alfred Kissinger, White House Years [1979]

STRUCTURE AND PROCESS

	Individual	Group	Cheap	Expensive	Together	Spread Out	Need it Fast	Have Time
Individual			Performance Appraisal Job Interviews	Staffing		Performance Appraisal Staffing Job Interviews	Performance Appraisal Job Interviews	Staffing
Group			Conflict Management Process Leadership Process Redesign	Culture Reshaping	Process Leadership	Conflict Management Culture Reshaping Process Redesign	Conflict Management Process Leadership	Culture Reshaping Process Redesign
Cheap	Performance Appraisal Staffing	Conflict Management Process Leadership Process Redesign Job Interviews			Process Leadership	Conflict Management Performance Appraisal Process Redesign Job Interviews	Conflict Management Process Leadership Performance Appraisal Job Interviews	Process Redesign
Expensive	Staffing	Culture Reshaping				Culture Reshaping Staffing		Culture Reshaping Staffing
Together								
Spread Out	Performance Appraisal Staffing	Conflict Management Culture Reshaping Process Leadership Process Redesign Job Interviews	Conflict Management Process Leadership Performance Appraisal Process Redesign Job Interviews	Culture Reshaping Staffing	Process Leadership		Conflict Management Process Leadership Performance Appraisal Job Interviews	Culture Reshaping Staffing Process Redesign
Need it Fast	Performance Appraisal	Conflict Management Process Leadership Job Interviews	Conflict Management Process Leadership Performance Appraisal Job Interviews	Culture Reshaping Staffing		Conflict Management Performance Appraisal Job Interviews		
Have Time	Staffing	Culture Reshaping Process Redesign	Process Redesign	Culture Reshaping Staffing		Culture Reshaping Staffing Process Redesign		

17

CONFLICT MANAGEMENT

Sivasailam Thiagarajan

WHAT IS CONFLICT MANAGEMENT?

A conflict is a clash between two parties (individuals or groups) with opposing perceptions, opinions, goals, ideas, needs, values, or styles. Conflicts are usually accompanied by feelings of hostility and other negative emotions. Conflict management is a process that enables the conflicting parties to achieve a collaborative win-win outcome. This intervention involves identifying incompatible elements and arriving at a decision that satisfies both sets of needs through dialogue and negotiation.

RELATED INTERVENTIONS

- ◆ Culture change is designed to bring about fundamental changes in an organization by involving large numbers of people at different levels. Most culture change efforts produce conflicts among people's perceptions, opinions, mental models, needs, and goals. Successful culture change involves identifying and managing these conflicts.
- ◆ Meetings and dialogues facilitate shared thinking, reflecting, problem solving, and decision making. In one sense, a dialogue is the opposite of conflict. Effective conflict management incorporates a dialogue between two apparently opposing parties.
- ◆ Team building increases the effectiveness of an intact team whose members regularly work together to achieve a common goal. The process of team building typically involves identifying multiple conflicts among members and between the needs of the team and the needs of its members. Effective team building involves establishing and implementing ground rules for managing conflicts.
- ◆ Feedback systems (such as performance appraisals) provide timely and accurate information about the performance of an individual, team, or organization. Often, there are differences in perceptions and opinions about a performance and its impact. Conflict management procedures provide effective tools for discussing feedback elements.

♦ Violence prevention may keep unresolved conflicts from eventually turning into workplace violence. For additional suggestions on the prevention of violence, refer to the violence prevention intervention in chapter 6.

WHEN TO USE CONFLICT MANAGEMENT

Conflict management is most effective:

♦ when there is increasing occurrence of unhealthy reactions to conflicts (such as lack of accountability, sabotage, and workplace violence)

♦ when there is an increase in costs associated with unresolved conflict (such as legal costs, professional arbitration costs, fines and penalties, lost time, and lost opportunities)

♦ when teamwork suffers due to reduced trust, lack of participation, increased tension, and disregard for diverse perspectives

♦ when decision-making efforts are delayed due to unresolved conflicts among people

♦ when communication problems increase.

This intervention may also be useful in dealing with the following:

♦ *Mergers and acquisitions:* Major organizational changes increase stress levels among employees and also increase the frequency and intensity of conflicts. Training and support for conflict management efforts can provide an effective proactive measure to reduce the negative impact of these conflicts.

♦ *Cultural diversity:* As organizations become more global, cross-cultural conflicts increase. Instead of conducting training workshops focused on specific national groups, such as "How to Do Business With the Japanese," we can provide more generalizable principles by equipping people with conflict-management skills. These workshops can focus on basic cultural values and the management of cross-cultural conflicts.

♦ *Resource management:* Budgeting and personnel allocation are examples of areas where conflicts arise due to the disparity between supply and demand. Conflict-management models provide effective tools for use during resource-management negotiations.

WHEN NOT TO USE CONFLICT MANAGEMENT

♦ Do not use conflict management when you are not prepared to open a Pandora's box. An essential outcome of a conflict-management program is to reexamine past unresolved conflicts that have been ignored, denied, suppressed, or buried. Rehashing these conflicts requires time and emotional energy.

♦ Do not use conflict management if you are not prepared with conflict-containment strategies for maintaining peace in the workplace.

The focus on managing conflict may detract us from paying attention to the earlier and essential procedures for preventing conflicts in the first place. Also, not all conflicts can be managed (on a short-term basis) because of genuine differences in values and preferences.

♦ Do not use conflict management if you cannot handle a redistribution of power. A critical element of conflict management is respect for everyone's perspective. An organization with a culture of top-down management may not be ready for this drastic shift. Without an appropriate increase in empowerment and accountability, people with higher status (and greater insecurity) are likely to sabotage conflict-management initiatives.

EXAMPLES

♦ *Clashing Cultures Problem:* A software engineering company headquartered in California spread its manufacturing, consulting, and marketing operations around different parts of Europe and Asia. After an initial honeymoon period and successful establishment of the technical infrastructure, the number of interpersonal conflicts in overseas facilities increased. Performance analysis indicated that these conflicts were frequently between expatriate managers and local employees. Initially dismissed as examples of the inevitable labor-management disputes, these conflicts were further probed by a cultural anthropologist. Her analysis suggested that the root causes lay among clashing cultural values.

— *Intervention:* A special conflict-management procedure was established. After presenting a systematic model for jointly identifying and analyzing conflicts, employees at all levels were trained to identify hidden clashes among cultural values in such areas as individualism and collectivism, structure and freedom, status and democracy, patriotism and globalism, long-term and short-term results, and gender roles and equality. Each facility also established a cross-cultural team of ombudsmen to mediate in major conflicts. This program resulted in an increase in job satisfaction scores and decrease in the number of unresolved conflicts.

♦ *Beyond Symptom Management Problem:* When a large insurance company announced a policy to prevent sexual harassment, the number of reported cases actually increased. Performance analysis suggested that the root cause was that there were different interpretations of the policy. Attempts to clarify the policy by adding more guidelines and imposing a zero-tolerance clause reduced sexual-harassment complaints but increased the cross-gender conflicts of other types.

— *Intervention:* The company implemented a conflict-management program with special emphasis on gender differences in values, preferences, and communication styles. A series of dialogues among men and women in different departments across different levels produced several practical guidelines. Eventually, the sexual harassment policy was incorporated into a broader set of guidelines for managing clashes that arise from gender differences. The dialogues are still in progress, now exploring conflicts that arise from differences in sexual orientation.

DESIGN GUIDELINES

Conflicts involve both content ("I need more money") and relationship goals ("I want you to trust me"). Content goals pertain to the substance of the conflict: what the people want when the conflict is resolved. Relationship goals pertain to the interdependence between the two people: how they want to interact with each other in the future. There are five types of conflict management, each of which differs from the others on the basis of the emphasis placed on these two types of goals. Each type has its own advantages and disadvantages:

- *Avoidance* places low emphasis on both content and relationship goals. It is characterized by a sense of powerlessness, denial of conflict, and indifference to the outcome. While this strategy enables you to save time with unimportant issues, it may inflame the conflict to a higher level.

- *Compromise* places moderate emphasis on both content and relationship goals. It is characterized by a search for trade-offs and for splitting the difference. While this strategy enables you to achieve some of your goals, it requires you (and the other person) to give up on other goals.

- *Accommodation* places low emphasis on content goals and high emphasis on relationship goals. It is characterized by giving in and smoothing over differences. While this strategy enables you to maintain the relationship, it requires you to sacrifice your content goal.

- *Competition* places a high emphasis on content goals and a low emphasis on relationship goals. It is characterized by a win-lose orientation and aggressive behavior. While this strategy enables you to achieve short-term content goals, it damages your relationship with the other person.

- *Collaboration* places a high emphasis on both content and relationship goals. It is characterized by creative problem solving and long-term partnership. While this strategy enables you (and the other person) to achieve mutual goals, it requires a lot of time and effort.

Follow these tips as you design the intervention:

- Don't ignore emotions. Emotion is a key element in conflict. Although we have been admonished to leave our feelings out of our professional conversations, unexpressed feelings can abruptly disrupt the discussion. Train and encourage conflicting parties to identify negative feelings (such as anger and powerlessness), share them with each other, and acknowledge them.

♦ Don't ignore logic. If emotion is a key element in conflict, then logic is a key element in effective conflict management. A conflict is successfully resolved only when it appears to be fair and equitable in both parties' logic. The classic "you-cut-I-choose" strategy and other logical approaches can be used to resolve conflicts. It is important, however, to remember that one person's logic could be perceived as another person's subjective judgment.

♦ Use a systematic approach. A step-by-step approach calms people down and ensures that critical elements are not ignored in the resolution process. We recommend the following six steps for effective conflict management:
   — calming ourselves
   — analyzing the conflict
   — establishing mutual goals
   — brainstorming options
   — selecting and implementing the best options
   — reflecting and learning from the process.

♦ Use an intuitive approach. Effective conflict management requires breakthrough ideas that satisfy apparently incompatible perceptions and needs of the two conflicting partners. The brainstorming step in the systematic conflict-management process requires you to deviate from traditional modes of thinking and to come up with creative approaches for achieving a win-win solution.

IMPLEMENTATION GUIDELINES

♦ Flaunt the benefits. Conflict management becomes second nature when individuals, teams, and organizations realize the costs of unresolved conflict and the benefits of effective conflict management. Point out that conflict management accelerates decision making, facilitates teamwork, fosters communication, reduces tension, and results in continuous learning. Also emphasize that conflict management helps employees to share a common vision and to utilize diversity among themselves.

♦ Create a culture of collaboration. Healthy management of conflicts requires a change in the traditional organizational paradigm. Encourage employees to move away from thinking of conflict as negative disruptions to thinking of it as positive opportunities; from weakening relationships to strengthening relationships; from preventing growth to facilitating growth; from toughness to vulnerability; from finding fault to seeking the truth; from scarcity to abundance; and from competition to collaboration.

♦ Provide third parties to mediate conflicts. Even a conflict between two individuals affects the entire organization. It is easier for people to be objective and neutral with other people's conflicts than with their own. So encourage the organization to train and support peer mediators who can provide help in observing, refereeing, healing, equalizing, and managing conflicts.

♦ Reflect and learn. The best way to learn conflict-management skills is to do it on the job. Train, encourage, and debrief people after they have successfully resolved a conflict to reflect on their interaction, come up with insights, and share them with each other.

REFERENCES AND RESOURCES

Publication

Stone, Douglas, Bruce Patton, and Sheila Heen. (1999). *Difficult Conversations: How to Discuss What Matters Most.* New York: Viking. Filled with everyday examples, this book presents a step-by-step approach for understanding the underlying structure of the conflict, identifying the role of emotions, and discovering the impact of conflicts on self-image.

18

CULTURE RESHAPING

Tom Devane

WHAT IS CULTURE RESHAPING?

Culture reshaping is an intervention designed to bring about changes in an organization's shared, usually tacit, assumptions. By altering these assumptions, we can alter the way that people think, behave, interact, and subsequently perform in an organization. Because these assumptions are often learned, our objective in a culture reshaping initiative is to have people unlearn them. Culture reshaping initiatives typically have these seven characteristics:

- ◆ They involve large numbers of people at different levels for design and implementation of the reshaping effort.
- ◆ They clearly articulate the organization's vision. Sometimes senior management develops the vision, other times organization members co-develop it.
- ◆ They use participative planning methods to broaden understanding of the vision and energize people around it.
- ◆ They redefine working relationships among organization members. Often this is accomplished by changing the formal organizational structure.
- ◆ They incorporate whole-systems thinking so changes in one part of the organization are not inconsistent with actions and directions in another part.
- ◆ They radically increase the dissemination of critical information—downwards, laterally, and upwards.
- ◆ They establish processes and mindsets for continuous renewal and improvement.

RELATED INTERVENTIONS

A variety of interventions can be used to reshape culture. Many well-known single events address one or two of the necessary criteria, as the following example shows. (Italicized words correspond to the preceding criteria.) For example, search conferences and future search conferences focus on *participatory visioning* and action plans. Other interventions, such as participative design workshops, focus on changing organizational *structure* and *working relationships*. Dialogue and appreciative inquiry use learning conversations to change existing *mindsets* and day-to-day work practices. And training games can help disseminate critical information and build mindsets for *continuous improvement*.

WHEN TO USE CULTURE RESHAPING

Use this as a primary intervention if the organization requires new ways of thinking about:

- how the organization interrelates with the outside world
- how organizational members relate to, and interact with, each other.

Culture reshaping initiatives are often used when leaders, either formal or informal, have determined that serious, major changes are needed in the day-to-day thinking and actions of members of the organization. Examples include

- The organization needs to increase innovation.
- People should take more personal initiative for improvement.
- The organization should move from a "fire fighting culture" to one of quality and continual improvement.
- Management styles and structures need to make a transition from a command-and-control environment to one in which people are intrinsically motivated and informed to take the best actions for the organization.

A good litmus test question for determining if culture reshaping is necessary is, Do people need to change their choice principles when facing organizational options? Culture deals at the level of deep-rooted assumptions and forms the foundation for the choices people make at work. For example, an organization's culture can help answer an employee's dilemma of whether or not to ship a product to meet the monthly shipping schedule even if the product is defective.

Many practical-minded managers ask about cost-benefit analyses. Because culture operates at such a deep level, it is often difficult to directly link costs and benefits. For example, it is difficult to answer these questions: What financial returns have we gained from abandoning our command-and-control style of management? and What is the ROI of discarding our fire fighting mindsets and practices?

WHEN NOT TO USE CULTURE RESHAPING

Do not use culture reshaping initiatives unless you have a well-thought-out plan on what you want to accomplish, the methods you will use to get you there, and the results you expect.

- Do not try to change culture one person at a time. Research has shown it is easier to change mindsets and behaviors of groups than individuals (groups can provide learning and practice support, peer coaching, peer pressures, and a variety of other forces that help initiate and sustain the culture reshaping).

♦ Do not cancel the initiative if results are not immediate. It takes time to change a culture.

♦ Be careful about announcing a culture reshaping program. Instead, focus on demonstrating, practicing, and reinforcing targeted new behaviors and thinking styles.

EXAMPLES

♦ *HiTechCo Problem:* HiTechCo's market share was plummeting. This multibillion dollar company had historically used a command-and-control management style and was inwardly focused. Management realized it needed a new product line and a new way of working together that would lead to faster decisions. Since management could not turn the entire company around overnight, it opted to create a new division with a new culture.

— *Intervention:* The company conducted a three-day off-site strategic planning session with all 35 employees of the spin-off division. The results: six vision points to pursue, an organization that understood and was committed to the new strategy, learning about others in the group, and a cultural shift toward participation and appreciation of diverse viewpoints that had not existed before.

Once strategic direction had been set, the company organized itself to execute the strategy. All members participated in a one and one-half day workshop and designed the following:

- an organization with six self-managing teams and two centers of excellence (each with goals to support strategy)
- a plan for rapidly integrating new members consistent with aggressive growth plans
- interdependent goals among teams, external customers, and suppliers
- a plan to implement tools and mindsets of total quality within six months.

The new division was able to reach profitability in only one quarter, and employees of the parent company began clamoring to work for the new division. Turnover in this division remained constant at about 5 percent per year, compared with a nearly 30 percent turnover rate in the parent company.

DESIGN GUIDELINES

♦ Planning interventions help reshape an organization's culture by involving more people, increasing the diversity mix, and energizing people to implement.

- Structuring interventions alter reporting relationships on an organization chart and change the way people collaborate, problem solve, and resolve conflict.
- Skill-building interventions provide members with an arsenal of new actions, tools, and thought processes.
- Learning conversations provide opportunities to think together and mutually explore deep-seated beliefs and alternative ways of acting.
- Microworlds are computerized simulations in which members experience the results of their choices in a safe practice environment while learning about new culture mindsets and behaviors.

Follow these tips as you design the intervention:

- Be clear in your mind what you want to change to, what you want to change from, and what you are prepared to do to bridge the gap. Senior management may say it wants to increase innovation, for example, but is it willing to free an entrepreneurial group from everyday pressures? Or create an environment that does not stigmatize failure?
- Tie your culture reshaping initiative into other existing projects so it is less confusing for the workforce and viewed as a part of an ongoing business imperative, not just a one-time touchy-feely exercise.
- Keep in mind your culture pool has inflows and outflows that help bolster—or dilute—the strength of an organization's culture. When hiring, screen for culture fit as well as technical skills. Consider a practice many high-tech firms adopted: an annual "pruning" process that removes individuals who do not fit the desired culture. Pruning targets typically constitute 2 percent to 4 percent of the workforce. While this practice is controversial, proponents believe their organizations are quicker to respond to market forces and their people are more motivated.
- Overcommunicate. Use a variety of channels like town hall meetings, joint planning sessions, one-on-ones, skill-building sessions, and learning conversations.

IMPLEMENTATION GUIDELINES

- Have a plan to implement the design, but do not be afraid to depart from it. Much in a culture reshaping effort is opportunistic rather than deterministic.
- Have senior and middle managers model the desired mindsets and behaviors. If the organization is trying to create a culture that uses data to make decisions, have managers establish metrics for themselves and hold themselves publicly accountable for results.
- Reward new ways of thinking and behaving. If the organization is striving for out-of-the-box thinking, reward innovative ideas. If it

is trying to emphasize teams, reward teams instead of just individuals. Remember, you probably have numerous compensation and reward structures that encourage old mindsets and behaviors.

♦ Take time to reflect on what is happening. Periodically assemble groups and ask, "How's it going? Knowing what we know now, is there anything we should have done differently? What happened that we thought would happen? What happened unexpectedly and why? How should we move forward?" Reflection time can be some of your best spent hours.

REFERENCES AND RESOURCES

Publications

Holman, P., and T. Devane (Eds). (1999). *The Change Handbook: Group Methods for Shaping the Future*. San Francisco: Berrett-Koehler. This book describes 18 proven group methods for changing mindsets and behaviors.

Leadership and Organization Development Journal. This UK-based journal and its international editors offer practical advice on change. Phone: 44 (0)1274.777700.

Schein, Edgar. (1997). *Organizational Culture and Leadership*. San Francisco: Jossey-Bass. This book provides a solid grounding in the elements of an organization's culture/.

Association

Organization Development Network. Conducts a large annual conference spanning several days with multiple tracks. There are numerous local U.S. chapters. Phone: 973.763.7337.

19

PROCESS LEADERSHIP

Andrew Kimball

WHAT IS PROCESS LEADERSHIP

Twelve people in a conference room argue over the best way to reduce time to market. They voice their views vigorously. Two camps seem to be squaring off against each other. Kim, a new hire invited at the last minute, listens closely to each side, until she finally steps in: "Let me see if I understand your view, George." Kim proceeds to summarize the ideas and feelings of the first camp. "Is that correct?" George looks at his group, nods. "Good. Now let me see if I understand Nguyen's view." Kim summarizes the opposite camp's ideas and feelings, emphasizing where it intersects with the first camp's view. "Is that correct?" Nguyen nods.

"So it sounds like the primary difference between your two views is that George thinks we should find a way to reduce design cycle time and Nguyen thinks we should focus on increasing design capacity. Is that an accurate summary of the two positions?"

The two camps nod their heads in concert. "So perhaps we should reframe the problem," suggests Kim. "Perhaps we should focus on how to increase design capacity in a way that will reduce design cycle time? Any ideas?"

Kim is practicing *process leadership*. Any interaction, whether it is a chance encounter over the water cooler, a sales call, or a creative problem-solving meeting, requires two elements to succeed:

- ◆ *content:* the ideas or critical information offered to achieve the objective
- ◆ *process:* how the meeting is structured and facilitated to achieve the objective.

Most meetings do not fail because of the lack of ideas. Most meetings fail because of the lack of effective meeting process.

Process leadership is an intervention used to solve this problem. It is a set of practices and strategies for maximizing the probability that an interaction or a meeting (we will call these simply "meetings" hereafter) will reach a successful conclusion. A process leader may be someone in a predefined role, such as a formal facilitator or someone who acts spontaneously, like Kim, because the person realizes that the meeting needs to be more effective.

Successful process leadership has the following features:

♦ *process awareness:* the ability to identify how successful meeting process looks, sounds, and feels to oneself and others
♦ *positive intention:* the profound desire to move an interaction forward to achieve a defined result
♦ *process skill:* the consistent and efficient use of core communication skills and strategies to achieve the positive intention.

RELATED INTERVENTIONS

Process leadership is similar to facilitation and meeting management. In most group interactions, a neutral party may play the role of facilitator or meeting manager. Typically, this neutral party's job is to support the person who called the meeting. Like the process leader, the facilitator's role is to optimize the meeting process. The facilitator does not determine the meeting objective, offer feedback, suggest his or her own ideas, influence the selection of ideas, or make any decisions.

A neutral facilitator may employ many of the strategies and practices of process leadership. Anyone in the meeting, however, neutral or not, may employ the practices and strategies of process leadership to lead the meeting to a successful conclusion. The process leader may be the meeting owner or a disinterested participant in the interaction.

By employing process leadership skills, the person can influence any group to define and achieve the goals of the meeting in a way that is clear and compelling for all parties.

WHEN TO USE PROCESS LEADERSHIP

You should use process leadership anytime it is important for a meeting to progress efficiently or more rapidly toward a successful outcome. For example, you might use process leadership when you:

♦ are leading a meeting in which there is no designated process facilitator
♦ are participating in a meeting in which you experience a lack of clarity regarding the goals, roles and responsibilities, meeting process, participant communication, decision-making process, agreements, or next steps
♦ think a meeting's success is in jeopardy due to participant conflict or poor communication skills
♦ are a participant in a meeting or an interaction with a topic in which you have little content expertise or experience.

Process leadership skills and strategies can be used in any interaction in which it is important that all parties move efficiently toward an objective. Such interactions might include sales calls, negotiation meetings, conflict resolution interactions, and crisis management discussions.

WHEN NOT TO USE PROCESS LEADERSHIP

Do not use process leadership if there is a designated process facilitator or a meeting manager. A designated facilitator will define and manage the process of a meeting. Your process leadership practices and strategies might be different than those the facilitator prefers and might diminish that person's credibility and effectiveness to the detriment of the meeting and the meeting owner.

EXAMPLE

◆ *Professional Services Partnership Problem:* A group of professional services partners met every Monday to discuss the state of the partnership. All of the partners were bright and quick to voice their opinions. Meetings tended to degrade quickly into loud, energetic parallel monologues with little understanding or resolution. Partners regularly left these meetings feeling angry, and frustrated. They universally accepted that the meeting was a waste of time.

— *Intervention:* A new partner joined the group. She had been trained in group-process facilitation. At the outset of the meeting, she asked for clarification of the meeting objectives, agenda, roles and responsibilities, and ground rules contract. At first the partners had to admit they had not done much thinking about these questions. They discussed her questions at length, and the meeting proceeded. During the course of the meeting, as opinions became energetic and critical, the new partner invited clarification and then summarized her understanding of both sides views. At the end of the meeting, several participants commented that it was the most successful Monday meeting they had ever attended.

DESIGN GUIDELINES

Process leadership is a powerful tool to use in the heat of discussion. For this reason, there may not be time to design the intervention beyond the implementation tips that follow. When there is time to prepare for a meeting in which you will be the process leader, you might be able to maximize the meeting success by asking yourself or the meeting owner the following questions:

◆ Why:
— are we meeting?
— is this problem important to solve?

◆ What:
— is the desired deliverable from our meeting today?
— is the meeting agenda?

— are the meeting ground rules?
  — time limits should we place on each segment?
  — hidden agendas might participants bring to the meeting?
  — is the problem we are trying to solve?
  — ideas have we tried or thought of trying to solve this problem?

- Who:
  — is the meeting owner?
  — are the key stakeholders who might be affected by the result of this meeting?
  — is the facilitator?
  — is the scribe?
  — is the timekeeper?
  — are the best participants to invite to the meeting as resources?
  — are the decision makers for each problem?
  — will likely implement any decisions from this meeting?

- Where:
  — is the best place to meet?

- When:
  — are we meeting?

- How should we:
  — frame the meeting?
  — introduce ourselves?
  — structure the meeting for optimal results (for example, in an information meeting structure, a creative problem-solving meeting structure, or a dialogue structure)?
  — frame the problem to be solved?
  — introduce roles and responsibilities?
  — make decisions?
  — communicate action items?

IMPLEMENTATION GUIDELINES

There are five different types of process leadership:

- *meeting framing:* to give participants the information they need to participate fully and successfully in the meeting
- *need clarification:* which clarifies where we are, where we wish to go, and what challenges we must solve to move from our current state to the desired state
- *solution development:* which involves two group thinking processes: divergence (the process of generating as many ideas as possible) and convergence (the process of determining which ideas are most likely to yield a solution or an action step)
- *decision-making clarification:* to specify who has the authority to make a binding decision and who should provide input into the decision

♦ *action planning facilitation:* to make clear agreements and action steps, including the initiator's communication, the respondent's communication, and the follow-up.

Tips for real-time use of process leadership might be organized as follows:

♦ *Framing the meeting:*
— Clarify roles and responsibilities.
— Clarify the intention of the meeting.
— Clarify the agenda and meeting process.
— Clarify the ground rules.
— Clarify who are the decision makers and who are the input-providers.

♦ *Defining the need:*
— Clarify the desired state (the vision and outcomes).
— Clarify challenges.
— Use "double-clicking" questions (such as How do you feel about that? and Can you be more specific?) to help meeting participants reveal deeper, more meaningful facts, needs, ideas, or feelings.
— In priority order, confirm understanding of the most critical elements of each party's feelings, vision, objectives, and challenges.
— Clarify and summarize considered solutions.

♦ *Developing solutions:*
— Facilitate the generation of ideas.
— Clarify the selection process to determine the best ideas.
— Refine ideas by reviewing each one's appealing aspects and challenges and then brainstorming.
— Clarify who the decision maker is and what the decision-making process is.
— Resolve objections by using double-clicking questions to clarify the need underlying the objection, followed by empathetic listening to confirm understanding of the need (such as, "When you say too expensive, can you be more specific?" "Let me make sure I understand what we need to figure out how to solve...").

REFERENCES AND RESOURCES

Publications

Edelman, Joel. (1994). *The Tao of Negotiation.* New York: Harper Business.
Carkhuff, Robert R. (1983). *The Art of Helping.* Amherst, MA: HRD Press.

Association

International Association of Facilitators, http://www.iaf-world.org.

20

PERFORMANCE APPRAISAL

Stewart Hickman and Jacqueline B. Visnius

WHAT IS PERFORMANCE APPRAISAL?

Performance appraisal is the system of identifying, describing, evaluating, and developing human performance in organizations. It involves looking at the individual employee's performance in the context of the organization's goals and objectives. Performance appraisals serve two purposes: They may be the basis for making human resource decisions, and they may be for employee development. The approach that an organization takes to its performance appraisal process depends on the purpose it serves within the organization.

The process of conducting performance appraisals is an integral part of most organizations, yet it is often the most maligned and disliked management process within the organization framework. If properly designed and implemented, performance appraisals can be valuable tools for employees, supervisors, and the organization.

RELATED INTERVENTIONS

Counseling, coaching, and mentoring are all part of an effective performance appraisal aimed at developing employees. Like performance appraisal, these interventions are focused on an individual's performance and future potential.

If designed to provide the basis for making human resource decisions, the performance appraisal process is most closely related to motivational interventions such as rewards and recognition, compensation and incentive systems, and overall motivation systems.

WHEN TO USE PERFORMANCE APPRAISALS

- ◆ *Human resource decisions:* The performance appraisal can be used as the basis for making personnel decisions. Decisions regarding raises, promotions, demotions, and firing are often based on the results or outcome of an individual's performance appraisal.

♦ *Employee development:* Typically, supervisors document employees' performance under headings such as strengths and weaknesses, developmental plans, and measurement against work goals and standards.

— The appraisal can provide valuable feedback to let an individual know how he or she is performing on the job.

— The process can also establish goals and objectives and provide a method of charting an individual's progress in meeting those goals.

— Performance appraisals also provide information with regard to an individual's need for further training, clearer objectives, or more feedback and encouragement.

— In the long term, performance appraisals can be used for planning an individual's career path.

Performance appraisals may also benefit an organization by:

♦ establishing congruence between organizational goals and individual performance
♦ increasing communication within an organization
♦ fostering a spirit of cooperation and teamwork
♦ increasing employee commitment, competence, and development.

WHEN NOT TO USE PERFORMANCE APPRAISALS

♦ Performance appraisals should not be implemented if the organization has not thoroughly researched and designed the process to be part of the overall organizational management plan. This helps guard against the many pitfalls that come into play when individual and organizational objectives, as they relate to performance appraisal, are in conflict. For example, individuals want to portray positive self-images and obtain rewards, whereas organizations want individuals to be open to negative feedback so they can improve their performance.

♦ Performance appraisals should not be the basis for salary, dismissal, or other negative decisions if the employee has not been appropriately selected, placed, and trained for the job.

♦ Performance appraisals will not be effective if the method, standards, and the like are not congruent with the particular appraisal objective. Many of the techniques used in performance appraisals (ranking methods, forced-choice rating, and so forth) do not achieve all of the objectives of performance appraisal.

EXAMPLES

♦ *Upstart Firm Problem:* Shawney has been managing a group of 10 project managers for a very small upstart firm for nearly two years. During that time, she has prided herself on her coaching and counseling abilities and feels that she has open, free-flowing communication with all of her employees. Lately, however, her workload has interfered with her ability to circulate, observe, and talk with her employees. She is concerned that certain staff members may be slacking off and that this is creating more work for the others. A few employees have also approached Shawney about salary increases and promotions. Because the firm is so young and small, Shawney has never had to worry about these issues before.

— *Intervention:* Shawney decided to implement a formal performance appraisal system. She realized that her employees needed to have career objectives that were in line with the goals of the company. Because her time was so limited, she decided to have the employees write a first draft of their own performance appraisal. She provided each of them with a list of the organization's and the department's goals and asked them to base their appraisal on these. She then reviewed all of these appraisals and chose certain items that needed to be consistent across all of the reviews. After updating the first drafts, she had all of her employees read and respond to the changes. Within two weeks, she had the appraisal forms done, and the employees had completely bought into the process. To begin with, everyone agreed that quarterly performance reviews were appropriate. The level of performance began to increase before the first performance review even occurred.

◆ *Sam's Performance Problem:* Kwanchai has been concerned about Sam's performance. They have spoken several times about his lack of motivation and inability to meet project deadlines.

— *Intervention:* During the performance review, Sam expressed surprise at not getting a rating of satisfactory. Kwanchai acknowledged Sam's confusion, and suggested that one way forward is to focus on the future. Together they identified the problems that they had previously discussed, determined where they were in agreement, and decided to establish some fresh goals for Sam. They agreed to meet formally in six months to share what they both hoped would be good news. Kwanchai hoped that the appraisal, which they both felt was very productive, would be an effective tool for turning around Sam's attitude and performance.

◆ *Salespeople Problem:* Yvette supervised a group of six salespeople for a small investment banking firm. A new sales territory, one that could prove to be very lucrative, just opened up. Yvette is having a difficult time deciding which of her employees should get it.

— *Intervention:* At first, Yvette's clear choice was George. He was the most outgoing and flamboyant of her employees. He was also the most attractive. Lynette was modest, hardworking, and had good sales. Ahmed, another seasoned salesperson, was very serious, stoic, and rather humorless. Yvette began to review the journals that she kept on her employees and relied on at performance review time. While personalities, looks, and likability had a strong effect on Yvette's thinking, she based her final decision on the facts alone. Her documentation and performance appraisal forms helped her make a fair and informed decision on who should get the new territory. In the final analysis, Yvette determined that Ahmed deserved the territory most. When she announced this to the department, she was careful to mention the specific reasons why she had chosen Ahmed. While a few of the other salespeople were a bit disappointed, they all agreed that Ahmed was an excellent choice for this new territory.

♦ *Engineering Research Department Problem:* Kazuo was asked to head a new project group for the engineering research department. This new job would involve a lot of travel and would be Kazuo's first management job. He was quite excited about the prospect. After two months, Kazuo was tired and quite frustrated. Before he had taken the new management job, he had been promised training as well as two new staff members. He had reminded his boss of his training and resource needs to no avail.

— *Intervention:* Kazuo happened to be at the home office during the semiannual performance appraisals. He was stunned to learn that he was receiving an unsatisfactory job rating. In the past, Kazuo had never received anything less than above average. Kazuo was angry and let his supervisor know that the only reason he got a low rating was because the company did not come through for him with training and resources. In this case, the performance appraisal was a poor substitute for an overall lack of organizational support.

DESIGN GUIDELINES

Various types of performance appraisals are possible, including 360 feedback reviews, peer reviews, management by objectives, and assessment centers. Once an organization determines the overall objectives for a performance appraisal system, it can begin to take the steps to develop the system.

The process of appraising an employee's performance begins with establishing specific performance goals. These goals must be achievable and measurable. Performance goals can be written to achieve four general outcomes:

♦ improving an aspect of the person's work that is not meeting expectations
♦ maintaining current levels of performance

- enhancing some aspect of the work the person is doing but needs to improve
- developing additional skills.

Next, a set of measurable standards, detailing how the job must be done or when a task is performed in an acceptable manner, is critical to a performance appraisal system. Performance standards are as follows:

- *Job based (not person based):* It is important to remember that performance standards are entirely different from the specific goals and objectives that are established for the individual.
- *Achievable:* The individual must be reasonably able to meet the standard with the skills he or she brings to the job.
- *Understood:* Just as the supervisor should have a clear understanding of the performance standards, the employee must have an understanding of, and if possible agreement on, the standards to be measured.
- *Time oriented:* Each of the standards must be specific in terms of what needs to be accomplished during a certain period of time.
- *Clearly written:* A copy of the standards should be in the hands of both the supervisor and the employee.
- *Subject to change:* Organizations change, and so do the performance needs. Performance appraisals evolve along with the organization and should be reviewed periodically. Standards should not be changed solely because an employee is not meeting them.

One of the first steps in the development of performance standards is a job analysis. This is accomplished through a number of methods, such as task analysis to determine the component tasks of a job; critical incidents that describe behavior of job holders that typify satisfactory and unsatisfactory performance of a task or job; and job elements, which outline employee characteristics required to perform a job. Regardless of the type of job analysis selected, the methods must be systematic and measured.

Another important step in establishing performance criteria is the selection of an appropriate system for measuring performance. Systems may be objective or subjective:

- Objective measures look at an employee without reference to another. Criteria may be, for example, units of work output and sales revenue targets. These types of performance measures are often quantifiable and always measurable. This results-oriented approach is often credited with helping to eliminate rater bias or opinion.
- Subjective systems largely involve human judgment. These relative rating systems compare one employee with another in the same job category or department. It is important to note that subjective measures of performance are often much more complicated and often have different meanings for different people. Absolute rating

systems, however, do not compare one employee with another. Examples of absolute rating systems include behavioral checklists, forced-choice system, and critical incident reports.

IMPLEMENTATION GUIDELINES

◆ Train supervisors in effective techniques for conducting effective performance appraisals.

◆ Communicate the standards and rating systems to the employees so it is clear on what basis they will be evaluated and how the results of the appraisal will be used.

◆ Obtain legal advice and follow federal regulations prior to implementing any formal appraisal process.

◆ Periodically review performance against the established standards.

◆ Keep forms simple.

◆ Use other raters (peers or customers, for instance) who are familiar with the employees' performance to increase the number of inputs to the performance appraisal system.

REFERENCES AND RESOURCES

Publications

Berke, George B. (May 1990). "How to Conduct a Performance Appraisal." *Info-line,* Issue No. 9005. Alexandria, VA: ASTD.

HR Magazine. Publication of the Society for Human Resource Management.

Sachs, Randi T. (1992). *Productive Performance Appraisals.* New York: AMA-COM.

Smither, James W. (Ed.). (1998). *Performance Appraisal: State of the Art in Practice.* San Francisco: Jossey-Bass.

21

STAFFING

Margo Prator

WHAT IS STAFFING?

Staffing is the process by which individuals are hired into, or exchange, positions within a company. The process comprises the following steps:

- *planning:* process in which the recruiter meets with the hiring manager to discuss what skills, knowledge, and abilities are required for the job
- *sourcing:* front-end process in which candidates are searched for
- *screening:* process in which an individual's skills are measured against position requirements and company culture
- *interviewing:* process in which the candidate meets members of the team who have the ultimate, hiring decision or have cross-functional relationships, or both
- *selection:* process by which final candidate is selected
- *offer:* a verbal or written process, or both, whereby the company gives an offer of employment
- *acceptance or decline:* process in which candidate accepts or declines offer. If offer is declined, revert back to sourcing process
- *new hire assimilation:* process after a candidate's acceptance that involves first-day readiness and assimilation
- *performance and retention:* if done correctly, retention of employees is a good measurement of successful staffing.

The staffing process ensures that a company continues to replenish the skills necessary to begin new projects and maintain competitiveness within their respective industries.

RELATED INTERVENTIONS

Other names for staffing include *recruiting, hiring, headhunting, contingency search,* and *retained search.* Interviewing is also an important part of staffing that is often seen as a separate intervention.

Often the foregoing process and methods for staffing are outsourced to agencies that specialize in those practices.

WHEN TO USE STAFFING

Staffing is used during times of company growth or when the organization experiences employee turnover. Knowing when it is time to hire more employees can be more complex than it at first appears. These are some key elements you should look for before agreeing that staffing is the appropriate intervention:

- Document that the amount of work has increased within that department and that this increase warrants addition of another position. Managers often add positions simply because they are falling behind schedule. Make sure a detailed performance-and-cause analysis has been performed that validates the need for additional personnel.

- If the request is prompted by the departure of an employee, verify that that person's position is still well defined and relevant. When a position becomes vacant, that is a great time to reexamine the distribution of work in it. Perhaps redefining this position and filling it with a person who has a different skill set than the person who vacated the position makes more sense than just filling the position as it is currently structured.

- Also, determine the actual reasons why this position was vacated. It is important to have some type of exit interview before a person leaves. You should also talk with the former employee's manager and a few of the employee's peers to uncover the true reasons for the departure. You need to make sure that the structure and the environment surrounding this job are not preventing anyone from succeeding at the job. Again, it is best if all of this information has already been obtained for you during a performance-and-cause analysis. However, the need for staffing is often independent of HPI projects, and so you must do your own assessment of why this need exists.

Another indicator that tells you whether staffing is appropriate is how well the manager who made the request for staffing has articulated what he or she is looking for. All of this information should be incorporated into a hiring plan that you help the manager develop. This hiring plan must include the department's and the company's objectives. It should also include the following components:

- *External sourcing plan:* Simply posting a job in the newspaper or contacting a recruiting firm does not constitute a valid sourcing plan in most staffing situations. You must carefully consider where and how to find particular skill sets and how well these skill sets meet the hiring goals. Sources for external candidates may include online advertising, job fairs, open houses, and professional networks.

♦ *Internal sourcing plan:* A company's existing employees are often the best pool of resources for finding qualified candidates. Hiring people from within the organization is a less risky venture, and it helps to build a corporate image that values promotion and advancement within the company. Employee referral programs are another great resource for staffing initiatives. These can either be formal or informal programs. Sometimes just asking people who hold a similar position to the one you are trying to fill if they know anyone who is looking for this type of job is a great method of finding candidates. Remember that many people in the organization may belong to professional associations or other types of networks for people in their line of work. You can also use more formal referral programs that pay bonuses to employees who refer qualified candidates. This may include companywide employee referral programs or just departmentwide incentives. The only drawback to these types of programs is that you are never sure if the referral is because the employee believes this person is qualified to hold this job or because the employee wants to collect the referral bonus.

♦ *Incentive plan:* How are you going to attract the talent you want? As described in the compensation section of this book in chapter 2, you need to make sure that the package of salary and benefits is competitive in the marketplace. Never forget that the company's reputation is also part of the perceived value of working for a particular organization. Candidates will often accept a little less compensation to work for an organization that they perceive to be progressive and humane.

WHEN NOT TO USE STAFFING AND RECRUITING

If the company does not have a hiring plan and does not see its business growing, hiring will just cause additional problems. You need to see the future in order to staff appropriately.

Companies may continue to staff so that they appear to be doing well. Not hiring (that is, a hiring freeze) is a red flag to employees and often causes turnover and morale issues.

Companies that hire as a reaction to an influx of money or projects often find themselves having to consider extreme options to meet their bottom line. These companies are often left with employees looking for work internally or having to lay off employees, many times at the company's expense.

EXAMPLES

♦ *E-Business Problem*: A local e-business company is experiencing high turnover rates in the sales and marketing areas, with four out of seven sales representatives resigning in the last six months. This has been the trend in this department since the company's inception two years ago. While it is not difficult to hire new employees to replace those who left, it normally takes about six weeks for a new employee to get up to speed with the company, product line, and customers. This constant turnover is resulting in sagging sales that are beginning to be seen in the company's bottom line. Sarah, the hiring authority, has been assigned to look into the issue.

— *Intervention:* Sarah met with the hiring manager for the sales and marketing department to discuss what knowledge, skills, and abilities are required for someone to be successful on the job. Some of the questions she asked included:

- How many years of sales experience are necessary to be competent in this position?
- Is a technical background required?
- Would someone with a technical background be able to get up to speed more quickly? Would that person be able to better identify a client's needs to grow its existing business as well as to develop leads for new clients?

Sarah also did some exploration on her own. She reviewed the exit interviews of the last few people who have left the department to try to identify any trends in their reasons for resignation. Three out of the four people who resigned most recently felt pressure to perform and did not feel qualified for the job. Sarah also found that sales representatives were being hired with strong sales experience, but no technical background. Sarah and the hiring manager were able to identify a skill set required for the position that included a strong sales background coupled with some technical savvy. The employees hired under the new set of criteria were able to shorten their learning curve significantly. As an added measure, Sarah followed up with the new employees once they started with the company to make sure they felt welcome and were transitioning well.

♦ *Manufacturing Company Problem:* One of the first assignments given to Penny, the new manager for the transaction processing team at a small manufacturing company, was to increase the retention rate of the accounts payable and accounts receivable clerks. She has been informed that on several occasions newly hired employees have come to the manager of the department with complaints that the job was misrepresented during the interview and that they are having a hard time feeling like part of the team.

—*Intervention:* Penny began by investigating the recruiting practices of the previous manager of the department. She found that the manager was making the final hiring decision on her own, without involving any other members of the transaction processing team in the interview process. Penny began to involve as many potential team members or other co-workers in the interviewing process as possible. As a team, they decided on interview questions for candidates. After meeting with candidates, the transaction processing team met to discuss the candidate and ultimately make a decision on a final candidate. Penny also set up new employees with a "buddy" to help them acclimate to the new working environment. Morale on the team rose and turnover decreased significantly.

♦ *Human Resource Problem:* Carl is the human resources manager for XYZ company. Each time an employee leaves the company, he simply advertises for the position based on the qualifications of the last incumbent, sets up the interviews, and fills the position. For new positions, Carl meets with the hiring manager to discuss the qualifications of the position and set a recruiting strategy. The business has not been growing lately, and it has been some time since Carl has met with the managers of his company to discuss staff planning.

  — *Intervention:* This scenario represents a lack of strategic planning in the recruiting function. If Carl does not help his managers determine a hiring plan, simply filling every open position may cause additional problems down the road. Carl began setting up meetings with his managers to discuss whether they actually needed to fill this position, since there has not been a lot of company growth, and what new skills would be required of the candidates if they do decide to fill it. Carl began collaborating with his managers during the recruiting process, allowing them to screen the resumes of candidates he brought in. The managers' increased involvement helped reduce the time to fill each position. Also, as a result of the conversations, there were a few positions that were not filled at all.

♦ *Pet Supply Distribution Company Problem:* Betty is the manager of operations at a Web-based pet supply distribution company. Business has not been strong lately, and, to make matters worse, Betty has lost several of her star performers in the past two weeks. Betty is concerned about losing any more of her employees. Her employees are starting to notice that there is less product going out the door, and have approached her with questions about it. In the past, the market has not taken a downturn for long, and she needed to be ready when the market picked up again.

  — *Intervention:* So far, Betty has been able to calm her employees' concerns about the future of the business. After all, she knew downturns in the business have never lasted long. Privately, she is concerned that not filling these open positions will make the employees worry more, thus increasing the potential for more openings. Because she knows that they have a great product and this downturn is temporary, Betty begins the interviewing process. To her surprise, she quickly found two great candidates who were near the minimum of the salary range. This is the best scenario possible, filling the positions inexpensively and quickly in anticipation of the market turning around.

DESIGN GUIDELINES

Companies may handle staffing in different ways. Organizations may have in-house recruiters, contractors may be brought on-site to perform this work, or companies may choose to outsource the entire process to a staffing agency.

Effective staffing requires understanding the following:

- ◆ workforce planning
- ◆ technology trends
- ◆ effective staffing strategies.

It is also important to form a partnership with hiring managers.

IMPLEMENTATION GUIDELINES

- ◆ Know the skill set you are looking for and where to find it.
- ◆ Be sure that you have a knowledgeable recruiting team.
- ◆ Make sure the organization has common staffing goals.
- ◆ Create a recruitment strategy that articulates where you are going to find these individuals and what methods you will use for selecting the right applicants. The strategy should address long- and short-term plans.

REFERENCES AND RESOURCES

Publications

Fast Company magazine.

Fein, Richard. (2000). *101 Hiring Mistakes Employers Make.* Manassas Park, VA: Impact.

HR magazine.

Kaye, Beverly, and Sharon Jordan Evans. (1999). *Love 'em or Lose 'em: Getting Good People to Stay.* San Francisco: Berrett-Koehler.

Tulgan, Bruce. (2001). *Winning Talent Wars.* New York: W. W. Norton.

Internet

www.shrm.org.

erexchange.com.

wetfeet.com.

Associations

Society for Human Resource Management.

Corporate Leadership Council.

Saratoga Institute.

22

PROCESS REDESIGN

Tom Devane

WHAT IS PROCESS REDESIGN?

Process redesign is an intervention designed to change the flow of activities and decisions that are associated with generating a specific business output. Examples of business outputs include a design for a new product, a purchase order, a product, and a service. Although business outputs may often be produced in one department, many of an organization's most mission-critical processes span departmental boundaries.

In addition to changing the flow of activities and decisions, a process redesign intervention often relocates departmental responsibilities. Well-executed process redesigns tend to have the following characteristics. They:

- involve groups of people who will be responsible for executing the new work
- use a diagramming method (such as process maps or flowcharts) to pictorially display current and future flows of activities and decisions among departments
- use metrics to establish performance baselines and measure progress
- incorporate whole-systems thinking so that process performance is aligned with other organizational variables such as overall strategy, competitive pressures, and activities in other parts of the organization
- include more than small representative design groups in the formulation and implementation of the new process
- consider nonprocess factors in the redesign that affect process performance such as organizational culture, intrinsic motivation, reward systems, and organizational structure
- encourage redesigners to set stretch goals (that is, goals that require considerable effort and challenge organizations to reach higher levels of performance).

RELATED INTERVENTIONS

Other interventions that seek to redesign processes include total quality management (TQM), business reengineering, and gemba kaizen. In addition, systems thinking projects often result in changes to organizational processes. Each of these related interventions may address several of the characteristics, but usually not all of them.

WHEN TO USE PROCESS REDESIGN

Use it as a primary intervention if the organization is experiencing poor performance attributable to one or more of the following root causes:

♦ Department exchanges of information or materials are slow, cumbersome, and inefficient.

♦ Decisions take longer than they should and are of low quality.

♦ A string of process activities that span departmental boundaries is not managed well because of turf issues that arise in the execution of the process.

♦ Bottleneck areas are causing delays for customers, weakening competitive position, and increasing the organization's costs.

♦ Benchmarking data, either from inside or outside the company, suggests that process outputs might be generated faster, cheaper, or with higher quality.

♦ The spirit and culture of continuous improvement exists in the organization, and people actively seek opportunities to redesign existing workflows.

WHEN NOT TO USE PROCESS REDESIGN

♦ Do not use process redesign initiatives unless at least one person in the process redesign group is familiar with a diagramming technique and principles of process redesign.

♦ Do not let just a few people redesign a process for an entire department.

♦ Do not skip the task of mapping the current process before starting the future process. (This first step can be a valuable team-building activity, and it often yields useful insights that would not have been available if this step had been skipped.) Groups should not make changes to their own process without consulting with other organizational groups that may be affected by their process.

EXAMPLE

♦ *Electronic Assembly Company Problem:* Demand for products made by the LMNO Electronics Assembly Company doubled in 1999. By November the company could not keep up with product demand and was beginning to lose market share to its top two competitors.

Management looked at the overall product flow through the plant and determined there was a bottleneck in Manufacturing Department 3.

— *Intervention:* The company convened a meeting of all the employees in Manufacturing Department 3 and presented the problem. LMNO provided process redesign training principles and chartered the entire department to embark on an increase throughput project that would critically examine how work was done, and then redesign a better process. For two weeks the group met for three hours each day about the project. Employees started by identifying internal customers and suppliers, and checking to see if all their expectations about the department were being met. They drew a diagram of the current process and were shocked to see the convoluted nature of the product flow among stations in their own department. They brainstormed ideas on how to speed up the product flow so they could achieve their aggressive self-imposed target of "an increase in throughput by 40 percent in two months." They then established metrics around five key areas that they could monitor to determine if they were on track to achieving their stretch goal. After designing a preliminary solution, they invited members of other manufacturing departments, purchasing, and production planning to comment on their design. After receiving some excellent input from the production planning department that the team had not considered, they incorporated those ideas into the final design.

Within two months they exceeded their goal. They posted a 50 percent increase in throughput. In the year 2000, LMNO Electronics Assembly Company launched process redesign projects in two other departments and for three processes that spanned several departments. These efforts helped them increase their throughput by an additional 42 percent.

DESIGN GUIDELINES

Process redesign efforts come under two major criteria: their purpose or work type, as table 4-1 shows.

The following tips can help in the design of process redesign initiatives:

♦ Involve as many people who will be affected by the redesign as is practically possible. In early reengineering efforts we found that members who did not participate in the redesign tended to resist the designs produced by the select few members of the representative design team.

♦ The design group should periodically check with other groups in the organization as well as external customers and suppliers to ensure that what the group is redesigning will not adversely affect the overall work system.

TABLE 4-1. PROCESS REDESIGN INITIATIVES.

Criteria	Examples	Implications
1. Purpose	• Reduce cycle time • Cut costs • Improve quality • Increase throughput • Enhance flexibility	The purpose of the process redesign effort will guide what participants look for, what they seek to achieve, what metrics they establish, what stretch goals they set, and how they go about redesigning. In short, the purpose focuses their attention on one or two of the key variables, while often de-emphasizing others.
2. Work-type	• Manual work • Knowledge work • Hybrid	While most work today contains aspects of both manual and knowledge work, it is a good idea to understand their mix in a process because different improvement principles may need to be invoked for each type. For example, the non-repetitive, information-based realm of knowledge work may call for less process mapping and a greater use of principles checklists to guide workers through complex decision branches not easily shown on a process map.

- ◆ Senior management should encourage the design group to set stretch goals, but should avoid setting specific goals for the group as this practice tends to be disempowering.
- ◆ Set aside a specific segment of the process redesign session to address implementation barriers resulting from the current culture, the current compensation system, and potentially self-limiting factors of the redesign participants.

IMPLEMENTATION GUIDELINES

- ◆ Monitor metrics and take corrective action when performance strays outside acceptable boundaries.
- ◆ Have senior and middle managers support the new process by providing necessary resources and showing their support through actions.
- ◆ Compensate and reward people in a manner consistent with the new process design and metrics.
- ◆ Do not assume that all process action can be represented on a process map. Knowledge transfer activities among process participants and relationship building can also have dramatic effects on overall performance, so make sure to nurture them.

REFERENCES AND RESOURCES

Publications

Rummler, Geary, and Alan Brache. (1995). *Improving Performance.* San Francisco: Jossey-Bass. This book, considered by many to be the seminal work in the area of process redesign, provides an exceptionally clear mapping technique and practical suggestions for implementing process changes.

Journal for Quality and Participation. The journal, from the Association for Quality and Participation (AQP), provides an excellent set of tips and best practices for those seeking to improve productivity by redesigning business processes. Phone: 1.800.733.3310.

23

JOB INTERVIEWS

Matthew S. Richter and Andrew Kimball

WHAT IS A JOB INTERVIEW?

Traditionally, interviewing is a process for gathering specific information about a candidate's past experiences and behaviors in such a way that they act as predictors of that candidate's future behaviors. This tried-and-true process, however, leaves out a key component of evaluation: the integration and matching of a candidate's current state of knowledge, skills, attitudes, and beliefs with the candidate's vision of where he or she wants to be, what he or she wants to do, and how he or she wants to achieve those goals.

The interview intervention, done successfully, does not require you to be a rocket scientist, but it is necessary to be prepared, know your objectives, and ask the right questions. Finally, interviewing, like any communication skill, is rooted in the psychology of human relationships. Any time you see the words *psychology* or *relationships* in the same sentence, you can bet what follows will be a simplification of an extraordinarily complex and convoluted subject. So it is with any interviewing process.

RELATED INTERVENTIONS

Job interviewing is a vital part of staffing. Therefore it deserves additional emphasis in comparison with other phases of the staffing process. Competency-based interviewing is a process by which competencies are predetermined and become the focus for the interviews. Competencies are the knowledge, skills, and abilities required for performance. This interviewing format is the parent of the process we define.

Behavioral interviewing, which uses questions that get at a candidate's past behaviors, is a popular format for selection. It is, however, a limited process that ignores the gathering of specific evidence (evidence that can be seen, felt, and personally experienced) of the candidate's capacity to perform.

Testing is an ineffective, often illegal process of using psychological, knowledge, and aptitude exams as criteria for selection. Many of these tests are great for personal development, coaching, and psychological diagnosis. They are not valid for the specific use of selecting candidates.

WHEN TO USE JOB INTERVIEWS

♦ When the ultimate goal is to hire the most effective and productive employee.

♦ When there is a clear understanding of the requirements for the job position and the job description. (Note the two are not always the same.)

♦ When time and money are important.

Effective job interview techniques are also valuable for coaching employees (that is, in finding out their needs and development areas through an interview), in needs assessments of any kind, for recording best practices, in dating, for conflict resolution, and for win-win negotiations.

WHEN NOT TO USE JOB INTERVIEWS

Do not use job interviews as the sole criteria for selecting candidates. Sometimes it is impossible to avoid thinking that the information gathered is a complete picture of the candidate. Even though we intellectually know how hard it is to learn everything there is to know about another human being in 60 minutes, we tend to act as if what we do learn is the whole truth. So we must be vigilant at recognizing when our assumptions about the candidate, our own beliefs, and our preconceptions influence our decisions. We should always remember to focus on the observable behaviors and objective data that validate the candidate's qualifications for the job.

♦ Do not forgo preparation. We cannot emphasize enough the need to prepare the interview. Having delivered countless interview training programs, we have discovered that most managers do not spend nearly enough time prepping the interview.

♦ Do not forget to record your thoughts and finds after the interview. Whether you take notes during the interview or immediately after, it is imperative that documentation exists from the interaction. Legal ramifications and faulty human memories are two very good reasons for the notes.

EXAMPLE

♦ *Telecommunications Problem:* A telecommunications call center based on the East Coast had an annual turnover rate of 120 percent. Given the management dynamic and the tendency for turnover in the telecommunications call center industry, the rate was at least explainable. However, this firm had a philosophy that helped it fill seats. If the candidate could fog a mirror, he was hired. This ideology also contributed significantly to the company's turnover problem. The annual cost of recruiting new employees and training them and the cost of lower productivity due to empty seats were estimated at millions of dollars.

— *Intervention:* The first step was to acknowledge that there were other contributing factors to the problem. Management issues certainly had an impact on employee morale as did poorly implemented strategic initiatives. However, this company's approach of hiring just anyone could not continue. Therefore, managers got together with a consultant and brainstormed all possible knowledge areas they wanted a prospective employee to have. Once that activity was complete, the knowledge areas were prioritized. For instance, knowledge areas necessary for successful performance were how the telecommunications industry works, knowledge of the consumer market, and knowledge of product trends. Questions were developed to discern whether the candidate would have this information. Skills were identified and prioritized, as well. For instance, customer service skills, communication skills, and organizational skills were labeled as being of the highest priority. Activities, scenarios, and questions were developed to have the candidates demonstrate their position of these skills. The same process happened for attitudes and beliefs that were desirable for the job. Environmental questions were designed. Then the managers were trained in how to ask the questions and facilitate the scenarios and discussions. They were trained how to analyze the answers. This interviewing process has decreased the turnover rate by over 30 percent.

DESIGN GUIDELINES

Interviews may be in the following forms:

- ◆ *The one-on-one interview:* This is the traditional interview at which the candidate meets with an HR recruiter, hiring manager, or decision maker to determine the selection for that position. Often the interviewer will meet with the candidate two or three times before making a decision.

- ◆ *The team interview:* This is a sequential interview process at which there are multi-interviewers who meet with the candidate one after the other, each making a determination based on his or her own strengths and contributions. We like this process more since it incorporates more perspectives on the candidate's capabilities.

- ◆ *The panel interview:* Utter hell for both the candidate and the interviewers! No one on the panel has an opportunity to truly dig in and probe thoroughly. The candidate is nervous, and questions are rarely answered more than superficially.

Based on your understanding of the position's requirements, there are four areas in which to discern information. You should prepare questions, activities, and scenarios in each of these four categories to develop the most expansive understanding of a candidate's potential:

♦ *Knowledge:* To discern whether a candidate possesses required and specific knowledge, you should ask questions that permit the candidate to demonstrate fluency with a topic. Since knowledge is something that can be memorized, the candidate will either know the answer to the question or not. Therefore when testing for knowledge, you should ask questions that get at explanations and recitations of information.

♦ *Skills:* When trying to ascertain a candidate's apparent skill for a task, it is often best to get a demonstration. Too often we make the mistake of asking candidates whether they can do a particular task. When candidates say they can, often there is no follow-up. There are two approaches for measuring a candidate's skill: (1) Ask the candidate how he or she accomplished a task in the past or might handle a particular situation in the future. Ask for specifics and probe into the details of the process the candidate describes. (2) Get a demonstration. Have the candidate role-play, solve a problem, write a sample, edit a document, maneuver through a software design flow, and the like. Then you can learn firsthand how the candidate performs on a particular task.

♦ *Attitudes and beliefs:* Attitudes and beliefs are probably the most difficult attributes to evaluate. Candidates today are trained to know the answers we are looking for and can recite whimsically the appropriate value at the right time. However, this display does not give you the necessary data to make a decision on attitudes and beliefs. Therefore, we recommend using what Joseph L. Badaracco Jr. calls *right versus right* scenarios and case studies. Right versus right refers to the idea that given a particular situation, there is no right answer, but potentially several, and those several potentially right answers could also be in conflict with each other. The trick with scenarios is that the answer is not important. You should not get caught up in a debate or judge the candidate for his or her answer. The ensuing discussion and the probing questions the interviewer asks for clarity provide a wealth of information about the candidate's values and beliefs. The discussion also gives you insight into the way the candidate thinks.

♦ *Environment:* Environment questions are those that get at a candidate's ability to meet job requirements. For instance:
  — This job requires some weekend work; will that be a problem for you?
  — This job requires that you pick clients up at the airport; will that be a problem for you?

IMPLEMENTATION GUIDELINES

- *Opening the interview:* The opening of any meeting sets the tone and dynamics for how the interaction will go. Many interviewers do not give enough attention and importance to the initial positioning. They assume candidates know why they are there. As a result, they briefly review the agenda and then jump right to the first topic without taking time to create an appropriate climate and to frame expectations carefully. Unclear expectations may lead to resistance and frustration on both sides.

- *Assessing the candidate:* One of the most useful ways to determine what a candidate's performance is likely to be in a new job is to determine the following:
  — the constellation of attributes that high performance in the job requires
  — the constellation of competencies the candidate already has
  — the interventions that would be needed to close the gap between job requirements and the candidate's attributes.

To answer these questions most successfully, it is useful to understand the knowledge, skills, attitudes and beliefs, and environment required for performance success. (These are the very same knowledge, skills, attitudes and beliefs, and environment questions you determined during your preparation.)

- *Framing the job and getting questions from the candidate:* This is your chance to talk about the job, the company, the products, the services, the team, and yourself in a way that moves the candidate to say, "Yes! I'll take the job!" During this phase of the interview, you should also sell your company. It is even valuable for candidates who do not get jobs to walk away feeling good about the organization. They will spread the word to others about their experience, and the people they talk to are potential candidates and customers. Now that you have completed most of the framing phase of the interview, it is important to provide the candidate some time to get answers to his or her questions. This is an opportunity for you to assess how the candidate thinks and processes information.

- *Wrapping up the interview:* Bad interviews often occur because the candidate and interviewer have divergent understandings about agreements, next steps, and roles and responsibilities. Research shows us that the most successful interviews should wrap up in such a way that both the candidate and interviewer:
  — leave with the same critical facts, understandings, and agreements
  — feel that their ideas and decisions were valued and appreciated
  — have an opportunity to provide feedback into how the interview process worked.

REFERENCES AND RESOURCES

Publications

Badaracco, Joseph L., Jr. (1997). *Defining Moments: When Managers Must Choose Between Right and Right.* Cambridge, MA: Harvard Business School Press. Not an interviewing book, but great for gathering scenarios to use in the interview. A must have!

Mornell, Pierre. (1998). *45 Effective Ways for Hiring Smart: How to Predict Winners and Losers in the Incredibly Expensive People-Reading Game.* Berkeley, CA: Ten Speed Press. I love this book!

CHAPTER 5

TELL ME:
IMPROVING INFORMATION

24. Knowledge Management
    by Mark Van Buren

25. Networks for Information
    by Patti Shank

26. Balanced Score Card
    *by Stewart Hickman
    and Jacqueline B. Visnius*

27. Meetings and Dialogue
    *by Ethan S. Sanders
    and Jacqueline B. Visnius*

28. Newsletters
    by Ethan S. Sanders

29. Public Relations Campaigns
    by Jennifer Homer

30. Debriefing
    by Sivasailam Thiagarajan

*"Knowledge is of two kinds. We know a subject ourselves,
or we know where we can find information upon it."*
—Samuel Johnson

	Individual	Group	Cheap	Expensive	Together	Spread Out	Need it Fast	Have Time
Individual			Debriefing	Knowledge Management Public Relations	Meetings/Dialogue	Debriefing	Debriefing	Knowledge Management Networks Balanced Scorecard Public Relations
Group		Networks Balanced Scorecard Meetings/Dialogue Newsletters	Networks Balanced Scorecard Meetings/Dialogue Newsletters		Meetings/Dialogue	Knowledge Management Networks Balanced Scorecard Newsletters Public Relations	Meetings/Dialogue Newsletters	Networks Balanced Scorecard
Cheap	Debriefing	Knowledge Management Public Relations	Meetings/Dialogue Newsletters Debriefing	Public Relations		Networks Balanced Scorecard Newsletters Debriefing	Meetings/Dialogue Newsletters Debriefing	Knowledge Management Public Relations
Expensive	Knowledge Management Public Relations	Meetings/Dialogue Newsletters Public Relations	Networks Balanced Scorecard	Knowledge Management		Knowledge Management Public Relations		
Together	Debriefing	Knowledge Management Networks Balanced Scorecard	Meetings/Dialogue Newsletters Debriefing	Knowledge Management Public Relations			Meetings/Dialogue Newsletters Debriefing	Knowledge Management Networks Balanced Scorecard Public Relations
Spread Out	Debriefing	Meetings/Dialogue Newsletters	Networks Balanced Scorecard		Meetings/Dialogue Newsletters			
Need it Fast	Debriefing	Knowledge Management Networks Balanced Scorecard Public Relations						
Have Time						Knowledge Management Networks Balanced Scorecard Public Relations Debriefing		

INFORMATION

24

KNOWLEDGE MANAGEMENT

Mark Van Buren

WHAT IS KNOWLEDGE MANAGEMENT?

Knowledge management is the explicit and systematic management of intellectual capital and the associated processes of creating, gathering, organizing, disseminating, leveraging, and using intellectual capital.

Knowledge is such a broad concept that we substitute the phrase *intellectual capital* to refer to a particular context. In the case of knowledge management in the workplace, intellectual capital refers to knowledge of value to an organization and excludes knowledge of value in other contexts.

Intellectual capital can be classified into three basic categories:

- ♦ *human capital:* the knowledge, skills, and competencies of people in an organization
- ♦ *structural capital:* the structures, processes, information systems, patents, and so forth that remain when employees leave
- ♦ *customer capital:* the value of an organization's relationships with its customers.

RELATED INTERVENTIONS

Organizational learning is a closely related intervention. The transfer of knowledge within an organization results in learning that supersedes the individual. Training, meanwhile, typically results in individual-level learning.

In practice, knowledge management refers to a whole category of different innovations that manipulate knowledge within an organizational context. Communication systems are an integral part of knowledge management in that they act as the mechanisms by which knowledge is shared across individuals and groups.

Knowledge management in its broader sense is related to a number of secondary interventions in the category of information. These interventions act to formally transfer knowledge throughout the organization, including

- ♦ Internet and intranet
- ♦ employee orientation

♦ dialogues and meetings
♦ feedback.

WHEN TO USE KNOWLEDGE MANAGEMENT

Knowledge management is a far-reaching intervention that can create significant benefits throughout an organization. On a fundamental level, knowledge management should be used when there is a need to have information and knowledge in a readily accessible, tangible form for the purposes of:

♦ sharing solutions and innovations
♦ determining best practices
♦ meeting customers' needs
♦ increasing responsiveness
♦ increasing collaboration.

Knowledge management can effectively transform an organization into one that has considerable competitive advantage. By integrating communications and learning, knowledge management can also contribute to a better overall understanding of an organization's vision, mission, culture, and values. This type of understanding has widespread implications for improving a company's structure and processes as well as its overall organizational health. When knowledge, communications, and learning are enhanced, beneficial carryovers to other performance improvement areas are inevitable.

WHEN NOT TO USE KNOWLEDGE MANAGEMENT

Do not let information technology be the driving force behind a knowledge management initiative. Knowledge is not always the result when the desire to increase information technology resources and uses is the key enabler behind the push for greater information. Knowledge management requires more than intranets, databases, and Internets; it often requires a shift in overall strategy. The emergence of information technology has been the driving force behind many knowledge management initiatives.

EXAMPLES

♦ *Computer Software Company Problem:* A large computer software company was concerned about a decrease in sales and profitability. Pulling salespeople out of the field for training on new products and services was usually the remedy when sales goals were not being met. In order to meet the learning and knowledge needs of its sales professionals, the company began exploring alternative ways of providing its employees with crucial information and resources.

— *Intervention:* The company developed intranet capabilities that consolidated sales training information, sales support resources, product materials, and an array of other information. Through a number of innovative interfaces, employees were able to access information that heretofore was only available during lengthy off-site training sessions. Via the company's new knowledge management software, the sales professionals obtained current information on products and information needed to increase sales capabilities. Even with this exciting new tool, the company knew that this was a first step in implementing knowledge management. The company plans to begin learning and communication strategy meetings in the coming months.

♦ *Innovation Problem:* Encouraging new ideas has always been a key component of business strategy for this manufacturing company. In recent years, the company has experienced rapid growth, and innovation has been at a standstill. Efforts to revive the creative juices within the company have been unsuccessful due in large part to inadequate communication channels. If it is to keep its entrepreneurial spirit alive, the company must determine what is needed to capture and restore the exchange of ideas that were once its mainstay.

— *Intervention:* After a number of months spent discussing the role of knowledge management and the value of intellectual capital, the company hired a chief information officer (CIO) to champion the knowledge initiative. Once hired, the CIO worked in conjunction with senior management to set up processes for creating, capturing, and distributing knowledge throughout the organization. A key component of its knowledge management program was establishing communities of practice to facilitate the exchange of information as well as instituting an evaluation and compensation strategy that rewards sharing behaviors. The company is committed to establishing an organizational and technical infrastructure that will continue to support the sharing and exchange of information.

♦ *Insurance Company Problem:* The customer service department of a large insurance company determined that its service representatives were not responding effectively to customer complaints and concerns.

— *Intervention:* The information technology (IT) department was consulted and determined that the group was most likely in need of a system that enabled the staff to respond to and resolve customer complaints by sharing information with each other. The IT consultant recommended implementing Lotus Notes to allow for discussion and dissemination of information. Based on the success in the customer service area, Lotus Notes was implemented on a companywide basis. Use of this new technology was effective in providing wide-ranging and broad solutions, but often required substantial user time to retrieve and synthesize the information. Even with regular enhancements, the system was not sufficient in and of itself to provide a total solution to the customer service department's concerns. The company was in need of a much larger strategy that would enable more effective decision making and increased collaboration.

DESIGN GUIDELINES

The broad category of knowledge management consists of five subcategories of activities based on the steps in the knowledge management process:

- ◆ identifying knowledge types, needs, and requirements
- ◆ creating new knowledge and uncovering existing knowledge
- ◆ compiling, gathering, representing, codifying, and re/organizing knowledge
- ◆ disseminating, distributing, and transferring knowledge
- ◆ applying, incorporating, reusing, exploiting, and leveraging knowledge.

These activities are combinations of processes and enablers that interact in unique ways and form critical leverage points for enhancing intellectual capital management capabilities.

Knowledge management is unique in that it is quickly becoming the primary source of competitive advantage within a growing number of industries. Despite the increased recognition of knowledge management as a critical element of organizational strategy, one thing is still certain: Knowledge management is not a well-defined process. The form and function of knowledge management depends to a great extent on how an organization chooses to define it. Even in the absence of universally accepted methods and procedures, there are certain critical elements that must go into the design of knowledge management initiatives in order to ensure widespread acceptance and ultimate success. Some of these elements include

- ◆ Communicating and educating organization members on the importance of knowledge sharing at all levels.
- ◆ Making certain that the knowledge management initiative is clearly and explicitly linked to business strategies.
- ◆ Determining the intellectual capital that is vital to the success of the core business strategy.
- ◆ Establishing knowledge managers, such as chief knowledge officer (CKO) or chief learning officer (CLO), to oversee the organizing, capturing, and disseminating of the organization's knowledge.

- Using pilot programs or prototypes that help to establish maps of the knowledge management process. The insight and understanding that is gained through these programs can be transferred to a larger knowledge management initiative.
- Systematizing and standardizing the technological infrastructure to support knowledge.
- Identifying and enlisting the support of key knowledge management champions from the ranks of senior management. Upper management sponsorship is critical to effective knowledge management.

IMPLEMENTATION GUIDELINES

Key components of an effective implementation of this intervention include the following:

- Understand and firmly grasp the processes and enablers that help or hinder the effective diffusion of knowledge.
- Develop sound methods for evaluating the impacts of intellectual capital.
- Establish benchmarking and best practices. Compare intellectual capital and training investments, practices, and outcomes with those of other organizations in similar industries, and compare with overall and leading averages.
- Promote and maintain a vigorous learning environment that allows for continuous development, adaptation, and evolution of intellectual capital stocks.
- Overcome the popular notion that knowledge is power.
- Recognize the tremendous role that culture plays in successful knowledge management and cultivate an environment that encourages and rewards the sharing and use of knowledge.

REFERENCES AND RESOURCES

Publications

American Productivity & Quality Center. (1996). *Knowledge Management: Consortium Benchmarking Study.* Houston, TX: Author.

Davenport, Thomas H., and Laurence Prusak. (1998). *Working Knowledge: How Organizations Manage What They Know.* Boston: Harvard Business School Press.

KM World.

Morey, Daryl, Mark Marbury, and Bhavani Thuraisingham. (Eds.). (2000). *Knowledge Management: Classic and Contemporary Works.* Cambridge, MA: MIT Press.

Newman, Amy. (March 1999). "Knowledge Management." *Info-line.* Issue No. 9903. Alexandria, VA: ASTD.

Van Buren, Mark E. (May 1999). "A Yardstick for Knowledge Management." *Training & Development.*

Internet

www.ASTD.org.

www.brint.com. The Business Researcher's Interest Website, filled with all the electronically available resources on knowledge management and links to where one can get everything else.

Association

American Productivity Quality Center (APQC), the first organization to hold conferences explicitly on knowledge management. Has a whole line of best practice studies that describes many of the better-known companies that have implemented knowledge management.

25

NETWORKS FOR INFORMATION

Patti Shank

WHAT IS A NETWORK?

Networked applications offer performance technologists powerful tools for sharing information across an organization. By using these tools, we can connect and share information through intranets, the Internet, and other avenues available through computer networks. How important is connecting and sharing (with or without the help of network applications) in an organization? Think of it this way, what happens when people do not share information and are not well connected? You get the picture.

By sharing and connecting, I mean all the things, formal and informal, that allow people and the organization as a whole to respond to business needs and adapt to change. Senge, in *Dance of Change* (1999), explains this well:

> *All organizations learn—in the sense of adapting as the real world around them changes. But some organizations are faster and more effective learners. The key is to see learning as inseparable from everyday work. (Training, by contrast, is typically episodic and detached from the context in which results are produced.)*

Network applications like email and discussion boards can make the type of learning that Senge describes more effective and efficient—and fun.

Every communications medium (talk included) has affordances. *Affordance* is a term coined by Donald Norman in his book *The Design of Everyday Things* (1988). According to Norman, *affordances* are "perceived and actual properties...that determine just how the thing could possibly be used." So, for example, what affordances does an upholstered chair have that make you want to sit a long while that a folding chair does not have? Comfort for one thing. Use this same idea to think about uses of media for sharing information. Table 5-1 lists several types of media and examples of the affordances for sharing information each of them offers.

TABLE 5-1. MEDIA AND THEIR AFFORDANCES.

Medium	Affordances for Learning
Talk (live)	Immediate feedback Emotion/subtleties of communication
Video	Visual Demonstration
Print	Usable anywhere Generally no training to use
CD-ROM	Portable Holds lots of data
Networks	People connections Any time, any place

Think about the things you do on the Internet that have become critical to you in the last few years: email, gaining and sharing information, online shopping, auctions, discussion boards, instant messaging, and so forth. Now, think about how that these things could improve sharing of information in organizations and individually. Here are just a few ideas: access to help, information, resources, mentoring, advice, training course ratings, peer review, collaborative work, and networking. Those things you choose are affordances.

The terms *interaction* and *interactivity* are used a lot to describe networked information sharing. Interaction can be with:

♦ content, such as text, hyperlinks, simulations, video, and quizzes
♦ other users, such as sharing favorite links, working together on documents, providing advice
♦ the instructor, subject matter expert, or facilitator, by, for example, answering questions, providing ideas and resources, listening to and evaluating plans
♦ technology, such as installing a browser, troubleshooting streaming media.

Interactivity can mean many things. Often it means interaction with content alone. Greg Kearsley and Ben Shneiderman (1998) describe true interaction as engagement. They say, "students must be meaningfully engaged in learning activities through interaction with others and worthwhile tasks. . . . By engaged learning, we mean that all student activities involve active cognitive processes such as creating, problem solving, reasoning, decision-making, and evaluation." This definition clearly holds interaction to a higher standard than simple content interaction.

RELATED INTERVENTIONS

Connections between people inside an organization (and outside too) are made all the time. People share information with colleagues in their department, people in other departments, people with similar jobs in other organizations, like-minded people in professional organizations. They also share information with people in their clubs and civic groups and with classmates. Network applications often make this process of sharing, helping, and communicating easier. A few of the common names for these applications include

♦ email
♦ listservs
♦ online courses
♦ discussion boards
♦ computer-mediated conferencing
♦ collaboration tools
♦ groupware
♦ online whiteboards.

WHEN TO USE NETWORKS

Networks make sense for connections when people are at a geographic distance from each other or when people are not able to regularly meet face-to-face. Even when people can meet face-to-face, electronic connections have additional affordances because they provide documentation of the connections (through the artifacts that remain afterwards, such as the text of a discussion or a list of URLs), and they enable people to communicate any time and any place. In many workplaces, it is difficult to find time to communicate. Even though geographic distance may not be a factor, lack of communication may be the norm. And in many cases, meeting face-to-face is optimized by continued connections with network applications.

WHEN NOT TO USE NETWORKS

♦ Do not use networks for information sharing unless there are goals. Let people know what to do with the tools. Tell them what is acceptable, what is not acceptable, and the norms for use.
♦ Do not use networks for information sharing without a moderator. If you are going to have a discussion board on performance management, for instance, it would be a good idea to have it moderated by someone who knows how to moderate and knows the topic. Otherwise, you may be asking for sharing of misinformation.
♦ Do not use networks for information sharing unless you provide training. Users need to learn how to use these tools so some training or performance support may be needed. Likewise, moderating in an online environment is not the same as moderating in-person. Both users and moderators need guidance.
♦ Do not use networks for information sharing unless the people who will use it want to. Forcing people to use it is rarely a good idea. It often works best to let the people who are most interested start the process and then let them sell others on the idea.

EXAMPLES

♦ *Performance Management System Problem:* A group of supervisors meet with a HR representative to discuss ideas on improving the performance management system in their organization. Not everyone could attend the meetings.

— *Intervention:* Between meetings, they send emails back and forth that further the discussion until the next meeting. Ideas are gathered and posted for those who could not attend the last meeting. Plan iterations are posted, and supervisors comment on them. Time at face-to-face meetings is optimized, and people who cannot travel to each meeting are a full part of the process.

♦ *Accounting System Problem:* An organization has just instituted a new accounting system. People who have different levels of knowledge have to learn it, and staff has to ensure that the software covers all necessary information.

—*Intervention:* A help board is established that allows people to post questions and gain quick help. People from the finance department might post frequently asked questions (FAQs). A monthly online software simulation demo might be posted to demonstrate specific features. Staff could be encouraged to send in suggestions for the next demo. Staff who are more comfortable with the software become mentors to those who are new to the company and others who need help. Supervisors in similar functional areas might work together to draft a memo about the system upgrades they desire.

DESIGN GUIDELINES

The use of networks for organizational and individual information sharing assumes a number of things:

♦ The people involved have the needed software and hardware.
♦ They are connected to the network.
♦ They know how to use the hardware and software and are comfortable with it.
♦ They have the time to use it.

These are big considerations. If they are not all true, some work will need to be done first to make sure these conditions are met.

Networked information typically occurs in one of two ways:

♦ interaction with content
— self-paced online courses
— information retrieval
— performance support
— resource lists
— catalogs

- interaction with people
  - email
  - polls
  - online collaboration
  - collaborative document writing
  - peer review
  - listservs
  - discussion boards
  - group-paced online courses.

IMPLEMENTATION GUIDELINES

The following tips can help in implementing network application for information sharing:

- *Discussion:* One of the easiest ways to foster interaction online is through online discussions using listservs or discussion boards. Figure 5-1 shows a Webpage from a Web Resource Collaboration Center (WRCC) discussion board. After a course on managing employee performance problems, for instance, an ongoing online discussion might ensue. A subject matter expert might foster a compelling discussion that truly engages the participants for the long term, which helps learners move from recitation of policies and procedures to application in their own situation. Examples of discussion questions might include:
  - If you are an experienced supervisor, what lessons have you learned about managing performance that new supervisors should know?
  - What kinds of supervisory actions would help avoid (many of) the disciplinary actions we've discussed?

Figure 5-1. Page from WRCC discussion board.

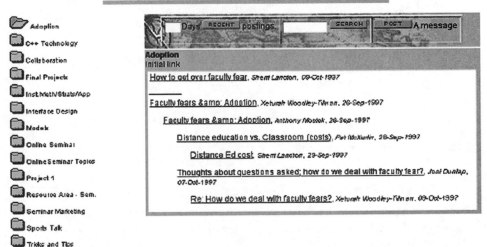

♦ *Sharing:* People often have information and resources that would benefit others. Through email, discussion boards, and online whiteboards, for example, colleagues can share information. Employee performance plans that one supervisor developed might be extremely helpful to a new supervisor who is unsure how to document problems. Another supervisor may share employment law URLs that others would find beneficial.

♦ *Collaboration:* Collaboration allows people to work together to accomplish a goal. Supervisors might work together to build templates for performance plans, for example. One supervisor might ask others to review her plans prior to implementing them. Network applications like email, discussion boards, and collaborative writing software could be used to facilitate this process. Figure 5-2 shows a WRCC Webpage on collaboration.

Figure 5-2. WRCC page on collaboration.

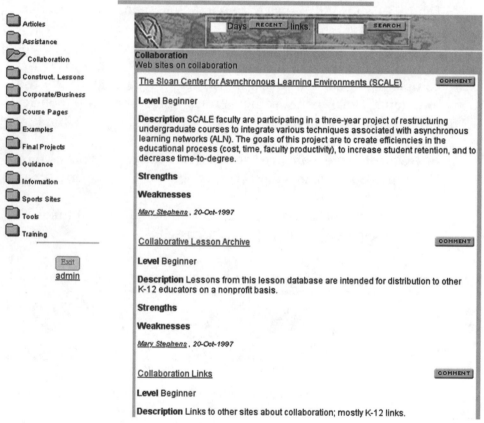

REFERENCES AND RESOURCES

Publications

Beer, V. (2000). *The Web Learning Fieldbook: Using the World Wide Web to Build Workplace Learning Environments.* San Francisco: Jossey-Bass/Pfeiffer.

Harasim, L., S.R. Hiltz, L. Teles, and M. Turoff. (1995). *Learning Networks: A Field Guide to Teaching and Learning Online.* Cambridge, MA: MIT Press.

Kearsley, Greg, and Ben Shneiderman. (1998, September-October). "Engagement Theory: A Framework for Technology-Based Teaching and Learning." *Educational Technology.*

Norman, Donald. (1988). *The Design of Everyday Things.* New York: Doubleday.

Senge, Peter. (1999). *Dance of Change.* New York: Doubleday.

Wenger, E. (1998). *Communities of Practice: Learning, Meaning, and Identity.* Cambridge: Cambridge University Press.

Internet

http://carbon.cudenver.edu/~tgibson/wrcc. The Web Resource Collaboration Center (WRCC) includes a discussion board, links/resource manager, and collaborative writing tools.

http://www.aln.org. Web of asynchronous learning networks.

http://www.co-i-l.com/coil/knowledge-garden/cop/index.shtml. Communities of practice.

http://www.emoderators.com/moderators.shtml. Resources for moderators and facilitators of online discussion.

http://www.lab.brown.edu/public/ocsc/collaboration.guide. Electronic collaboration.

http://www.myplaceware.com. My Placeware provides tools for live virtual meetings using a Web browser and a phone.

http://www.microsoft.com/windows/netmeeting. Tools for virtual collaboration.

http://www.psu.edu/cac/ets/presentations/Tlsites. Teaching and learning with technology.

http://thinkofit.com/pubs.htm. Links to many free and inexpensive asynchronous discussion tools.

http://groups.yahoo.com. Tools for asynchronous discussion, polling, and document sharing.

http://www.zaplets.com. Email-based tools for discussion, brainstorming, group calendars, and more.

Associations

The Association for Educational Communications and Technology. Website: http://www.aect.org/.

Society for Applied Learning Technology. Website: http://www.salt.org/.

26

BALANCED SCORECARD

Stewart Hickman and Jacqueline B. Visnius

WHAT IS THE BALANCED SCORECARD?

The balanced scorecard is a measurement system used to link performance with overall organizational strategy. It is best used as a strategic management system that provides a framework for translating a company's long-term strategic objectives into a set of coherent performance measures. The scorecard also serves as a tool for communicating the strategy and goals throughout an organization.

Use of the balanced scorecard enables organizations to move beyond the lagging financial measures such as return-on-investment and sales growth, typically used to evaluate performance, to a more well rounded set of indicators. Most important, the balanced scorecard aligns performance with overall strategy to achieve breakthrough performance.

A good balanced scorecard has a mix of measures that combine past performance with drivers for future performance. Robert S. Kaplan and David P. Norton, authors of *The Balanced Scorecard: Translating Strategy Into Action* (1996), suggest using the following categories for an effective balanced scorecard:

- ◆ *financial:* return-on-investment, earning, operating expenses, net cash flow, and the like
- ◆ *customer:* information about how satisfied customers are with the services and products you provide
- ◆ *internal business processes:* critical internal processes that determine customer satisfaction such as quality improvement, employee skills development, and complaint handling
- ◆ *learning and growth:* sales from new products and services, time to market of new goods and services.

By selecting a limited, manageable number of critical indicators or measures within each of the four categories, or perspectives, the scorecard will help focus strategic vision and provide a basis for establishing current and future organizational success.

To achieve success with the scorecard, the support and participation of top management is essential.

Related Interventions

Although it is unique, the balanced scorecard resembles other types of performance interventions, such as total quality management (TQM), reengineering, cross-functional teams, customer-supplier partnerships, and continuous improvement.

The scorecard is unique in its ability to communicate, monitor, and improve organizational performance through its integrated strategy formulation. These elements of the scorecard are closely related to other interventions such as culture reshaping, process redesign, motivation systems, feedback systems, and knowledge management. Linking the success measures to performance and compensation ties this intervention to performance appraisal, compensation, and incentive systems.

When to Use the Balanced Scorecard

The balanced scorecard is commonly used as a tool to measure and improve performance, while clarifying and providing consensus on the desired performance. More and more, organizations are using the scorecard as the framework for establishing an integrated strategic management system. As Kaplan and Norton (1996) describe, organizations are using the balanced scorecard to

- ◆ clarify and update organization strategy
- ◆ communicate strategy throughout the company
- ◆ align unit and individual goals with the strategy
- ◆ link strategic objectives to long-term targets and annual budgets
- ◆ identify and align strategic initiatives
- ◆ conduct periodic performance review to learn about and improve strategy.

The balanced scorecard is most effective in overall strategic alignment. Therefore, its success can filter into many areas of the organization, and it can have an impact on many areas of performance enhancement. For example:

- ◆ *Leadership development:* It gives organizational leaders experience in developing strategy and managing the process.
- ◆ *Team building:* A shared vision, accountability, and responsibility for achieving success can foster cohesiveness and collaboration in groups and among groups.
- ◆ *Motivation:* Working toward a common goal and achieving success with scorecard measures can prove to be unifying and energizing to members of the organization.

The balanced scorecard adds value because it focuses an organization on the output or accomplishment measures, rather than the process-oriented measures that may not be quantifiable.

WHEN NOT TO USE THE BALANCED SCORECARD

The balanced scorecard is not effective when it is tacked onto other organization initiatives that are considered fads or flavors of the month. Implementation of the scorecard calls for a commitment to breakthrough performance. It is not as effective when it is used solely as a measurement system.

EXAMPLES

♦ *Operating Expenses Problem:* The new CEO of a leading property and casualty insurer needs to cut $20 million in operating expenses in order to survive. One likely approach to reducing the company's costs was through a systematic downsizing program. Rather than simply laying off people, the company began by establishing a cross-functional team with the responsibility of coming up with a viable plan that would align the company's units with the organizational objectives. The ultimate goal was to both decrease expenses and create a climate that would allow the company to respond more effectively to the changing business environment.

— *Intervention:* The team, with the help of an external performance consultant, presented management with the balanced scorecard approach. After a thorough review process, management accepted the plan, giving it its full support, and the balanced scorecard was implemented. Over a period of one year, the company has become a more strategy-focused organization and has slowly begun reducing costs. Using the scorecard has differentiated the insurer from the competition, which has for the most part relied on reengineering and total quality management programs.

♦ *Sunlit Power Problem:* Sunlit Power has been feeling the effects of increased competition and a rapidly changing regulatory environment in recent months. Price volatility, pressures, and industry consolidation have challenged the company to become more directed and strategy focused.

— *Intervention:* The company established a steering committee to perform research and benchmark with other companies in the utility industry. With the assistance of a performance improvement specialist, the company decided to introduce the balanced scorecard. To achieve tangible business results, Sunlit split the company into five business units. Each unit was charged with defining the parameters for measuring according to the four perspectives as outlined by the balanced scorecard's architects, Kaplan and Norton. While conceding that the process can be difficult at times, the company has learned to refine its data collection processes and measures so that the process remains focused and accurate.

♦ *Regional Bank Problem:* A regional bank is implementing a major growth strategy through the purchase of many smaller banks and three companies that provide ancillary services to the banking and finance industry. As a result of the rapid growth, the company is concerned about its ability to integrate the new business lines and provide a clear focus for the company's future.

   — *Intervention:* The bank began small-scale implementation of the balanced scorecard in order to begin the process of aligning and integrating the new businesses and services into the company. Starting with one area, business processes, the bank has been able to test the scorecard and allow it to evolve. After achieving success in this area, the company began to roll the scorecard out to other areas. The bank has even begun to use the scorecard as a motivational tool by linking it to performance incentives.

♦ *Human Resource Department Problem:* The human resources department of a young, Web-based retailing firm has instituted the balanced scorecard program into the organization. The goal is to use the system both to measure the organization's performance and to justify the existence of the HR department. Many of the new Internet companies have begun outsourcing the HR function, and the staff of the company is concerned about losing their jobs.

   — *Intervention:* The director of HR started the program without the support of other members of management and assigned performance measures to each of the company's departments without their input. It turns out that the impetus for this program was actually the CEO who was trying to find a way of showing the rest of the organization that the HR department really did understand business measures. He had seen the balanced scorecard idea in a recent edition of *Forbes* magazine and thought this was a perfect way to build credibility for the HR department. The program never got off the ground.

DESIGN GUIDELINES

An effective balanced scorecard requires management to identify the areas that are viewed as a priority for measurement. The success indicators for each measurement must be congruent with the organization's overall strategy. A well-designed balanced scorecard uses the following guidelines:

♦ Know and understand the organizational mission and vision statements and translate them into a workable set of measures and objectives that management agrees to.

♦ Identify the strategic business units and learn about their business needs.

- Establish relevant links to the scorecard measures for each business unit.
- Begin with a manageable number of measures. For example, develop one measure for each of the four dimensions.
- Develop measures that are simple, easy to gather, and easy to interpret. Measures should also be specific and show signs of success or failure. The results of the measures should provide useful, timely information at a reasonable cost to the organization.
- Get feedback on the measures from stakeholders and management.
- Redraft the scorecard as necessary based on feedback and suggestions from stakeholders.
- Assemble a plan for data gathering.
- Implement the measurement plan and report on results. If goals are not being met, report on actions that are being taken to improve performance. Subsequent reports should show progress toward the performance goal.

IMPLEMENTATION GUIDELINES

- Obtain buy-in and support from leadership; these are critical to the success of the balanced scorecard.
- Establish a task force made up of senior management, or cross-functional teams, from each business unit to recommend measures for unit scorecards.
- Establish a communication network, both internally and externally, for all affected employees.
- Allow business units a high level of autonomy to establish measures and objectives as long as they fit within the prescribed guidelines.

REFERENCES AND RESOURCES

Publications

Balanced Scorecard Report. Harvard Business School Press.

"Implementing the Balanced Scorecard at FMC Corporation: An Interview with Larry D. Brady." (September 1993). *Harvard Business Review,* 143–147.

Kaplan, Robert S., and David P. Norton. (January-February 1992). "The Balanced Scorecard—Measures That Drive Performance." *Harvard Business Review,* 71–79.

Kaplan, Robert S., and David P. Norton. (September-October 1993). "Putting the Balanced Scorecard to Work." *Harvard Business Review,* 134–142.

Kaplan, Robert S., and David P. Norton. (1996). *The Balanced Scorecard: Translating Strategy Into Action.* Boston: Harvard Business School Press. This ground-breaking book by the architects of the Balanced Scorecard shows how managers can use this tool to mobilize their people to fulfill the company's mission.

Kaplan, Robert S., and David P. Norton. (1996, January-February). "Using the Balanced Scorecard as a Strategic Management System." *Harvard Business Review,* 75–85.

Manas, Todd. (1999)."Making the Balanced Scorecard Approach Pay Off." *ACA Journal,* 13–21.

Novak, Clare. "HPI Balanced Scorecard." *Info-line.* Issue No. 0010. Alexandria, VA: ASTD.

Internet

http://www.bscol.com. Balanced Scorecard Collaborative.

27

MEETINGS AND DIALOGUE

Ethan S. Sanders and Jacqueline B. Visnius

WHAT ARE MEETINGS AND DIALOGUE?

Meetings are a method of bringing people together to collectively solve problems, share information, plan, and make decisions. It is often best to have face-to-face interaction in order to promote clear communication between members of a group. Dialogues, like meetings, are interactions characterized by open-minded inquiry, active listening, and honest communication. Dialogues are an essential element of successful meetings. Effective meetings require planning and preparation, and must have a stated purpose. Decisions such as who will be included in the meeting and how the meeting will be run must revolve around the meeting's stated purpose.

Effective meetings have the following additional key features:

- ♦ a leader who defines the purpose of the meeting, decides on who will attend, sets the agenda, and runs the meeting
- ♦ participants who have a clear and valid reason for being included in the meeting, know the meeting objectives, and come to the meeting prepared to meet those objectives
- ♦ an agenda that is as brief as possible and a commitment from the meeting participants to adhere to the agenda
- ♦ objectives that are achievable
- ♦ a specific conclusion that documents what was accomplished and what items need to be acted on.

RELATED INTERVENTIONS

Meetings and dialogues are related to knowledge management, newsletters and announcements, and team-building activities.

Other methods of communication within an organization can include retreats, workshops, training and education, work groups, and teams.

WHEN TO USE MEETINGS AND DIALOGUES

Meetings and dialogues are held for a number of reasons, but most often they take place when the knowledge, experience, and opinions of several people are needed. A clear, demonstrated need should exist, and every meeting should have a specific, stated objective and a broad purpose. Dialogues often are particularly important if the meeting is called in order to solve some type of conflict between departments or between people. Meetings are a critical part of every organization and can often perform better than any other communication technique. Meetings are useful in the following situations:

- to share information or plan a project
- to receive information
- to analyze or solve a problem
- to reach group consensus
- to explain or gain support for a decision
- to make recommendations and seek feedback
- to generate new products and processes
- to motivate employees
- to demonstrate a new product or service.

Meetings can provide other benefits as well, including:

- *Motivation:* If the purpose is clear, meetings can be effective in building morale and promoting a sense of teamwork.
- *Group process:* Meetings can be vehicles through which human processes are studied and problem solving is facilitated.

When Not to Use Meetings and Dialogues

The loss of time and money that occurs when meetings are poorly planned or without purpose is quite high. Meetings may not be the most effective means of communicating for the following reasons:

- There is inadequate data or preparation.
- The subject matter is sensitive or confidential and should not be shared with some group members.
- Something can be communicated more effectively by one-on-one discussion, telephone conversation, written memo, or electronic mail.
- A decision has already been made by the management team, and the meeting is only intended to legitimize the decision.
- Conflict or hostility is high in the group, and collaboration is unlikely.
- The subject is trivial or of little interest to most group members.

Examples

- *Electronics Manufacturer Problem:* Sarah, head of data equipment sales for a large electronics manufacturer, has recently noticed that the sales staff has grown further and further away from the engineering services department. Without a good relationship with engineering, the sales staff is unable to adequately address customers' questions about technical issues and development problems. The result has been a number of customer complaints about the sales department's lack of knowledge, responsiveness, and expertise. Sarah was aware that the other sales departments (software, test equipment, and broadcast sales) were having some of the same problems.

— *Intervention:* The managers of each of the four sales departments for the company began holding weekly meetings with the director of engineering services. During these meetings, the group shared information about products, pricing, and functionality. The meetings were well planned with a specific agenda on what each meeting was to cover. The interchange of ideas, concerns, and knowledge was appreciated by both the sales and engineering departments. The increased communication greatly improved the salespeople's ability to more effectively address customer issues, and the engineering department began to understand customers' needs better. Several new products were developed in the next year to fulfill some unmet customer needs.

◆ *Sweets Pricing Problem:* One of the first programs assigned to Jonathan, the new vice president of finance for Sweets, Inc., was to implement a program of pricing and purchasing standardization across the entire company. This proposed policy would require a major change within the company because pricing decisions had previously been the responsibility of the regional directors. A result of the decentralized pricing and purchasing decisions was a wild variance in profits from region to region.

— *Intervention:* Rather than communicating this new policy through the company's email system or by memorandum, Jonathan decided to organize a meeting that would include all individuals whose jobs would be affected by this new policy. After a series of meetings during which the new policy was communicated and all company concerns were addressed, the standardized pricing program was implemented. Profits increased, and the variability across regions leveled off substantially.

◆ *Sales Staff Meeting Problem:* Ben meets with his sales staff each Monday afternoon. Although no one really knows why these regular meetings are scheduled, it is mandatory that everyone attend. Each week, the entire staff sits through the meetings while Ben holds court. Sometimes the group discusses sales activity or company matters, but for the most part, Ben just reviews the minutes from the senior managers' meetings, which is held each Monday morning. This is followed by a round robin at which each sales member describes what he or she has been working on during the preceding week. Even the sales secretary is required to share some aspect of his job during the round robin. The sales staff is convinced that Ben holds these meetings because it gets him points with his boss.

— *Intervention:* This scenario demonstrates a meeting without a purpose. If Ben feels the need to meet face to face, he has to prepare and plan for what is to take place in the meeting. The minutes of the senior staff meeting could easily be distributed through email. At the very least, Ben should synthesize the points down to the key information that the salespeople need to do their job properly. Instead of regularly scheduled staff meetings, it would make a lot more sense to have the sales staff email to Ben their weekly sales activity reports and their action plans for the coming week. He could then devote a specified amount of time during the week to discussing the sales activity with the staff. Currently, the time the staff spends in meetings would be much better spent following up on leads or making sales calls.

DESIGN GUIDELINES

Typically meetings are for one or more of these purposes: problem solving, decision making, planning, reporting or presenting, or evaluation.

Once a purpose and desired results for the meeting are determined, it is time to focus on planning the meeting. A well-planned meeting will have the following design elements:

◆ A set of specific objectives based on the broad purpose. These objectives should be clear, in writing, and communicated to the group in advance of the meeting.

◆ A list of potential participants who are chosen based on the following factors:
  — Who needs the information that will be shared
  — How important the information is to these individuals
  — How valuable the contribution of each participant is to achieving the meeting objectives.

◆ The number or participants determined by the meeting objectives. If the purpose of the meeting is to pass on information about a new policy or product, a larger group can be planned. If the meeting is for budget planning or decision making, however, a smaller group would be in order. It is important to assign the roles of facilitator and record keeper to specific participants who will attend the meeting.

◆ A well-formulated agenda that includes everything that must be covered. This will ensure that you will achieve all of your objectives. The topics should be prioritized in a manner that makes the most sense to the meeting leader (for example, most important to least important).

- A specific date and time that will allow for adequate preparation time for participants. The meeting should be scheduled for a day and time when participants will be most attentive (for example, Monday mornings and Friday afternoons are often the worst time to have a meeting). All meeting times should be scheduled around other organizational priorities, key participants' schedules, and the company's calendar. The length of the meeting is also important. Meetings that last longer than 90 minutes without a break often lose their effectiveness.

- A location chosen based on its proximity to the people attending, the number of participants, facility cost, set-up, and amenities. As much as possible, the location should be distraction-free and comfortable. It is, of course, possible to have a virtual meeting if your company has the proper technology in place. In general, this technology must allow face-to-face communication. Chat rooms, bulletin boards, and email are no substitute for situations that require complex collaboration.

- Established ground rules for use during meetings. Possible ground rules are:
  — Everyone must participate.
  — Respect others' opinions. Seek clarity but do not challenge other people's opinions.
  — Retain focus, maintain momentum, and reach closure on agenda items.

IMPLEMENTATION GUIDELINES

Meetings call for a strong, dynamic leader who normally functions as the group facilitator. The leader does not have to be the most senior staff member at the meeting, but it should be a major stakeholder in the project. The meeting leader must also have a strong sense of what needs to be accomplished during the meeting. A good leader will do the following:

- Adhere to the agenda.
- Maintain a productive climate by listening closely, speaking frankly, encouraging feedback, and accepting feedback professionally.
- Encourage and structure participation by calling on participants for input and allowing only one person to speak at a time. Participation should be equal, with no one individual, including the leader, dominating the meeting.
- Maintain control of the meeting to ensure order and productivity. Even with equal participation, someone must be in charge of the meeting to ensure that participants stay on track and are focused on the meeting objectives.
- Observe participants so that productivity reducers (boredom, frustration) can be spotted and dealt with quickly. Often an

energizing question, break, or an activity will effectively deal with the problem.

♦ Evaluate the success of the meeting through a ranking process or by obtaining feedback from participants.

REFERENCES AND RESOURCES

Publications

Alessandra, T., and P. Hunsaker. (1993). *Communicating at Work*. New York: Simon & Schuster.

Doyle, Michael, and David Straus. (1976). *How to Make Meetings Work*. New York: Berkley.

Journal of Organizational Change Management.

Spruell, Gerry. (1997). "More Productive Meetings." *Info-line*. Issue No. 8710. Alexandria, VA: ASTD.

Internet

http://www.astd.org. ASTD.
www.effectivemeetings.com.
www.iaf-world.org.

Association

International Association of Facilitators (IAF).

28

NEWSLETTERS

Ethan S. Sanders

WHAT ARE NEWSLETTERS?

Although it is somewhat strange to think of a newsletter as an "intervention," newsletters can be an extremely effective way to diminish an organization's communication problem, to publicize employee accomplishments, and to build a sense of community within an organization. A newsletter is any printed pamphlet, brochure, or small newspaper that contains news or information of interest chiefly to a special group. Although we have all read, and perhaps written newsletters, they tend to be one of the most misunderstood forms of communication. Too often, newsletters become dumping grounds for every minute piece of information that employees would like to tell the world. When done correctly, however, newsletters can be an important vehicle for keeping employees updated on current events within the organization and in educating employees on the marketplace surrounding the organization. Newsletters can also be used to communicate with customers, vendors, and other groups of people who are associated with the organization. For purposes of this chapter, however, we will focus on the use of newsletters for internal communication interventions.

RELATED INTERVENTIONS

Any form of internal communication that uses text and still images could be considered a newsletter. Intranet sites are a perfect example of an electronic newsletter. Even regularly scheduled emails that share a common format with newsletters (such as headings, topics, and articles) can be considered newsletters.

Related interventions include the following:

- ◆ Announcements.
- ◆ Brochures.
- ◆ Flyers.
- ◆ Bulletin boards.

- Rewards and recognition: Newsletters are a great place to celebrate people's accomplishments.
- Recruitment and staffing: Newsletters are a great way to educate new and potential employees about the company.

WHEN TO USE NEWSLETTERS

Although there are no golden rules about when to use newsletters, here are some indications that a newsletter may help the organization reach its goals:

- Employees feel that the organization is so departmentalized that they never know what is going on in other parts of the business.
- The organization is changing rapidly, and people are unsure of what decisions have been made, which ones are still pending, when decisions will be made, and who these decisions will affect.
- The organization is trying to build a certain culture and needs to get people to buy in to it.
- The organization has accomplished a lot in a given time period and wants to use these successes to raise the motivation level within the organization.

WHEN NOT TO USE NEWSLETTERS

- Do not use a newsletter if employees urgently need the information. A printed newsletter is not an efficient means for disseminating this type of information. In general, newsletters require a good amount of time for writing, editing, and distribution.
- Never use newsletters as a replacement for face-to-face meetings with employees. If organizations solely rely on newsletters as their communication device, they will find it difficult to consistently provide timely and relevant information.
- Never deliver bad news via a newsletter. Any type of news that is likely to elicit a strong emotional response in employees should be delivered more personally.

EXAMPLES

- *Bank Problem:* After being purchased by a much larger bank, employees of the acquired bank were concerned about the stability of their jobs. There were many decisions that would be made during the six months that the merger was expected to take. Announcements were made early in the process that certain positions, including tellers and branch managers, would be guaranteed, but positions in marketing, accounting, and other areas were in question. Within a few days of the announced merger, it was becoming increasingly difficult to determine which information was official and which information was a product of the rumor mill.

— *Intervention:* Along with several other communication devices, *The Transition Times* was born. It had a logo and look that would act as an official stamp for this information. The newsletter was printed once a month and coupled with a voicemail hotline that was updated daily, pay stuffers that acted like press releases and were included in employees' paychecks, and posters with bulletins attached to them. Although this intervention was not able to reduce all of the anxiety that accompanies a change of this magnitude, it reduced some of the uncertainly about the current status of the merger.

◆ *Moving Company Problem:* A moving company had added three new locations in the past 10 years, and all of these satellite offices were in different states. The company's vision was to build a network of agencies across the company and gain efficiencies through collaboration and teamwork. Each of these companies, however, had become their own little fiefdoms. Although they all bore the same name, each was competing to outshine the other. Many opportunities to share tonnage and gain operating efficiency were lost due to competition.

— *Intervention:* The problem required multiple interventions, of which one was to build a sense of community among the operations. A newsletter was used for this purpose, and employees of the different locations began to realize that they had a lot in common. The newsletter had a regular column that highlighted the accomplishments of employees from different locations who had worked together.

◆ *Employee Satisfaction Problem:* A recent employee satisfaction survey uncovered major issues of dissatisfaction with how employees were being treated, compensated, and managed. In particular, the data was clear that employees felt management never gave them feedback about their performance.

— *Intervention:* A misguided newsletter was begun to try and alleviate some of these concerns. While everyone in the senior management team thought this might help the situation, no one had the time to put it together. The managers asked HR to find someone to write the newsletter, and a vendor was chosen. The vendor received copies of the employee satisfaction survey and some hand-scribbled notes from the management team. HR asked the vendor to write a 15- to 20-page newsletter that would come out "as often as needed."

DESIGN GUIDELINES

Some of the different types of newsletters include those for employees, customers or vendors, and shareholders.

The following tips can help in producing newsletters and announcements:

♦ Before you begin producing a newsletter, carefully consider its intended purpose and its intended audience. To produce something of value to them, you must have a clear understanding of who is going to read it and why.

♦ Consider how frequently the publication will come out. Choose a frequency that matches the organization's needs. Most newsletters are either monthly, bimonthly, or quarterly. If it is less frequent than quarterly, question whether the organization really wants a newsletter. In general, you want to create a situation in which people recognize the newsletter when it arrives on their desk, and they look forward to its publication. Choose the frequency carefully. Nothing looks less professional (and less valuable) than a newsletter that comes out sporadically.

♦ Consider the size of the newsletter. In general, the smaller, the better. It is best from a financial standpoint if you can standardize its size. This will help to keep your printing costs down. However, some of the worst newsletters I have seen have obviously added material just to occupy the allotted amount of space. These fillers often include crossword puzzles, jokes, irrelevant graphics, and cartoons. While these items can add visual interest, they are usually perceived as thin attempts at filling space.

♦ Generating meaningful content will be one of your major challenges. Chances are your organization will not want to hire a full-time newsletter editor. Hiring a freelance editor will often be disappointing. Even excellent freelance writers have a difficult time finding subject matter and a writing style that fits your corporate culture. It is often best to find people within the organization who would like to write for the newsletter. Although their work may need a lot of polishing, the information will seem more credible if it comes from another employee. You can always hire a developmental writer to clean up the prose.

♦ Meaningful content generation can also be aided by a small editorial review committee. Each month (or however often is necessary) the committee can get together and decide on the theme for the next issue, the stories they have heard that will fit this theme, and people within the organization who can write about these ideas.

♦ Come up with a name and a look for the newsletter. Many companies fail to name their publication, which causes the publication to lack a focused identity. If the newsletter is just called the *XYZ Company Newsletter* and is printed on plain white paper, most people will not be able to distinguish it from interoffice memos and other paperwork. Put a lot of time into naming the newsletter. Be clever about it. Play with words and spellings. Words with double meanings can be very powerful if they are done correctly. The name should somehow reflect the company's ideals and the intent of the newsletter. Here are some names I have come up with and the situation they described.

— *The Transition Times* was a newsletter I wrote for a bank that was being acquired. We created a logo that showed the old bank's logo melding into the new bank's logo.

— *The Despatch* was a newsletter I wrote for a transportation company. Here the double meaning of the word *dispatch*—for the name of the department that dispatched the crews and for a news item filed by a correspondent—tied the newsletter together with the company's purpose. Since this was an international shipping company, we used the old English spelling of the word *dispatch* to create a sense of history and a connection to Europe.

— *Cornerstone* was another bank's newsletter that was closely reviewed by the bank's shareholders. They wanted a name that connoted stability and tradition. To also make it contemporary, we came up with a modern logo that made the name look like it was etched in a polished piece of granite.

♦ Do not allow your newsletter to become a hodge-podge of articles and notes. Make sure you have standardized sections to the newsletter (for example, the "mail bag" section that reprints the letters of satisfied customers, or "outlook on the future" that discusses trends in the industry). It is okay to have the cover story vary according to the theme of that particular issue.

♦ It is best if each issue of the newsletter has an overall theme. Find one that reflects the current interests of people in the organization and then select articles that fit that theme. Only columns that are ongoing should be exempt from fitting into that theme (for example, a section that announces recent marriages and the births of employees' children).

♦ Edit and layout are extremely important to the perceived value of a newsletter. No matter how good the content is, most readers will be highly critical of the publication if they find any typos, inaccuracies, or poorly formatted materials. Normally it is better to hire your own editors and designers. Although there are lots of companies that provide these services, you would normally pay a premium and have difficulty controlling the quality. I have frequently used relatives and friends who I know are professional quality nitpickers. Whatever you do, do not allow just anyone to edit your newsletter. Frequently, one of the authors or the person who lays out the newsletter will ask to do the copy editing. Normally, you need to have a fresh set of eyes and someone who is detailed oriented look at the text.

♦ Take a few risks with the newsletter. Take on subjects that are on employees' minds even though they may be politically sensitive. If you write honestly and objectively about a topic, most people will appreciate your bravery. Of course, it is wise to have a senior manager review the article before it is published. That manager can then advocate for the article in the event that some people become upset by the content.

♦ Try to include at least one human interest story in each issue. Employees love to hear about their colleagues' unique interests and hobbies. You will be amazed to learn about your colleagues' diverse talents once you start asking people what they do in their free time.

IMPLEMENTATION GUIDELINES

♦ It is essential that a newsletter come out in regular intervals. Take deadlines seriously. Do not allow the "spring newsletter" to arrive in July.

♦ Begin the production process at least two months before the newsletter is due out. It takes a long time to write and produce one.

♦ Always have a review committee look over the newsletter before it is published. It is often a good idea to have an HR person look it over in order to avoid legal problems with employees.

♦ Shop around for printers and renegotiate printing contracts at least every three years. As the technology for printing changes, the costs can drop dramatically.

♦ Print a lot more copies than you think you will need. If you do a nice job, you will be surprised how many other uses people will find for your newsletter. For example, the sales and marketing department will often use them to promote the company; employees who appear in the newsletter will want extra copies for friends and relatives; and HR may use them for recruiting. In general, the first 300 to 500 copies are the most expensive to print. After that the copies are only a few pennies each.

♦ Choose the paper stock carefully. I have found that glossy stock paper normally is not worth the extra money. Also, glossy stock cannot always be recycled. A heavy stock and muted color is normally your best bet. The heavy paper just makes the newsletter feel more "weighty" (pun intended), and readers tend to respond better to it. Of course, you will need to check if your company has style and identity guidelines on what colors the company logo is allowed to appear with.

♦ Do not allow the design to interfere with readability. First and foremost, the newsletter must be easy to read.

REFERENCES AND RESOURCES

Publication

Fanson, Barbara A. (1994). *Producing a First-Class Newsletter: A Guide to Planning, Writing, Editing, Designing, Photography, Production, and Printing.* Bellingham, WA: Self Counsel.

Internet
http://www.tedgoff.com/erlist.html.

Association
Newsletter and Electronic Publishers Association (NEPA),
http://www.newsletters.org.

29

PUBLIC RELATIONS CAMPAIGNS

Jennifer Homer

WHAT IS A PUBLIC RELATIONS CAMPAIGN?

Public relations (PR) campaigns are interventions designed to promote the exchange of influence and understanding among an organization's constituent parts and the public. Public relations is a management function that helps define organizational objectives and philosophy. Public relations campaigns attempt to communicate with all relevant internal and external stakeholders in the effort to create consistency between organizational goals and societal expectations, as Baskin and Aronoff (1988) explain.

RELATED INTERVENTIONS

Many interventions that stress the need for improved organizational communication include public relations team members and expertise. These interventions must involve communication with the public or other external stakeholders in order to be considered a form of public relations. For example, company Websites are a vehicle for public relations literature, although they are frequently attributed to marketing and sales functions.

WHEN TO USE PUBLIC RELATIONS CAMPAIGNS

Although they do not like to admit it, many organizations suffer from image problems. Many times, this image problem starts from the inside of the organization because employees do not fully understand what business the organization is in, what the organization's goals and objectives are, who the organization's customers and markets are, and how the organization will measure success. Many employees come to work every day, but do not know how their work and performance relates to the organization's bottom line.

The senior management of an organization often relies heavily on the PR department to fix an image problem. The problem could stem from a product recall, to a chemical spill, to some negative reports about the behavior of a top leader, or from poor customer service and fulfillment. The problem will affect the organization's customers, investors, employees, and everyone else who comes in contact with the organization. While the PR department is largely responsible for combating the negative press, everyone in the organization has to work to improve the image, especially the frontline staff who come in contact with customers every day.

Organizations must use a variety of tools to keep track of media placements and other mentions in newspapers, on the Internet, or on television. Media clipping services are an invaluable tool that will track an organization's name, acronym, or associated words and tell how often any of those appear in thousands of daily and weekly newspapers, on Websites, and on television news. Although it is relatively easy to gauge public opinion from media clips, organizations should also conduct regular satisfaction surveys to determine the opinion of another important group of stakeholders: customers and clients. It is important to point out that although an organization's image in the media may be positive, if customers or clients are not satisfied, the company still has an image problem to resolve. This is where the internal and external communication systems must work hand in hand. If the entire organization—from the frontline staff to the CEO—is not speaking with the same words and talking in the same language to the customers, the image problem will not improve. That is why it is critical that employees be engaged in the business, understand the goals of the organization, and be able to communicate up the chain of command and listen when communication is coming from the top.

In most organizations, the PR or communications department is charged with responding to media inquiries, disseminating news releases to the media, communicating companywide information to employees, writing speeches for the organization's top leaders, planning events, and so on. However, the role of PR and communications in an organization can be much more than just spreading company news. An effective PR or communications department can:

- ♦ help employees understand their role in the organization and how they can have an impact on the bottom line
- ♦ link together employees and senior management in a tighter, more strategic relationship
- ♦ use the organization's experts for speeches, events, and special writing tasks
- ♦ improve or enhance the organization's image in the minds of investors, industry leaders, employees, customers, and other audiences
- ♦ improve organizational performance.

WHEN NOT TO USE PUBLIC RELATIONS CAMPAIGNS

- ♦ Before drastically changing the way the department runs its PR campaigns, map the entire PR campaign process, from beginning to end, to determine ways to improve speed, response time, and message dissemination. Benchmark your PR campaign against several other organizations to gather and adopt best practices.

♦ Do not make assumptions about the audiences or media segments; instead, interview as many types of audiences as possible to gain a clear view of their information needs.

♦ Do not assume your PR campaign has all the relevant messages that will appeal to the media. Scan the newspapers, magazines, or other media outlets for trends in stories, headlines, and newsworthy information. Pick up on one or two trends that your organization has an expertise in and exploit them in your press materials.

♦ Always keep an up-to-date, comprehensive database of your key media contacts and reporters, and track their interview or information requests so you can follow up in the future.

♦ Never let an organizational spokesperson conduct an interview with the media without proper preparation and role-playing (practice questions, make sure key organizational messages are clear, and so forth). A spokesperson that gives a bad interview in the media can do a great deal of damage to the organization's reputation and public image!

EXAMPLES

♦ *Fulfillment Problem:* An organization has a negative image in the media due to a recent fulfillment problem: It was not getting enough inventory out to retail stores. The negative image hurt sales during the winter holidays.

— *Intervention:* The CEO, senior management, and PR department crafted an aggressive campaign of newspaper ads, radio commercials, and television commercials. The message from the CEO was clear and concise, admitting the problem, and explaining what the company is doing to fix it. The campaign also included an offer of $10 off the customer's purchase. The company worked to improve fulfillment following the holiday crisis to ensure that the same problem would not surface the next year. Throughout the year, the company communicated those improvements to customers so they would return during the coming holiday season.

♦ *Website Problem:* The employees of an organization are writing negative remarks about the company in a Website. The company's stock is suffering because of the employees' unrest.

— *Intervention:* The CEO and senior management held open meetings to discuss the negative remarks and why the employees were unhappy. After allowing employees to voice their concerns, the CEO (and senior management) immediately explained what steps they were going to take to resolve the issues. These steps included an immediate review of wage equity between male and female workers, the administration of a multirater 360 feedback assessment for all managers, and a review of the company's leave policy for workers with family emergencies. The key is making promises and keeping them. If the CEO were only interested in hearing the concerns, but not committed to resolving them, then the problem could surface again and become much worse. The PR department helped the CEO and senior management craft messages, explain clearly what the employees were unhappy about, and suggested a course of action. The PR department suggested implementing a new internal communications vehicle, an electronic newsletter, so that employees understand what's going on in the business, and have appropriate means for giving feedback and suggestions. They key to success was follow-through.

DESIGN GUIDELINES

The following tips will help you design a PR campaign:

♦ Establish the goals (including the purpose, mission, objectives, and strategies), determine the present situation, determine the aids and barriers to the goals, and forecast for the future.
♦ Establish strategic plans (long range) and tactical plans (specific decisions and actions) for your campaign.
♦ Consider your budgets carefully. Have a short-range budget and also project the costs through the duration of a campaign.

How you proceed will depend on the type of campaign. Baskin and Aronoff (1988) classify PR campaigns in the following way:

♦ *Media relations:* Reaching journalists, assignment editors, and producers through news releases, telephone interviews, face-to-face interviews, events, and press conferences.
♦ *Community relations:* Planned, active, and continuing participation within a community to maintain and enhance its environment to the benefit of the organization and the community.
♦ *Employee communications:* Help employees become well informed about their organization and encourage them to express their views to management.
♦ *Consumer relations and marketing:* Public relations and marketing functions should be supportive of each other. Public relation's support for the overall marketing mix, including product design, distribution, communication, and pricing, can greatly increase the effectiveness of any marketing strategy.
♦ *Financial (or investor) relations:* Provide prompt disclosure of corporate news that is significant to the financial community. Strong financial relations programs, characterized by responsiveness,

openness, and regular communication, help lower the cost of capital for businesses.

♦ *Government relations and public affairs:* Shape public opinion and legislation, develop effective responses to matters of public concern, and help adapt to public expectations. In addition, public affairs activities may be involved in monitoring public policy, providing political education for employees or constituents, maintaining liaisons with various governmental units, and encouraging political participation.

IMPLEMENTATION GUIDELINES

The following steps are recommended in implementing PR campaigns:

♦ Continually review the campaign designed to ensure that the objectives are being met. Also make sure you continually monitor and address the nonroutine procedures and decisions that are being made. Although some modifications to the original plan will always be necessary during implementation, it is important not to lose sight of the original goals of the campaign.

♦ Keep track of how well the campaign is addressing the stated problem, the needs of the audience, the allotted time frame, the projected costs, and the evaluation design.

♦ Build a PR infrastructure. Over time, many PR campaigns can become routine. Often similar situations will occur that will allow you to reuse PR campaigns that were implemented in the past. Be sure you are always debriefing and learning from past implementations so that future efforts can be carried out with minimal effort and maximum effectiveness. These "reusable" campaigns must be created with organizational policies, procedures, and rules in mind.

Public relations campaigns can make a significant contribution to a positive organizational climate by influencing organizational decisions and internal communications, and by establishing organizational communication policy based on a goal-oriented approach. If an organization is suffering from an image problem, for example, the PR department can help identify the source of the problem, the departments involved, and a communications solution that involves both internal and external vehicles. Take a chemical spill as a real-life crisis. An effective public relations campaign would already have a crisis plan in place. Here's how it would work:

♦ As soon as the event happens, the CEO, executive management team, and PR department meet to discuss the incident, employees involved, customers affected, effect on the local community or environment, and other stakeholders.

♦ The entire team chooses a media spokesperson as well as an internal spokesperson and begins to craft relevant messages.

- ◆ The entire team crafts a solution and plan of action for dealing with the crisis.
- ◆ An internal spokesperson (probably the president or CEO) communicates with the employees first, providing all relevant information, and the action plan for dealing with the crisis.
- ◆ The media spokesperson issues a news release or statement immediately following the incident, and conducts all media interviews.
- ◆ The PR team and media spokesperson follow up with media as necessary.
- ◆ The president or CEO, executive management team, and PR department debrief about the incident, and determine necessary steps to prevent the same crisis from happening again.

REFERENCES AND RESOURCES

Publications

Baskin, Otis, and Craig Aronoff. (1988). *Public Relations: The Profession and the Practice* (3d edition). Dubuque, IA: William C. Brown.

Communication World. A publication of the International Association of Business Communicators.

Shaffer, Jim. (2000). *The Leadership Solution*. New York: McGraw-Hill.

Internet

www.iabc.com. Website for the International Association of Business Communicators (IABC).

www.prsa.org. Website for the Public Relations Society of America (PRSA).

Associations

IABC.

PRSA.

30

DEBRIEFING

Sivasailam Thiagarajan

WHAT IS DEBRIEFING?

While experience may be the best teacher, raw experience alone does not automatically guarantee that people learn from it. People learn from experience only when they reflect on it, gain valuable insights, and share these insights with each other. Debriefing is the process of facilitating participants to help them reflect on their experience, gain valuable insights, and share them with each other.

RELATED INTERVENTIONS

- ◆ Action learning involves a combination of action and reflection by a team that solves complex, strategic problems in a real-world organizational setting. Team members apply existing skills and knowledge and create new skills, knowledge, and insights through continuously reflecting on and questioning the problem definition, the collaborative behavior, and the ensuing results. The debriefing procedure is built into the action-learning cycle.
- ◆ Coaching is an intervention in which one person improves the performance of another by interactive questioning, collaborative goal setting, systematic observation, constructive feedback, and positive guidance. Most coaching sessions incorporate debriefing of individual performers.
- ◆ Training games are interventions that improve participants' competency levels. In simulation games, the rules of the game reflect some workplace process and the play objects reflect real-world artifacts. Debriefing is an essential component of simulation games.

WHEN TO USE DEBRIEFING

- ◆ *Learning moments:* Organizational life is replete with important milestones such as completing a project, passing an inspection, and acquiring a new client. All of these milestones reflect the culmination of processes experienced by different people. These milestones provide appropriate opportunities for debriefing participants to capture the lessons learned during the experience.

♦ *Feeling the pain:* Organizational life is also full of painful tragedies such as accidents, downsizing, mergers, loss of clients, and discontinuation of product lines. Appropriate debriefing techniques can help people to process the impact of these events, discover useful principles, and move on to future activities.

♦ *Abstract and complex:* Debriefing also helps people to revisit large-scale events (both real-world and simulated ones), analyze the elements, derive cause-and-effect relationships, and decide the best course of future action.

♦ *Emotional involvement:* People feeling intense emotions—whether positive or negative—find it difficult to focus on logical patterns and root causes. In highly emotional situations, most people make mindless assumptions and acquire superstitious behavior patterns. Used appropriately, debriefing can support experiential learning by adding a rational component.

♦ *Slowing down:* In today's complex and dynamic workplace, critical events occur so rapidly that their significance is lost on the people affected by it. Debriefing enables us to take the time to reflect on what happened during these sudden events and to learn how to better cope with future events of a similar nature.

Other uses of debriefing include the following:

♦ *Human performance improvement:* Debriefing may reinforce different steps of the human performance improvement (HPI) process. For example, a focus group of employees can be debriefed to identify major performance problems and to analyze the root causes. Similarly, debriefing can be used as an effective technique for collecting, interpreting, and processing evaluation data about the effectiveness of the new intervention.

♦ *Performance improvement:* Debriefing can be used to strengthen any other performance-improvement intervention. It can be added to another intervention to ensure continuous improvement. For example, it could be used as the last step in the conflict management process to help the confronting partners reflect on their experience and learn from it.

WHEN NOT TO USE DEBRIEFING

♦ *When you are rushed:* Take your time. It is important to set aside ample time for the debriefing discussion. Do not make the mistake of ignoring the time required for debriefing while scheduling an experiential activity.

♦ *When you do not have qualified help:* Know your limits. Remember that you are not licensed to practice therapy. In situations that involve intense emotional trauma, seek the help of trained professionals instead of adding to the problem through inappropriate intervention.

EXAMPLES

♦ *Poison Problem:* Customers at a restaurant suffered from a mild case of food poisoning. This situation resulted in health inspections, media frenzy, confusion among employees, and a significant drop in the number of customers. The situation was handled in a somewhat sloppy manner, requiring a couple of months before things returned to normalcy.

— *Intervention:* Recognizing this experience as a learning opportunity, the performance consultant assembled a cross section of restaurant employees along with a few representative customers and suppliers. She facilitated an extensive debriefing session to analyze what happened during the situation and what factors contributed to the inefficiency in handling it. The group also played out various what-if scenarios involving fatalities, lawsuits, and permanent damage to the business's reputation. The resulting set of recommendations from this group was circulated to other employees for additional inputs. As a result of this debriefing, the restaurant now has a set of guidelines for preventing, managing, and containing future cases of food poisoning.

♦ *Reengineering Problem:* A large financial-services institution was planning to reengineer its processes and install a new information management system. Even before the change was implemented, rumors about its impact were flying around, distracting the employees, making them anxious about their future, and significantly reducing their productivity. After investigating the situation, the performance consultant decided to conduct a proactive debriefing exercise that involved all employees of the organization.

— *Intervention:* The debriefing session was conducted as a large group activity, involving nearly 600 employees, all assembled in the ballroom of a local hotel. This collection of participants was divided into breakout groups of 30, each with employees from different functions, job levels, and years of service. Facilitators conducted debriefing discussions with each breakout group, using the same set of questions, but in a flexible format. Results from each group were rolled up to the coordinating team, which presented this summary information to the entire group through a computerized slide show. The breakout groups were then reassembled into new groups to discuss the similarities and differences of the outputs from earlier groups. At the end of the second round of debriefing, each group came up with a set of recommendations. The session ended with members of the top management addressing major concerns identified during the debriefing and all participants preparing personal action plans for effectively coping with the forthcoming change.

DESIGN GUIDELINES

Debriefings vary according to the type of experience, size of the group, and type of facilitator.

- *Type of experience:* Reality debriefing involves real-world experiences in the workplace. Simulated debriefing involves experiential learning activities such as training games, role-plays, and corporate adventure exercises.
- *Group size:* Large group debriefing involves a discussion with hundreds of participants. This type of debriefing usually begins with discussions in subgroups, whose outputs are later analyzed by the entire group. Small group debriefing involves three to 10 participants who have shared the same experience (for example, completing a project) from different perspectives. Individual debriefing involves a single participant who has undergone a significant experience (for example, surviving an act of workplace violence).
- *Type of facilitator:* Typically, an external facilitator coordinates the debriefing discussion. In a different type of debriefing, a team may manage its own debriefing without depending on external facilitation. Sometimes, individuals may be debriefed through a questionnaire that is administered either in a paper-and-pencil mode or online mode.

Following are tips to help in designing a debriefing:

- Use a model. You can increase the effectiveness of a debriefing session by preparing a set of appropriate questions to probe different elements of the experience. In general, these questions should reflect the following topics for reflection:
  — How do you feel?
  — What happened?
  — What did you learn?
  — How does this relate to other aspects of your work life?
  — What if the situation were different?
  — What should you do differently in the future?

- Analyze the experience. The most effective way to prepare debriefing questions is to analyze the original experience into its components, including events and decision points, objects involved in the process, feelings and emotions aroused by the process, people involved in the process, principles associated with the process, and scenarios related to situational variables. You can use lists of these components to generate comprehensive sets of questions related to each of the topics suggested earlier.
- Integrate debriefing with other activities. For best results, incorporate debriefing discussions with team meetings. You can also

include debriefing as the final step in all technical and interpersonal processes.

♦ Do it regularly. Conduct a debriefing discussion at weekly or monthly intervals—even when no significant event has occurred. This type of periodical debriefing enables you to obtain information about multiple perspectives and helps participants develop fluency with the technique.

IMPLEMENTATION GUIDELINES

♦ Train facilitators. Successful debriefing programs in your organization depend on the availability of trained people who can facilitate these discussions. Begin your debriefing initiative by training a group of facilitators. Do not limit yourself to members of the training department. Include a variety of managers and team leaders in your group of facilitators.

♦ Encourage extreme flexibility. The real secret of converting managers into facilitators is to encourage a mindset that enables them to be simultaneously structured and flexible. While it is important for the facilitators to have an organized set of debriefing questions, it is equally important to encourage spontaneous comments from the participants. The general approach should be one of encouraging a freewheeling dialogue and falling back to the prepared structure when the conversation meanders in meaningless directions.

♦ Publish the results. Encourage people to reflect on their experiences by giving them samples of other people's reflections. Summarize insights and action plans from each debriefing session and make this summary available to a large audience through print and electronic channels. Solicit feedback and inputs from readers to continuously increase and improve the results of reflection.

♦ Preserve confidentiality. The effectiveness of debriefing sessions depends heavily on the participants' honesty, even when it is painful. Nothing dampens the authenticity of a debriefing session as the fear of being the only person to point out that the emperor is naked or the need to speak in politically correct conundrums. Protect the privacy of participants who make potentially controversial statements by publishing the results without individual attribution.

REFERENCES AND RESOURCES

Publication

Luckner, John L., and Reldan S. Nadler. (1997). *Processing the Experience: Strategies to Enhance and Generalize Learning* (2d edition). Dubuque, IA: Kendall/Hunt. Originally designed for use with outdoor experiential learning, the models, activities, and questions in this book can be adapted for use in any type of debriefing context.

Internet

http://www.reviewing.co.uk. Roger Greenaway's Website contains practical advice and useful information.

Association

North American Simulation and Gaming Association (NASAGA). Members of this professional organization frequently conduct research on different aspects of debriefing. NASAGA annual conferences feature several sessions on debriefing techniques.

CHAPTER 6

GET WELL SOON: IMPROVING HEALTH

31. Energy Management
    by Mark L. Berman

32. Work-Life Balance
    by Mark L. Berman

33. Employee Assistance Programs
    by Ethan S. Sanders
    and Jacqueline B. Visnius

34. Counseling
    by Kathy Kelly

35. Win-Win Negotiation
    by Kat Koppett

36. Violence Prevention
    by Todd Packer

"Early to bed and early to rise, makes a man healthy, wealthy, and wise."
—Benjamin Franklin

	Individual	Group	Cheap	Expensive	Together	Spread Out	Need it Fast	Have Time
Individual			Energy Management Work-Life Balance	Counseling		Energy Management Work-Life Balance Counseling		Energy Management Work-Life Balance Counseling
Group			Negotiating Violence Prevention	EAP	Negotiating Violence Prevention	EAP	EAP Negotiating Violence Prevention	
Cheap	Energy Management Work-Life Balance	Negotiating Violence Prevention			Negotiating Violence Prevention	Energy Management Work-Life Balance	Negotiating Violence Prevention	Energy Management Work-Life Balance
Expensive	Counseling	EAP				EAP Counseling	EAP	Counseling
Together		Negotiating Violence Prevention	Negotiating Violence Prevention				Negotiating Violence Prevention	
Spread Out	Energy Management Work-Life Balance Counseling	EAP	Energy Management Work-Life Balance	EAP Counseling			EAP	Energy Management Work-Life Balance Counseling
Need it Fast	Negotiating	EAP Violence Prevention	Negotiating Violence Prevention	EAP	Negotiating Violence Prevention	EAP		
Have Time	Energy Management Work-Life Balance Counseling		Energy Management Work-Life Balance	Counseling		Energy Management Work-Life Balance Counseling		

31

ENERGY MANAGEMENT

Mark L. Berman

WHAT IS ENERGY MANAGEMENT?

Energy management involves monitoring, preserving, and enhancing the three main types of personal energy: physical, emotional, and intellectual. A common purpose is to ensure sufficient energy to regularly and continuously achieve job-related goals. No one has an unlimited supply of energy, though some appear predisposed to have more than others. Even the most energized persons have their limits. Pushing past these limits for brief periods may produce temporary energy "outages." Consistently depleting one's energy supply over a considerable period of time may produce a condition referred to as burnout. The latter is characterized by lowered productivity, reduced mood, and minimal energy in one or more areas.

The foundation of energy management is built upon 10 key principles. All of these may have profound effects on energy supply:

1. What you do and think affects energy supply.
2. When you do things, including the order you engage in various tasks, affects energy supply.
3. How you do things (efficiently or inefficiently, for example) affects energy supply.
4. Expend the most energy on your most important tasks.
5. Reward actions or thoughts which contribute to effective energy management.
6. Reduce negative as well as increase positive self-talk.
7. Identify, monitor, and reduce sources of stress.
8. Modify and improve diet, sleep, and exercise programs.
9. Participate in as many energy-increasing activities as possible.
10. Secure others' support and assistance for your energy management efforts.

Related Interventions

Energy management, burnout prevention, stress management, and time management are all related to a greater or lesser degree. The main way that energy management relates to health is that extended periods of very low energy are not only a ticket for burnout, but also may contribute to or exacerbate physical illness, mental fatigue, and emotional distress. Energy management is similar to work-life balance in that lack of balance can produce excessive drains of one or more energies. Energy management relates to employee assistance programs in that low energy often is a root cause of employees' seeking help from such programs. Energy management relates to inside air quality improvement in that poor air quality can lead to reduced physical energy, which in turn could have a negative impact on both intellectual and emotional energy.

When to Use Energy Management

Energy management is most appropriately utilized in situations in which employees are hammered by demands to be more productive, but are provided with insufficient resources to fully accomplish their objectives in the time allotted. Long hours on the job month after month, coupled with having to engage in very demanding tasks will typically, over time, adversely affect productivity, mood, and other areas. Due to increased competition and other factors, it is getting harder to climb up at least some career ladders. Even very qualified and motivated workers may not be guaranteed a smooth upward ascent. In order to get ahead, workers generally have to acquire new skills and information bases. This often requires considerable energy expenditure, especially intellectual, but often emotional as well. In addition, new responsibilities and greater decision-making latitude are likely to place real demands on energy supplies. To stay in the hunt, workers will likely have to work harder, longer, and smarter. This probably will have a cost in terms of accelerated expenditures of all three energies.

Whether or not a particular individual will be counted among the select few who make it up the ladder may have as much to do with the amount of personal energy at the person's disposal as any other single factor, including native intelligence, training, formal education, on-the-job experience, and drive to succeed.

Energy management may be preferred over other interventions because it focuses on highly specific actions or behaviors, involves precise measurement of energy levels, and can generally be shown to play a significant role in improved job performance, mood, and the like.

When Not to Use Energy Management

Energy management is likely to have no impact when:

♦ the amount of personal energy available to an individual is not a relevant factor

◆ the person has a great deal of all three energies and utilizes techniques to effectively manage these energies.

Focusing on energy management in situations in which severe emotional or behavioral problems, or both, are the true culprits can, at the least, prove counterproductive and may even be destructive to the recipient.

EXAMPLES

◆ *Workaholic Problem:* John is a dedicated worker, essentially a workaholic. He puts in whatever hours a task requires to get it done, even if it means going without a single break all day. This approach to his job has earned John the admiration of his supervisor, but also has led to a number of days when he experiences energy outages.

— *Intervention:* A colleague advises him that taking one or two 15-minute tension-free breaks during the workday can lead to greater overall productivity than plugging along with no time out to relax and recoup his energy. John tries it. It works!

◆ *Glass Ceiling Problem:* Joan is a very bright, highly knowledgeable, and well-trained midlevel executive who is definitely on her way to higher and more responsible positions. She has run into and broken through numerous glass ceilings in her 10-plus years in the business world. Now, however, she has been promoted to a setting in which, for the first time in her experience, a number of her colleagues seriously ask, "Can a woman handle this job?" Their doubts are taking a huge toll on her emotional energy (which is involved, for example, in conflict resolution and in staying calm and focused under strong criticism).

— *Intervention:* Joan learns that her self-talk or internal dialogue plays a large role in determining the amount of emotional energy drain that she suffers. Through monitoring and modifying how she talks to herself about herself (that is, labeling and then reducing self-doubt), Joan is able to minimize this effect.

◆ *Inactivity Problem:* Paul is tired all the time, both at work and elsewhere. He is a rather inactive person, who spends considerable time trying to determine what is causing him to feel fatigued. An examination by a physician comes up negative (no significant medical problems). Paul decides that what he needs to do is to get more rest. He does precisely that, but his fatigue only increases.

— *Intervention:* A few months later a friend suggests that perhaps what Paul needs is to rest less and exercise more. Paul follows his advice, and with very good results.

◆ *Universal Donor Problem:* Mary is what is called a Universal Donor. This means that she will give of her time and energy to anyone who requests it of her, no matter how crucial the tasks she currently is working on are to the overall functioning of the organization that employs her. Simply ask Mary to do something for you, and she will take a break from what she is doing and help you out. What a great gal! Unfortunately, over time this always-help-the-other-person attitude inevitably causes Mary to miss deadlines on her projects. An insightful and understanding co-worker whom Mary trusts informs her that serving as the universal donor is counterproductive.

— *Intervention:* Mary's colleague suggests actions she can take to deal with this propensity. Mary learns to identify her most important activities and then to devote the bulk of her time and energy to them. She still helps out other workers, but only if doing so does not significantly impede her ability to accomplish her most crucial objectives.

DESIGN GUIDELINES

The primary categories of interventions involved in energy management are as follows:

♦ *Monitoring and measurement:* Monitoring and measurement need to be carried out in order to determine the amount of energy available in each of the three areas (physical, intellectual, and emotional). Without this knowledge, it is difficult if not impossible to know how much to focus on either energy conservation or enhancement. As a result, there is a higher likelihood of energy outages or, perhaps, burnout than if monitoring or measurement were regularly pursued.

♦ *Implementation of techniques or procedures:* It is necessary to have a careful matching of one's own energy management needs to the precise techniques or procedures that are most likely to have the most beneficial effect on energy supplies.

♦ *Prediction of energy expenditures:* The ability to accurately predict upcoming energy expenditures increases the chances that sufficient energy will be available when it is needed.

The following tips will help in designing an energy management intervention:

♦ Ensure that highly specific problematic behaviors (that is, those that are likely to be unnecessarily depleting energy) are targeted.

♦ Emphasize the need to use precise and fairly frequent measurement, at least early in the process of developing an effective energy management program.

♦ Encourage attention to the other energies (that is, intellectual and emotional), as these are more often responsible for outages or burnout than is physical energy.

IMPLEMENTATION GUIDELINES

♦ Consider the broadest range of key factors, conditions, and circumstances (for example, marital disagreements, children's behavioral difficulties) that likely affect energy supplies.

♦ Do not assume that because you experience fatigue, the cause is always depleted physical energy (or emotional or intellectual energy). Evaluate your supply of all three varieties in order to determine which are most relevant at the time.

♦ If possible, work with another person on your and his or her energy supply, in a sort of buddy system. This system includes occasional monitoring of the other's apparent energy level and advising your buddy when one or more energies appear low or to be dropping rapidly.

REFERENCES AND RESOURCES

Publication

Cooper, Robert K. (1986). *High Energy Living.* Emmaus, PA: Rodale. *Journal of Occupational Health Psychology.*

Internet

OnHealth.Webmd.com.

Association

American Psychological Association.

32

Work-Life Balance

Mark L. Berman

What Is Work-Life Balance?

At first glance the concept of work-life balance may call to mind the old saying, "All work and no play makes Jack a dull boy." The latter conveys a time-honored belief that you require a fair amount of recreation in your life, or else you will drown in boredom, tedium, overwork, and the like.

My experience as a consulting psychologist is not in keeping with this truism. What I have found is that the Jacks (and Jills) of the world vary greatly in what constitutes an effective balance between work and the rest of their life activities. Simply put, an arrangement that is beneficial for one person may be highly detrimental to another person.

An important consideration in assessing work-life balance is the contribution that employment makes to our lives in general, beyond income, status, or power. For example, how does our work affect our personal energy (physical, intellectual, emotional) supply? Does it allow us to have a sense of accomplishment in what we do and to take pride in our achievements? Do we look forward to going to work, and do we enjoy most if not all of the various tasks it involves?

For those whose jobs are energy enhancing and provide feelings of pride and accomplishment, work clearly is a major plus. Persons in this position may find that, up to a point, the more they work, the better they feel physically, mentally, intellectually, and in other aspects of their life as well. For them the optimum work-life balance may be highly skewed toward a substantial workload.

The bottom line is this: Some people can put in a great deal of time on the job and yet maintain a viable work-life balance. They can do this if their work is essentially energy enhancing. If work is quite energy depleting, stressful, and otherwise debilitating, however, then a very different work-life balance is likely going to be required, one where considerable time away from the job is crucial. Keep in mind that it is not always the number of hours we work that really matters, but how these hours affect us over time.

Here are some indicators that a work-life situation may be out of balance:

♦ We suffer chronic mental, physical, or intellectual fatigue.
♦ We experience deteriorating relationships with family members, friends, or co-workers.
♦ Our work productivity declines substantially over time.
♦ We develop emotional or behavioral difficulties, such as low mood.
♦ We display a tendency to engage in avoidance behaviors at work, rather than working to achieve positive outcomes.

Such indicators should be monitored often and closely enough to detect significant changes in their status. In the absence of hard data, try not to automatically assume that an out-of-balance work-life situation is the result of too much work or work that is too challenging.

RELATED INTERVENTIONS

Energy management (see intervention 31 in this chapter) is related to work-life balance in that methods to minimize energy depletion and to maximize energy enhancement will increase the likelihood that an optimal balance is achieved and maintained.

WHEN TO USE WORK-LIFE BALANCE

Use this intervention when you determine that there is a significant imbalance between work and the rest of your life. By monitoring such things as the quality of your relationships with family, friends, and co-workers, you will be able to assess the balance and determine procedures to improve it.

WHEN NOT TO USE WORK-LIFE BALANCE

Changes in work-life balance may be difficult if not impossible to make under a variety of conditions, including the following:

♦ when rigid employer practices preclude modifications in key aspects of the job
♦ when time constraints are very pronounced, limiting the availability of enjoyable, energy-enhancing, and stress-reducing nonwork activities.

EXAMPLES

♦ *Tedium Problem:* Bill has worked 60-plus hours a week for the past 30 years. In fact, most of his time is spent at work. Until about two years ago, Bill had a highly varied and exceptionally interesting workload. Then things changed drastically. His work routine more and more became the same old, same old. Repetition and tedium replaced freshness and excitement. Now working long hours became a real drag. What formerly functioned as a good work-life balance now was way off the mark.

— *Intervention:* Bill considered several possible options. He could try to reduce his work hours or increase his off-work time, or both. The demands of his job were such that Bill could not easily cut back the time he spent at work. He could and did, however, develop several new leisure time activities. Implementation of the latter helped Bill again achieve a good work-life balance.

◆ *Physically Ill Problem:* Betty constantly felt physically ill. Her visits to physicians were becoming more frequent, though doctors could not find anything wrong with her. She was working but 24 hours a week, so burnout did not loom as a strong explanatory concept. What was going on?

— *Intervention:* It turns out that Betty had absolutely no recreational outlets. Over time, a number of her closest friends had moved away. Betty decided to join several organizations, whereupon she made new friends, and opened up a new world of recreational opportunities.

◆ *Energy at Work Problem:* Sam expended a great deal of energy at work. His basic philosophy was quite simple. The more hours he devoted to his job, the greater his income, kudos from management, and pace of advancement. Sam felt that an effective work-life balance meant that he worked many hours, with little attention paid to anything else. One day he decided that he could likely boost his feelings of self-worth if he added another hour to each work day. After implementing this schedule, Sam found that he experienced a serious energy shortfall. Why?

— *Intervention:* Because he already was expending a lot of energy on the job, meaning that his increased work hours resulted in even more energy depletion than before, without increased recreational time to offset these losses. Sam made a negative impact on his work-life balance.

◆ *Recreational Activities Problem:* Helen's friend engaged in numerous recreational activities that served to keep her well-balanced in terms of work versus nonwork activities. Helen, who engages in only a few such activities, decided to follow her friend's broad-scale approach, but nothing happened. Her work-life balance remained far from ideal. Why is this?

— *Intervention:* What works for one person may not work for another. Helen learned that she really does not enjoy a lot of recreational activities that many other persons avidly pursue. She then turned her attention to changes on the work side of the equation and with good results.

DESIGN GUIDELINES

Your benefits will be greater the more you know the precise mix of work-life balance activities that best serves you.

♦ Discuss with others how they go about achieving an optimal work-life balance.

♦ Enlist others to assist you in monitoring your personal work-life balance.

♦ Think about your main work-related tasks. Determine how each generally affects such things as your energy, stress, and mood levels. If you find that your work-life balance is not optimal, it may be that excessive work involvement plays a significant role. If so, consider increasing your involvement in energy-enhancing, mood-elevating, and stress-reducing on-the-job activities, while decreasing your participation in tasks that are energy-depleting and the like.

♦ When your work-life balance is less than ideal, and you suspect that insufficient or ineffective nonwork activities may be an important factor in this, assess how each of them typically affects energy, stress, mood, and so on. Consider becoming more involved in those activities that are stress-reducing, mood-elevating, and the like.

♦ Especially for women: It is often the case that female workers are expected to go flat out in performing whatever other roles—mother, wife—they may have. Any woman who wears two or more such hats is likely no stranger to this situation. They know that the demands on them can be very high, which may make achieving a positive work-life balance a far greater challenge than it is for men in general. There is, of course, no quick-and-dirty solution for this state of affairs. However, there are a number of avenues to pursue in this regard. Here is one example: The nature of one's self-talk often has a considerable effect on energy supply. Monitoring this internal dialogue and reducing the amount of time spent thinking negatively should help achieve a greater supply of personal energy, which is often a key factor in maintaining a desirable work-life balance.

IMPLEMENTATION GUIDELINES

Achieving a good work-life balance does not necessarily mean a 50-50 split between the two (or 75-25 or 90-10). The key is what works for you. If non-work activities are generally not energy-enhancing, and if work is highly augmenting of personal energy, then, all things being equal, a higher percentage of your time likely can be devoted to work without adversely affecting the balance.

REFERENCES AND RESOURCES

Publications
Blanchard, Ken, D.W. Edington, and Marjorie Blanchard. (1999). *The One Minute Manager Balances Work and Life: A Healthy Lifestyle Is the Key to Success*. New York: Morrow.

Dunn, Gloria. (1998). *From Making a Living to Having a Life*. Fairfax: CA: Violin Publishers.

Internet
www.sparksdevelopment.com.
www.stanford.edu/dept/acr/worklife.

Association
University of Pennsylvania, Division of Human Resources.

33

EMPLOYEE ASSISTANCE PROGRAMS

Ethan S. Sanders and Jacqueline B. Visnius

WHAT IS AN EMPLOYEE ASSISTANCE PROGRAM?

An employee assistance program (EAP) is a workplace benefit designed to assist in identifying and addressing performance and productivity problems associated with myriad personal, lifestyle, and work-related issues. It is a consultation service that provides free counseling and referral service for employees, but is not a replacement for mental health benefit services. An EAP can address workplace concerns centered around health, marital, family, financial, alcohol, drug, legal, emotional, stress, and other personal situations that may affect worker performance.

The EAP benefit may include substance abuse counseling, mental health therapy, marital therapy, financial crisis counseling, career counseling, and child-care and elder-care services. These programs may be expanded to include sexual harassment and workplace violence as well as many other contemporary issues that can adversely affect an employee's ability to focus on work-related issues.

RELATED INTERVENTIONS

Counseling, coaching, mentoring, work-life balance, and peer-to-peer counseling are often critical elements of many EAPs. These types of interventions are centered on the constructive (not punitive) treatment of individuals who have special needs. Like EAPs, these programs help to ensure employees' well-being and health.

WHEN TO USE EMPLOYEE ASSISTANCE PROGRAMS

In certain situations, counseling and coaching do not provide a remedy for an employee's declining or poor job performance. An employer can then make a formal referral to the employee for further confidential, professional services.

An EAP benefit is appropriate when an employee is experiencing difficulty with a personal issue, such as a serious illness or a death in the family, that causes that individual significant concern. When brought to an employer's attention, this type of situation often results in an informal referral to an EAP. Normally, the employee must initiate participation in the EAP.

Certain extreme situations, such as emotional instability, may signal a serious and more critical problem that prompts an immediate formal supervisory referral to the EAP.

Some added benefits of EAPs include the following:

♦ reduced turnover and absenteeism
♦ reduced costs associated with health care, recruitment and training of new employees, and workers' compensation
♦ reduced number of on-the-job accidents or injuries
♦ improved overall health and morale for employees.

WHEN NOT TO USE AN EMPLOYEE ASSISTANCE PROGRAM

Referral to an EAP may not be an appropriate intervention if the condition or problem confronting the employee has escalated to the point at which there are significant health, safety, or other high-risk concerns for the employer. Timing is an important factor in the EAP referral process. If a situation appears to be escalating into a crisis situation, the employer may be forced to take other more serious measures to resolve the situation.

EXAMPLES

♦ *Account Representative Problem:* Judith is an account representative with a recruiting firm. Lately she has had trouble sleeping and has lost her appetite. She also realizes that she has been short tempered and impatient with many of her colleagues. She attributes many of these symptoms to high stress associated with her job of finding employees for high-profile technology firms. Judith is concerned about her loss of interest in a lot of activities and is finding it more and more difficult to get out of bed each morning. She knows her work performance is beginning to suffer, and she is tired of feeling so down.

— *Intervention:* Judith decided to set up an appointment with an EAP counselor at her company. The company promoted the program widely, and Judith hoped it could help her find out why she felt so much stress. Judith began a course of assessment, counseling, and treatment that helped her discover that the source of her stress, which was diagnosed as depression, was the declining health of her ex-husband.

♦ *Plant Closing Problem:* General Discoveries was about to face massive plant closings. The schedule was for 10 plants to shut down in nine months, with five to follow by the end of the year. It was essential, however, that the remaining plants continue to run at peak efficiency. The organization's leaders were concerned not only about employees who were losing their jobs but also about those employees who would remain with the company. Survivors' guilt and other phenomena could compound the organization's ability to perform. Frederica, the manager of EAPs and life management services, knew that it was her job to help the employees deal with this major transition.

— *Intervention:* Frederica began to work on a number of issues including training supervisors to listen to troubled workers and providing counseling service during the entire shutdown period. Stress management classes, career counseling, and liberal leave policies were all provided to displaced workers. New corporate communication programs began to help workers who were not displaced to see the benefits of the changes.

♦ *Work Performance Problem:* Nancy was beginning to see some serious problems with Kelly's work. Kelly was missing deadlines, coming in late, and making serious errors in the publications that she edited. Nancy received two complaints from clients regarding Kelly's performance and attitude, and felt it was time to confront her before the problem became more serious.

— *Intervention:* During a meeting with Kelly, Nancy learned that Kelly had been driving 300 miles to her parents' home each weekend to help care for her father who was suffering from Alzheimer's disease. Nancy realized that Kelly was responsible for her own two children, and she was working full-time and caring for her elderly father. Nancy suggested that the company's EAP could help ease the burden by providing information, resources, and referral for care providers. Counseling was also available to help Kelly cope with this life change.

♦ *Personality Change Problem:* Brad had been severely irritable lately. His clothing was disheveled, and he took no pride in his personal appearance. Many of Brad's co-workers had expressed concern about his complete change in personality. Some of them thought Brad had been hanging around with a new group of friends who were heavily into drugs. Brad had also been driving a brand new BMW and had recently purchased an expensive home on the beach. One day, a co-worker saw Brad in the lobby exchanging a paper sack for a wad of bills.

— *Intervention:* Brad's manager had been monitoring Brad's activity and performance lately and had made a formal referral to an EAP. Brad was not adhering to the treatment program and was now using the office as a place to buy and sell drugs. The situation had escalated beyond control, and it was time to take serious action. In this situation, the company's EAP services were not sufficient to deal with Brad's serious drug problem.

Design Guidelines

EAPs may provide a number of different services:

- legal and financial consultations
- work-life programs
- critical incident stress debriefings
- workplace violence seminars
- peer-to-peer consultation.

The following guidelines can help in designing an EAP:

- Consider the costs and benefits of each service and its relationship to performance.
- Clearly identify those services that your organization is willing to offer its employees.
- Establish procedures that help managers assess whether short-term resolution or outside professional resources are needed.
- Maintain confidentiality and respect the privacy of all employees who make use of an EAP. This will both protect the information that an employee discloses and increase credibility and support of the EAP process.
- Communicate with employees and their families about the availability of EAP services and educate them about the services.
- Train organization management in early problem recognition and identification, timely intervention, and appropriate referral to the EAP.
- EAP services are integrated into the overall benefit plan of the organization, but the service delivery system is separate and apart from other organizational processes and functions.

Implementation Guidelines

- A referral is made for employees for problem diagnosis, treatment, and assistance.
- An action plan is established that addresses the unique needs of the employee.
- The goals and objectives of the action and treatment plan are supported and followed up on regularly.

References and Resources

Publications

EAPA Exchange. Journal available through the Employee Assistance Professionals Association.

"EAPs Adopt Broad Brush Approach to Helping Employees." (October 1999). *Employee Benefit Plan Review,* 44–46.

Employee Assistance Professionals Association. (1999). *EAPA Standards and Professional Guidelines for Employee Assistance Professionals.* Arlington, VA: Author.

Oher, J.M. (1999). *The Employee Assistance Handbook.* New York: John Wiley.

"Quality of Care Is Primary Concern in Delivery of EAP Services." (September 1999.) *HR Focus,* 4.

Solomon, Charlene M. (February 2000). "Behavioral Health: The Forgotten Benefit." *Workforce,* 47–51.

Vernarec, Emil. (June 2000). "The Best Defense." *Business and Health,* 29–37.

Yandrick, Rudy M. (October 2000). "Getting By With a Little Help From Friends." *HR Magazine,* 102–109.

Internet

Collins, Kenneth. "A Manager's Guide to the EAP." *Workforce.* Available at Workforce.com at archive/article/001/15/58.xci www.eap-association.com.

Association

Employee Assistance Professionals Association: www.eap-association.com.

34

COUNSELING

Kathy Kelly

WHAT IS COUNSELING?

Counseling is the process by which two people, working one-on-one, meet to address one of the person's life issues that are having an impact on productivity and workplace performance. Counseling looks at the relationship of an individual's personal and emotional responses to his or her on-the-job practices. Discussion topics may involve one or more of the following:

♦ interpersonal conflicts
♦ self-esteem problems
♦ stress management
♦ supervision issues
♦ poor time or task management skills
♦ balancing work and family
♦ clarification of priorities
♦ abuse issues.

Effective counseling requires open, direct, and honest communication so the counselor can accurately record expectations, success measures, and consequences of continued poor behavior.

Counseling provides

♦ support for the resolution of behavioral and emotional challenges that affect one's workplace life
♦ tools managing difficult behaviors, critical assignments, work relationships, and work-related stress.

The key activities of counseling involve

♦ regular discussions of one's beliefs, feelings, perceptions, and viewpoints in the context of workplace performance
♦ self-examination of behaviors, beliefs, feelings, perceptions, and viewpoints and their impact on one's workplace performance
♦ planning and goal setting to help one adjust his or her personal and emotional responses to workplace events and environments.

The focus on training highlights these additional features of counseling:

♦ As with training, performance is the key indicator of success in counseling.
♦ People set their own goals and take responsibility for their improved performance.
♦ Aspects of counseling that are correlated with effective learning include goal setting, problem identification, problem solving, active participation, self-assessment, and learning through experience.

The results of counseling include

♦ improved productivity
♦ improved self-esteem
♦ improved work environment.

Counseling can improve intrinsic motivation by raising one's feelings of self-worth, enhancing one's belief systems, and providing one with the tools for increasing self-awareness and self-concept, thus improving work performance.

RELATED INTERVENTIONS

Coaching, mentoring, and peer counseling are related to counseling. Counseling is similar to coaching and mentoring in that they all use incidences of an individual's performance to make improvements.

WHEN TO USE COUNSELING

Counseling is best used when there is a personal, emotional root to an unsatisfactory workplace performance. Most often counseling will help an employee see the connection between his or her personal situation and work behaviors. It may involve discussions about feelings, attitudes, stresses, and personal growth.

In addition, counseling can help employees develop strategies for enhancing career opportunities and job satisfaction. The emphasis here is on providing employees with the tools, information, and resources they need to set goals and seek opportunities that will enhance their careers. Employees learn how to use their skills and interests for personal growth and increased job satisfaction.

WHEN NOT TO USE COUNSELING

♦ Counseling is not an efficient strategy when the amount of effort required will probably not result in a significant improvement in work function. Ask yourself whether the time invested will likely result in significant performance upgrade.
♦ Sometime counseling situations warrant the assistance of human resource counselors and mental health professionals, such as crisis

services and mental health counseling. Whenever a counseling situation involves high-risk situations, hazardous or violent incidents, serious trauma, or substance abuse, professional assistance should be sought.

EXAMPLES

♦ *Creative Meeting Problem:* Kahisa's Webpage editorial staff has a creative meeting once a month. The purpose of this meeting is to discuss new ideas for the site, brainstorm possible innovations, and introduce new ways to grow the site creatively. The team established ground rules to promote open dialogue and free expression of ideas without fear of ridicule from others. Jack just doesn't get it! At every meeting he either makes inappropriate comments about others' ideas or surfaces issues that are not within the scope of the meeting. As a result of his conduct during these meetings, the team has become openly hostile to Jack. In return, he has become obstinate and uncompromising in his team interactions. Kahisa spoke informally to Jack about his behavior after several of the meetings but that has not helped.

— *Intervention:* Kahisa decided to try a counseling approach with Jack. The first step was to get Jack to see the problem, so during the first meeting Kahisa asked open-ended questions to gain an understanding of his perspective, what he thought about his behavior, and why he thought he was getting the reactions he was from his teammates. It seems that Jack thought his ideas were usually better than the rest of the team's but that they never listened to him. He also had little respect for either Kahisa or the rest of the staff. Kahisa was able to help Jack see how his behavior in the meetings was contributing to the problem, how lack of respect was overshadowing effective communication, and what part he played in the problem situation. They were able to come to some agreement about the cause of the problem: that Jack's poor communication skills and his lack of connection to the team were impeding successful expression of his ideas. They agreed on a plan of action (Jack took some communication training and met with each team member individually to strengthen his work relationships and find some common working ground with his colleagues) and a meeting schedule so that they could monitor Jack's progress. This resulted in more appropriate participation and better meeting dynamics.

♦ *Change in Performance Problem:* Damien started to notice a change in Deb's work performance. During the first four months on the job, Deb demonstrated excellent time and project management skills, had good working relationships with her colleagues, and consistently performed above expectations. Recently, however,

Damien noticed that things had changed significantly. Deb's attendance and punctuality were slipping, and she was missing deadlines with no warning or explanations. Damien set up a meeting with Deb to find out what was going on.

As soon as Damien asked Deb if there was a problem she started to cry. She explained to Damien that she had some personal problems that were causing her to be distracted. Damien asked Deb for specifics and spent the rest of the meeting trying to help Deb find a way to get her daughter to stop using drugs. At the end of the meeting, he offered to get together with her regularly to lend a sympathetic ear. Over the weeks Damien learned more and more about Deb's personal situation. He understood why her work performance was not up to par and made allowances. When others from his team complained about Deb, he made excuses. This continued for several months. Deb's performance continued to deteriorate and Damien picked up the slack.

— *Intervention:* After one of their counseling sessions, Damien realized he had gone beyond his role as boss and was not making the work situation any better. In fact, he was making it worse! His team was now complaining about him as well as Deb. So he decided to gets some assistance from human resources. HR explained to him that the people in that department would assist Deb with her personal issues and that he had to refocus his discussions with Deb on her work performance. Damien realized that he was not well prepared for this, so he asked HR to provide him with some mentoring as he counseled Deb.

He worked with his mentor and Deb to set up new guidelines for their interactions. They agreed that in the future, she would discuss only work-related issues with Damien and see a trained counselor for help with her personal problems. They created an action plan to establish work performance standards that Deb would have to meet to keep her job. Thereafter, their counseling sessions focused on workplace issues. This solution allowed both Deb and Damien to improve their work performance.

DESIGN GUIDELINES

Counseling may take one of the following forms:

♦ Nonpunitive disciplinary action is focused on getting employees to acknowledge their performance gap, identify the underlying cause, and agree to bring performance to minimum standards or higher.

♦ Skills counseling is to help employees understand what new skills are required to advance their careers. This type focuses on developing new skills in anticipation of the next career step, rather than handling current performance deficiencies.

♦ Support may be for personal and corporate performance in the areas of risk management, behavioral health care costs, productivity, turnover, corporate culture, critical incidents, leadership development, and workers' compensation. Professional assistance is highly recommended for this type of counseling.

The following tips may help is designing counseling:

♦ Articulate the difference between actual and expected performance.
♦ Identify the cause of the problem and win agreement that there is a need for a change.
♦ Develop a plan with specific actions the employee will take to bring performance to acceptable standards.
♦ Follow up regularly to ensure goals are being met and recognize accomplishments to reinforce correct behavior.

IMPLEMENTATION GUIDELINES

♦ Create a supportive environment that allows employees to discuss reasons for their performance deficit. Practice active listening, probe and question, and gain agreement for action.
♦ Follow a consistent process:
— Have an open-ended discussion to raise the problem.
— Identify the underlying cause or causes.
— Gain agreement on an action plan.
— Follow up.
— Acknowledge performance improvements or carry out consequences.
♦ Make sure you are prepared to counsel: Get training! Beware of traps, such as making allowances or accepting poor performance, disagreeing about the existence of a problem or the solution, having preconceived notions, acting more like a parent or personal counselor than a boss, dominating the discussion or dictating solutions, moving too quickly to problem-solving phase, following through on warnings and consequences.

REFERENCES AND RESOURCES

Publications

Journal of Workplace Learning, Employee Counselling Today.
    http://www.swets.nl/backsets/catalogue_result_1366-5626.htm.
Stone, Florence M. (1999). *Coaching, Counseling, and Mentoring: How to Choose and Use the Right Technique to Boast Employee Performance.* New York: American Management Association.

Internet

http://www.counseling.com.

35

WIN-WIN NEGOTIATION

Kat Koppett

WHAT IS WIN-WIN NEGOTIATION?

Negotiation is a process of back-and-forth communication with the intention to reach an agreement between two or more parties when they have shared and differing interests. *Win-win* refers to the goal of achieving a positive outcome for all sides with each party seeking solutions that maximize mutual gain.

RELATED INTERVENTIONS

- ◆ *Mediation* is a nonbinding, facilitated negotiation in which a neutral, third party assists opposing parties toward agreement. Mediation is especially useful when participants have relatively equal status and the conflict is sticky enough to benefit from an outside eye, but not so adversarial as to make communication impossible.
- ◆ *Arbitration* is a formal, legally binding mediation in which the interested parties pledge to honor any agreements the arbiter crafts. Arbitration can be a useful alternative to going to court when conflicts have escalated.
- ◆ *Conflict management* is often identified as the more emotional, interpersonal cousin of negotiation. Conflict management techniques include assertiveness training, team building, cultural awareness, and communication skills.
- ◆ *Creative problem solving* is a set of techniques for generating, evaluating, and selecting win-win solutions. Without the ability to come up with mutually beneficial agreements, successful negotiation is doubtful.
- ◆ *Cut-throat negotiation* is the old-school approach to negotiating agreements. Cut-throat negotiators begin with the assumption that there is a fixed pie and that more for you means less for me. They may also believe that they will benefit from dirty tactics. Often, however, agreements reached through these methods may damage long-term relationships and be hard to enforce.

When to Use Win-Win Negotiation

Use this intervention:
- ♦ when you value the relationship
- ♦ when you and the other party share some interests and differ on others
- ♦ when you are willing to invest time in reaching the best agreement
- ♦ when a solution is not obvious
- ♦ when a solution is obvious and you wish to explore better ones
- ♦ when your alternative to reaching an agreement is not better than what you can negotiate.

Win-win negotiation has a broad range of applications, including many not related to work, such as interpersonal conflict resolution, customer service interactions, and even shopping at flea markets.

When Not to Use Win-Win Negotiation

- ♦ *The other party does not want one:* Not all negotiators believe that searching for a win-win solution is in their best interest. One or more of the parties may choose to use methods designed to maximize their individual gain, rather than reach the best agreement for mutual benefit. If you do not recognize and counteract power plays, dishonesty, and manipulation, you may get taken advantage of.
- ♦ *The agreement is not an improvement:* Sometimes the best agreement that you can hope to reach with another party is not as good as what would happen if you failed to reach one at all. It can be difficult to walk away from a negotiation. Be sure that you do not consent to an arrangement that will leave you in a worse position than if negotiations broke down. Know your alternatives and use them as comparison.
- ♦ *There is a power differential:* As valuable as formal negotiation procedures can be, they can also be used to take advantage of weaker parties. As a negotiating party or a mediator, take great care to take into consideration the status relationships between the parties, and beware any negotiation in which one or more parties is denied respect or freedom to act in their own best interest.
- ♦ *Emotions are too high:* As well-prepared as you might feel, as reasonable as you may trust the other parties to be, remember that when people's needs are on the line, emotions may run high. And when individuals get emotional, their best intentions to reach mutually beneficial agreements may fly by the wayside. Find ways to diffuse your own and others' emotions when interactions become too contentious.
- ♦ *Not all parties are involved:* There may be constituents other than those individuals sitting at the negotiation table. In order for an agreement to last, the needs of those parties must be taken into

account as well. Investigate and take into account the pressures put on the negotiators by those they represent and others that will be affected by your decisions.

♦ *When it is not fair to all parties:* There are different ways to define and determine fairness, and human beings tend to seize upon the definition that supports their personal interests.

EXAMPLE

♦ *High-Tech Problem:* A high tech company in Silicon Valley, Complicated Technologies, is desperate to recruit new programmers. It has found an excellent candidate. He has told him that he has two other offers. Complicated can pay the going market rate, but no more in salaries. Dot-coms have been stealing away Complicated's potential recruits with wild stock options and a more autonomous work environment. Complicated is a large and much-more established company, but without a lot of the bells and whistles of the dot-com industry. The managers that Harry, our recruiter, reports to are getting desperate for bodies. Every day they are losing money because they do not have enough qualified people working on development.

— *Intervention:* Before the negotiation, Harry makes sure to review his own desires and limitations and those of his constituents— the managers. He also tries to anticipate what will be important to the recruit, Gil. Because Complicated is under such pressure, Harry worries that his BATNA—not hiring Gil and waiting to find someone else—is not very strong. He believes that with the economy softening, however, Complicated will be more attractive as a stable, established venture.

When the negotiation begins, he asks Gil what is most important to him and what Gil sees as the pros and cons of working for Complicated. Gil volunteers that he has been hopping from small company to small company and would like to settle down since he and his wife are planning to start a family. Harry is able to offer Gil a lower compensation package than he might have gotten elsewhere, but guarantees him more vacation, more manageable work hours, and some sense of stability. Each side is very pleased.

DESIGN GUIDELINES

There are myriad different solutions and strategies involved in negotiation, but they fall into two major categories: distributive (or zero-sum) and integrative (or expanding the pie):

♦ *Distributive negotiation:* Most people think of distributive negotiation when they think of negotiable situations. It involves dividing up a fixed amount of resources with the assumption that more for you means less for me. A famous distributive negotiation example goes like this. Two people have a cake. They each want as much of the cake as possible. How do they make sure that the cake is divided equally? The recommended solution is that one of them cuts the cake in half, and the other chooses a half. One-time interactions with a narrow focus in which the future relationship is not an issue tend to be distributive. Although win-win negotiation tends to focus on integrative possibilities, many negotiations have some aspects that are distributive. That said, there are often integrative possibilities to be found by combining and trading distributive points.

◆ *Integrative:* The classic illustration of an integrative solution involves the division of an orange. Both parties are adamant that they need a whole orange. One possible solution is to divide the orange in the same manner as the cake in the preceding example. Upon further exploration, however, we find that one party wants the orange to make orange juice, and the other needs the peel for a cake. In this situation, a compromise in which a distributive solution is used would leave all sorts of untapped value on the table. By exploring the real needs of the parties involved, the "pie" to be divided was expanded, and the total value of the negotiation rose. In this case, more for you does not mean less for me. The foundational principle of win-win negotiating is the search for integrative solutions to seemingly distributive scenarios.

The following tips may help in designing a win-win negotiation:

◆ Prepare, prepare, prepare. The most valuable commodity to a successful negotiator is information. You must know your own interests, strategies, and alternatives, and whatever you can find out about the other side's interests and alternatives. In addition, gather as much data as you can about who else might be involved in and affected by your negotiation and what the generally accepted standards are in terms of price, and contract clauses.

◆ Remember that there are more than just substantive needs. Substantive needs are the ones that we generally think of when we plan for a negotiation. A substantive need is a need around the literal content of the negotiation. For example, if you are renegotiating a contract with a client, the substantive needs might include price, availability of consulting services, and timelines for delivery. Parties also have needs that involve the relationship, however: I want to trust you; I have a need to feel respected; I want to feel competent and as if I am getting a good deal. Finally, process needs must be taken into account: How we reach a decision will affect how I feel about it, how I can sell it to my constituents, and how likely I am to follow through.

- Know your best alternative to a negotiated agreement, or BATNA. You must be willing to walk away if BATNA is better than whatever you can agree to in the interaction. If you do not have a good BATNA, however, you may be forced to settle for less than your optimum outcome. The same is true for the other side. Explore both BATNA's before you begin negotiating. Remember, if you take advantage of the other party, it may come back to bite you.

IMPLEMENTATION GUIDELINES

- Always think win-win. Some people enter negotiations with a strong win-lose attitude: "I'll get as much as I can for myself and to heck with anyone else." There is a price to pay for this approach. Agreements that are win-lose are harder to implement and can irreparably damage relationships. Other people may be too willing to settle for a lose-win scenario because they do not believe they have the power or the right to get more. This is obviously less than optimal. Finally, it is possible, through escalating emotional conflict or competition, to end up with a lose-lose agreement. Entering the agreement laden with good information, respecting yourself and the other party, and beginning from an assumption of collaboration will reduce the chance of this happening.

- Think interests or needs, not positions. Although you will want to enter a negotiation with some idea of your bottom line, target, and bliss line positions—the lowest, expected, and wishful out-comes—remember to focus on the parties' actual needs, rather than on specific solutions that you might have thought about ahead of time: "The selling price of the house must be $200,000," is ultimately just a position. What if you could get the buyer a lower interest rate on the mortgage? What if the house had a guest cottage that could be rented out?

- Collaboratively generate integrative solutions. Rather than think of the parties in a negotiation as sitting opposite each other in an adversarial fashion, imagine the parties on one side of the table and the problem on the other. Then collaboratively come up with solutions designed to maximize the value for each party. Some places to start include
  — Identify shared needs.
  — Identify different but compatible needs (for example, the orange).
  — Expand the pie by integrating additional interests over time, projects, methods of payment, and so forth.

- Take breaks. When people get tired or emotionally overwrought, negotiations become less effective and tend to break down. Build in breaks to refresh yourself, and regroup.

References and Resources

Publication

Fisher, Roger, and William Ury. (1983). *Getting to Yes: Negotiating Agreement Without Giving In.* New York: Penguin. The classic bible of win-win negotiation.

Internet

http://www.pon.harvard.edu. PON, the Program on Negotiation, is a consortium of Harvard, MIT, and Tufts Universities that specializes in negotiation in all arenas. Training courses and materials available.

36

VIOLENCE PREVENTION

Todd Packer

WHAT IS VIOLENCE PREVENTION?

Accepting the detrimental impact of violence on employee morale, health, safety and productivity, trainers and others can use their unique skills to prevent violence and mediate the impact of stress, trauma, and violence on workplace performance. Critical aspects of the cycle of violence and recovery that have an impact on training and development include

◆ miscommunication: perceptions that manifest in inappropriate and inflammatory interactions
◆ stress: psychological pressures from dynamics internal and external to the work context
◆ voicelessness: repeated experiences of silencing
◆ fear
◆ shame
◆ anger
◆ access to weapons
◆ despair.

RELATED INTERVENTIONS

Individuals and organizations have approached managing interpersonal behavior that can escalate into violence through a variety of interventions, including

◆ stress management
◆ conflict resolution
◆ counseling and therapy
◆ coaching
◆ team building.

Environmental aspects of violence prevention are related to other general environmental management efforts, including

◆ general physical safety analysis and preparation
◆ sociotechnical design

♦ security systems implementation
♦ environmental crisis prevention and preparation.

WHEN TO USE VIOLENCE PREVENTION

Ideally, violence prevention is a continuous effort that becomes infused into other interventions. Unfortunately, organizations often implement efforts only after an incident (sometimes catastrophic) of violence has occurred. In this context, the efforts may be hampered by the impact of the trauma on the workers.

Violence prevention becomes particularly useful when the following occur:

♦ Multiple organizational systems (for example, human resources, physical plant, training, public relations, union and staff representatives, and executive staff) work together to create a comprehensive approach.

♦ External or internal events occur that sensitize participants to the impact of violence.

♦ Strategies are presented in a fashion that does not overwhelm members (that is, avoiding the "scare tactic" approach that can cause participants to distance themselves from phenomenon).

♦ Concerns may be aired or gathered in a confidential manner.

♦ Statistics are presented in a context of relevance to the particular work setting.

♦ Participants use creative problem solving to develop effective strategies that have meaning in their unique setting, and their leaders support the recommendations.

♦ Organizational members can evaluate options calmly, out of a crisis context, and develop a critical incident response mechanism to respond swiftly, compassionately, and professionally to any situations that may arise.

♦ All participants, including facilitators, recognize fears about violence but remain committed to creating a realistic and hopeful plan of action.

Because of the unfortunate prevalence of violence in multiple levels of human interaction, lessons from the workplace can be useful in settings as varied as among one's family and religious community, at school, and in one's neighborhood.

WHEN NOT TO USE VIOLENCE PREVENTION

Effective interventions must proceed from a point of safety. If one is in a conflict situation that seems out of control, do the following to the best of your ability:

♦ Maintain calm.
♦ Seek escape.
♦ Alert others to the danger.

- ◆ Isolate the violent offender.
- ◆ Only intervene with the help of specially trained professionals (such as mediators, hostage negotiators, police, and mental health professionals).

Always be aware of—and research—the history of violence in a particular work context prior to beginning violence prevention efforts. Given the nature of this topic, even relatively neutral case examples and training sessions can spark heated emotions if there has been a previous incident in the setting. Be sensitive to possible traumatic reactions of individual participants and be prepared with referral materials (such as mental health hotlines) should there be reactions that you are unable to handle.

The drama of this issue can lend itself to a certain sensationalism. Case examples can be gruesome and attention-getting. Avoid the temptation to spice up a training session with irrelevant but dramatic examples of violent outbursts. It is possible that in discussing actual or fictitious cases, members may experience paralyzing despair. Debriefing is critical to ensure that participants use hope to build actionable steps to secure a safe work setting. Never leave a work setting overwhelmed by awareness of violence.

Always, always take all threats seriously. Whether threats to others or threats of self-harm or suicide, acknowledge the seriousness to the one who voiced the threat. Seek counsel of appropriate organizational members (through human resources, employee assistance program staff, and supervisors, for example) and document threats as well as incidents.

Brief and debrief all members continuously throughout the intervention.

Be aware of and successfully manage with appropriate experts issues of legal liability, media exposure, community relations and organizational reputation during the course of the intervention.

EXAMPLES

- ◆ *Packing-up Problem:* Mike Breen, the owner of Mike's Mail House, was getting concerned about all of the negative press that the U.S. Postal Service was getting following three shooting rampages by postal employees. Although his company was an independent, retail packaging store, many of his employees had worked for the Postal Service in the past, and many were subjected to the same types of stressors as its employees. Even more concerning were the comments he had heard from several of his customers. They would jokingly refer to the fact that they needed to be nice to Mike's employees, for fear that they would "go postal." To Mike, this was no laughing matter.
  - — *Intervention:* Mike hired Janice Wilhelm, a specialist in violence prevention. She came in and did a careful study of Mike's employees and found that in general they were pretty happy with the working conditions. A few of them were facing personal crises at home (such as a divorce, a terminally sick child, and a set of alcoholic parents). More important, there was an

unhealthy rivalry starting to develop between the people who worked the front counter and those in the shipping and receiving department. Apparently, each time a customer's order ended up with an error on it (for example, a misspelled address), the workers would blame each other. Janice recommended that the company begin an employee assistance program (EAP) and that a weekly mediation meeting be conducted to uncover the root causes for the errors. Furthermore, Janice recommended that all workers be involved in coming up with new processes to ensure the accuracy of information. Janice helped Mike to create a violence prevention plan using the DEFUSE model, and this plan was posted in each of Mike's four locations where customers could see it. There was even a tag line at the bottom of the violence prevention poster that said "Workplace Violence is No Laughing Matter." After three months with the new EAP program in place and the order processing greatly improved, Janice came back and conducted another study. She found that nearly all of the employees were reporting higher levels of satisfaction, that the employees with home-life issues had adapted nicely to their situation, and that Mike himself was feeling more comfortable in his own company.

♦ *"Oh Mercy" Problem:* Mercy Hospital had faced a problem that it never thought would darken its doorstep. A month ago, one of its security guards and a maintenance worker had gotten into a terrible argument. Apparently the guard had denied the maintenance worker access to the drug storage room, but the maintenance worker's supervisor had told him to make sure the floor was mopped in there before he left for the evening. The maintenance worker asked the guard to open the door and watch him while he cleaned the floor. The guard refused stating that he had more important things to do. As the argument ensued, the maintenance worker threatened the guard with a broom handle, and the guard pulled his gun in what he claimed was self-defense. Two of the doctors on duty overheard the argument and ran to try to diffuse the situation. It took them nearly 30 minutes to get the guard to put his gun back in its holster and to get the maintenance person to go home for the evening. The next day, both employees were fired. The hospital had a strict policy on workplace violence. As both men left the HR department, they vowed to get even with the other.

— *Intervention:* Polly Manstin, the HR director, felt that the hospital needed to get to the bottom of this situation, She was convinced that there was more to it than just an interpersonal problem between these two employees. Polly interviewed all of the security guards and maintenance workers over the next few weeks. She discovered that there had been tensions between these groups for years. Sadly, some of this tension was caused by racism. Most employees on the maintenance crew were South American Hispanics, whereas all of the guards were either African American or Caucasian. Also, the guards had held a particular grudge again the maintenance workers for refusing to clean the surveillance equipment including the closed-circuit cameras, monitors, and alarm devices. The maintenance workers claimed that this equipment was too expensive and sensitive for them to clean. There had been an incident about a year ago in which a camera stopped functioning after it had been cleaned and the maintenance department was forced to pay for its repair. The guards said cleaning their own equipment was "beneath us." To solve these problems, Polly began with the managers of each department. They were required to sit down with one another and work out a plan for getting all parts of the hospital cleaned. This included secured areas as well as all of the security equipment. Fortunately, both managers felt so bad about what happened, they eagerly worked to reach a compromise. A regular schedule was created for cleaning secured areas of the hospital, and a nurse was appointed to observe the maintenance people while they cleaned these areas. The hospital decided to rehire both men involved in the conflict, but to have them work on opposite schedules. The guard was reassigned to front desk duty, which did not require him to carry a gun. Both men were placed on probation for two years, forced to apologize to each other in front of their peers, and required to attend counseling for one year. This decision was made because it was determined that their firing was becoming a polarizing issue in the two departments (in effect, they had become martyrs) and because they had each been excellent employees prior to this incident. Finally, the hospital began a regular violence prevention program that included cultural diversity training.

DESIGN GUIDELINES

The DEFUSE model is a helpful tool for understanding various approaches to violence prevention. The six facets of this model include

- ◆ *Disarm*
  - — Remove weapons of destruction.
  - — Engage safely—verbally and nonverbally (for example, smile).
  - — Negotiate with confidence and knowledge.

- ◆ *Educate*
  - — Access information for yourself.
  - — Design educational aspects of training and interventions that respond to workplace violence.
  - — Inform by spreading the word of safety and defusing.

♦ *Focus*
  — Reflect: Gain awareness of your own reactions.
  — Connect: Seek support and alliances with influential decision makers to create a safe workplace.
  — Direct: Identify simple, manageable next steps.

♦ *Understand*
  — Respect diversity in people and their reactions to stress and conflict.
  — Listen to people and learn from books and other resources.
  — Acknowledge your limits.

♦ *Secure*
  — Assess dangerous locations as well as safe havens.
  — Protect: With colleagues, create systems to ensure staff safety.
  — Prevent: Build and avoid abuse in monitoring systems.

♦ *Empower*
  — Renew strength and awareness.
  — Collaborate: Ask for help, offer support.
  — Transform: Actively participate in nonwork efforts for peace.

The following tips are helpful in designing a violence prevention initiative:

♦ Make it meaningful and relevant. Since violence can be a vast topic with multiple approaches to prevention, take time to research a setting so you can ensure that interventions are grounded in the needs, experiences, limitations, and culture of a particular setting. Continually seek input through confidential mechanisms (such as employee suggestions during evaluations).

♦ Develop strategies through creative problem solving. Often the most effective approaches are already in place informally in particular settings. Also, staff can apply strategies that work in other settings (such as at home or school) to the workplace. There is no single approach that will always work, so encouraging people to actively engage together in creating a safe workplace can be highly beneficial.

♦ Collaborate with appropriate organizational and external experts. Identify who will be responsible in an organization for maintaining policies and procedures regarding workplace violence prevention and response. Develop strategies with input from research and expert advice, particularly from legal and mental health professionals.

IMPLEMENTATION GUIDELINES

♦ Recognize the basic unexpected aspect of violence. No effort can guarantee that violence will never occur in a particular setting.

Building confidence through education and an effective response system can ameliorate the impact of potential incidents, but violence is inherently chaotic and to a large extent unpredictable. However this does not preclude employees from maintaining productivity or from developing effective strategies in the face of a violent environment.

♦ Document, document, document. Whether it is preparing personnel evaluations or gathering evidence for police authorities, it is essential to have clear, accurate, and detailed written information. It can be helpful to design forms that can help gather critical information quickly. This is particularly important when responding to threats.

♦ Maintain hope. Violence can seem to be a hopeless aspect of our human identity. Take encouragement from the fact that violence is the exception, rather than the rule, in human interactions. Individuals, workplaces, and nations have successfully found nonviolent strategies to ensure safety and prosperity for themselves and others.

REFERENCES AND RESOURCES

Publication
Ury, William. (1999). *Getting to Peace: Transforming Conflict at Home, at Work and in the World.* New York: Viking/Penguin Group.

Internet
http://www.osha-slc.gov/SLTC/workplaceviolence/index.html. The United States government agency, the Occupational Safety and Health Association (OSHA), has produced several reports and statements on this subject. This site also contains links to other organizations.

Association
Amnesty International.

CONCLUSION

Sivasailam Thiagarajan

My 25 years of experience as a performance consultant reinforces my previous 15 years of experience as a physics teacher: Nothing (whether it is the universe or this book) ever comes to an end. Conclusion is just a convenient delusion.

The book-writing project has come to an end for Ethan and me. Or has it? In one sense, this is just the beginning. The project has ended (because the publisher has wrested the manuscript from our clutching hands), but the product is far from being complete. The book is not even up to date because every week we see thousands of new entries when we search the Internet with our key terms. Our authors have not stopped doing their job either. I still get email notes from them asking if it is too late to make just one small change in their chapter. We even get notes from our nonperforming authors who feign innocence and inquire about the due date for the delivery of the completed manuscript. Very soon we will begin receiving notes from readers pointing out our stupidity in leaving out The Most Important Intervention. Ethan and I will have our second thoughts, debrief ourselves, and decide what we should do next. (How about some mugs and T-shirts, Ethan?)

If you are reading this page, you have probably completed the book. Or have you? Perhaps you are one of those people (like me) who read from the back of the book or read the shorter sections first. And whether you read the book from cover to cover or just reviewed the chapter on a specific intervention, you are not yet done. This is just the beginning—because inert knowledge is a huge waste. The real learning is yet to begin. This occurs when you translate this knowledge into something useful. True learning occurs only when you apply the principles and procedures, tips and tricks, facts and figures to a real-world performance improvement project. You need experiential reinforcement to complete the book learning.

This book contains 36 different interventions. Yes, there are many more interventions. This book describes 36 interventions, and the glossary following this conclusion lists many more. And, yes, there are still more interventions. However, let me share with you a wonderful piece of advice that was given to me by my mentor: Don't count your interventions; make your interventions count!

GLOSSARY

This glossary represents the most comprehensive list of interventions we could think of. We carefully selected which interventions to describe in detail in sections in the book and which to merely reference in this glossary. An asterisk appears next to those interventions for which there are sections. It would be impossible to definitively capture all activities that could be considered interventions in the workplace. We hope you will find this list useful as you search for new and creative solutions to your organization's problems.

IMPROVING KNOWLEDGE

*Accelerated learning is an intervention that is based on the scientific knowledge and understanding of the human brain to provide effective learning experiences. This intervention takes into consideration all aspects of the learning environment, uses music and arts to create positive emotional states, builds the learner's self-confidence and personal expectations, enriches information with imaginative metaphors, encourages collaborative learning, and presents positive suggestions through body language, attitude, and choice of activities. Accelerated learning also honors and utilizes people's different intelligences and learning styles.

*Action learning involves a combination of action and reflection by a team solving complex, strategic problems in a real-world organizational setting. Team members apply existing skills and knowledge and create new skills, knowledge, and insights through continuously reflecting on and questioning the problem definition, the collaborative behavior, and the ensuing results.

*Coaching is an intervention in which one person improves the performance of another by interactive questioning, collaborative goal setting, systematic observation, constructive feedback, and positive guidance. Most coaching sessions improve levels of competency and motivation.

*Electronic performance support systems (EPSSs) are software programs that provide just-in-time, on-demand information, guidance, examples, and step-by-step dialogue boxes to improve job performance without the need for training or coaching by other people.

*Job aids are storage places for information other than memory that performers use while performing a task. A job aid provides a signal—audio or visual—to the performer about when to carry out the task and steps, reducing the amount of recall necessary and minimizing error.

Learner-controlled instruction is an intervention in which the performer is given a set of learning objectives and a menu of resources. The learner selects, schedules, and uses the appropriate resources (including access to subject-matter experts, training materials, and learning activities). The learner also selects and controls how and when she or he will be tested for achieving the objectives.

*On-the-job training (OJT) is an intervention that improves an employee's work performance. It is conducted on a one-on-one basis by an experienced practitioner at the work site while the learner is engaged in performing a work task.

*Self-directed learning is a general term that usually refers to self-paced training programs that use a wide variety of delivery media. These delivery media can range from print products to Web-based systems. Self-directed learning can also refer to less formalized types of learning such as learning in teams, knowledge management systems, and self-development programs.

*Training games are activities that improve people's competency levels. Most games feature conflict (such as competition among teams), control (rules for making moves and scoring points), closure (a special rule that specifies how the game ends and who wins), and contrivance (an element of artificiality). In simulation games, the rules of the game reflect some workplace process and the play objects reflect real-world artifacts.

IMPROVING MOTIVES

Ceremonies are events undertaken to celebrate progress toward the achievement of different milestones. These celebrations help energize the performers, savor their achievement, review their activities, and re-commit themselves to progressing toward the next milestone. Ceremonies that are spontaneous, immediate, and directly related to a work task are very effective in maintaining and improving employee performance.

*Compensation systems are policies and procedures related to payment made by organizations to individual performers for their work-related achievements. In addition to direct salary payments, compensation systems may include insurance, pension, and stock ownership.

Flow-state maintenance is an intervention that adjusts the difficulty level of a work task to the competency level of the performer so that it is neither frustrating (because it is beyond the capacity of performer) nor boring (because it is beneath the capacity of performer). By maintaining an optimum level of challenge, this intervention increases the performer's interest and attention.

Incentive systems are interventions that include a collection of incentives and a set of procedures for using them. All incentive systems are intentional: They are deliberately developed for the purpose of influencing employees' performance to be aligned with the business strategy. Incentive systems are also standardized to identify categories of employees, activities, incentives, and relationships among them. Incentive systems typically include a variety of monetary incentives (such as salaries, differential pay, allowances, deferred income, and other perquisites) and non-monetary incentives (such as working conditions, training, facilities, management, and career opportunities).

*Motivation systems increase the amount of commitment and persistence of performers. An intrinsic motivation system increases the meaningfulness of work, sense of competence, availability of choices, modification of negative moods, and feelings of progress. This intervention typically involves empowerment, trust, the freedom to make mistakes, a clear purpose, information, positive feedback, skill recognition, an exciting vision, whole tasks, collaborative climate, milestones, celebrations, feedback from end user, and removal of task barriers.

*Playfulness is an attitude that finds (or creates) amusement and enjoyment in all situations. On the basis of the principles of play therapy, research on recreation, and studies on flow state, playfulness emphasizes that a performer's job is too important to be taken seriously. This intervention, associated with fun, optimism, and a sense of humor, helps people not to sweat over the small details and suggests that everything is a small detail anyhow.

*Rewards and recognition are the act of highlighting a performer's accomplishment by having an important person personally deliver to the performer objects or activities that he or she values as an immediate reward for measurable achievements related to organizational goals. Typical types of recognition include employee-of-the-month awards, trophies, plaques, announcements in the company newsletter, lunch with the president, certificates, personal notes from the CEO, gift certificates, and photographs displayed on the bulletin board.

*Team building is an intervention that increases the effectiveness of an intact team whose members regularly work together to achieve a common goal. The process of team building typically involves analyzing the strengths and improvement opportunities in a team, building on the current strengths, reducing ineffective practices, and preparing a plan for ongoing team effectiveness. Guided by a facilitator, team-building activities involve clarifying the goal, specifying roles of different team members, providing mutual feedback, and increasing the levels of cohesiveness and trust.

IMPROVING PHYSICAL RESOURCES

*Automation and computerization are interventions that augment or replace human performers to obtain improved, reliable, and consistent outputs. Automation involves the use of mechanical, electrical, and robotic devices to perform large-scale or microscopic tasks that require strength and precision. Computerization involves the use of hardware and software (including expert systems) to process huge amounts of data in a rapid, reliable, and objective fashion.

Collaborative spaces are containers, or virtual spaces, designed to facilitate and promote working together using a process that involves voicing insights, shedding assumptions, and noting common directions, goals, and energies of the group. It is a "place" that encourages risk taking and thinking outside of the box in order to explore innovative ways in which to move an organization toward its desired future. Collaborative spaces can take the form of a Website, conference call, shared models, notes databases combined with email, and the like. The value of collaborative spaces is in the relationships that develop and can lead to subsequent collaborations.

Display systems are tools used for training, sharing, and presenting information in real or lapsed time. A wide variety of systems exist (such as, large venue projectors, whiteboards, and plasma/flat panel display screens) with a variety of uses, including virtual reality, simulation, and digital cinema.

*Ergonomics and human factors are interventions designed to improve human performance through physical support. Ergonomics uses principles from human physiology and cognition to design equipment in such a way as to improve the productivity and comfort of performers. Ergonomics and human factors engineering are concerned with workplace layout, equipment controls, instrument design, furniture and furnishings, and environmental conditions, such as lighting and noise, and how these elements can be adapted to the physical, mental, perceptual, sensory, and esthetic attributes, capacities, and preferences of people.

Food and beverage services are provided to enhance employee comfort, convenience, and morale, to protect employee health, and to reduce travel time and time away from the workplace. Typical food and beverage services include beverage and snack vending machines, coffee bars, cafeterias and contract catering service or lunchrooms, and mobile food units or snack bars for large plants or widely dispersed work areas.

Input/output systems use input/output processing to transform data and information. Examples of such systems include technological innovations such as voice and handwriting recognition systems and computer touch pads. As interventions, these systems help individuals improve their performance by enabling and empowering them through the use of devices that facilitate and adapt work processes to individual needs and preferences.

Mobile office design is an intervention that is used to support employees, such as consultants, salespeople, and management who often do business at a distance from office locations. In these situations, employees must rely on technology and telecommunications to link and collaborate with clients, employees, and colleagues. In essence, the individual's laptop, voicemail, personal digital assistance (PDA), pager, and cell phone become his or her office. Mobile office design is often married to other forms of flexible office practices, telecommuting, and virtual offices.

Occupation safety involves intervening in the workplace to provide safe and healthful working conditions and protection against hazards that might cause illness, injury, or death, including hazardous work conditions, methods, materials, and substances.

Office equipment includes fax machines, telephones and communication equipment, shredders, clocks, desks, racks, janitorial equipment, copiers, and the like. When implemented as an intervention, office equipment is relied upon for its ability to facilitate and enable work processes. Optimal location, ease of use, infrequent downtime, and accessibility are important elements of office equipment utilization.

*Physical resource management interventions control and direct tangible assets such as equipment, raw materials, facilities, and end products. This activity involves planning, budgeting, scheduling, and controlling components. Many of these resources are in limited supply and in great demand. Specifically, the performance consultant helps the organization determine what (and when) resources to procure, identify potential sources, select the best source, integrate new resources with existing ones, optimize the use of these resources, and eliminate unwanted resources.

Simulator is an intervention that utilizes a machine, device, item, equipment, or system that replicates real life or real systems. The simulator assumes the appearance, characteristics, or capabilities of the real device, equipment, or system. Simulator activities are primarily used in training activities (flight simulators, laboratory learning).

Tools design is an element of the physical workspace that is used to support employee performance. When integrated with physical space, design, and features, electronic and other office tools will be more aligned with employees and the work they need to accomplish. Examples of tools design include workstation setup, computer and network configuration, laptop and docking stations, electronic whiteboards, and video conferencing. To be effective, these tools require holistic integration with the physical space and environment.

IMPROVING STRUCTURE AND PROCESS

*Conflict management is an intervention that enables two people (or two groups of people) to achieve a collaborative win-win outcome. This intervention involves identifying incompatible concerns of different people and—through direct negotiation—finding a solution that satisfies both sets of concerns.

*Culture reshaping is an intervention designed to bring about large-scale change in organizations by involving large numbers of people at different levels. This intervention involves planning or setting a direction for the organization and structuring or redefining working relationships among organization members. Most culture reshaping efforts incorporate future vision, whole-systems thinking, public dissemination of critical information, integration of feeling, thinking, and action, participation of all individuals, and continuous processing.

*Job interviews are processes for gathering specific information about a candidate's past experiences and behaviors in such a way that they act as predictors of that candidate's future behaviors. These interviews should also include the integration and matching of a candidate's current state of knowledge, skills, attitudes, and beliefs with the candidate's vision of where he or she wants to be, what he or she wants to do, and how he or she wants to achieve those goals.

*Performance appraisal programs are an ongoing management process that includes defining and developing performance criteria, designing appropriate appraisal formats to measure the criteria, implementing the appraisal system, evaluating the success of the appraisal system, and using the results of the appraisals in HRD practices. Performance appraisal systems serve many purposes including feedback and recognition, personal development, goal setting, and career development.

*Process leadership programs are interventions that seek to improve the process of influencing, motivating, and persuading people to take a desired action that is in their and the organization's best interests. These improvements are normally realized through executive education programs such as courses, coaching, and advanced communication skills.

*Process redesign is an intervention that begins with the development of a map to graphically depict the flow of work as a sequence of activities toward the achievement of an organizational goal. Beginning with the customer's requirements as the final output, a process map identifies different inputs, decisions, actions, and outputs. The map is then reviewed and analyzed to remove redundancies, nonvalue-added activities, and delays so that high-quality outputs are obtained at a lesser cost and a faster rate.

Scheduling is an intervention that plans for allocating people, time, space, facilities, equipment, and materials to various activities and projects, monitoring the progress of those activities and projects, and ensuring the smooth operation of the organization or program. Examples are work schedules, production schedules, and annual class schedules (Tracey, 1991).

*Staffing is an intervention that surveys all sources of personnel, inside and outside the organization, to locate and attract the best possible candidates for new or vacated positions. The organization actively seeks candidates by advertising both internally and externally in newspapers and professional and technical publications and through search organizations, notices, and personal contacts (Tracey, 1991).

IMPROVING INFORMATION

*Balanced scorecard (BSC) is a multidimensional framework for describing, implementing, and managing strategy at all levels of an enterprise by linking objectives, initiatives, and measures to an organization's strategy according to Kaplan and Norton (1992). The scorecard provides an enterprise view of an organization's overall performance by integrating financial measures with other key performance indicators around customer perspectives, internal business processes, and organizational growth, learning, and innovation. The BSC is not a static list of measures, but a framework for implementing and aligning complex programs of change and, indeed, for managing strategy-focused organizations.

*Debriefing is the process of facilitating participants to help them reflect on their experience, gain valuable insights, and share them with one another. People learn from experience only when they reflect on it, gain valuable insights, and share these insights with others.

Employee orientation is an intervention designed to provide new employees with complete and uniform information about the company, its organization, mission, functions and policies, compensation, benefits, services, work requirements, standards, rules, safe work habits, and desirable employee-management relations (Tracey, 1991). The objective of these programs is to develop confident, loyal, effective, and productive workers.

Feedback is an intervention in which an individual purposefully provides timely information about a performance and its impact in order to improve individual, team, and organizational accomplishment. Positive feedback that is given soon after a performance increases the frequency of the performance, especially when given in a public setting. Constructive feedback that is given immediately before the next opportunity to perform increases the quality of performance. Effective feedback should fit the type of performance and the expectations of the performer. It should also focus on specific elements of the performance.

*Knowledge management is the process of creating, identifying, capturing, and distributing organizational knowledge to the people who need it. Knowledge management is an important factor for today's organizations for several reasons. First, it increases their competitive advantage by allowing them to quickly convert their combined knowledge of a subject into products, services, and strategies that outperform others in the marketplace. Second, it increases the organization's ability to adapt to change by making knowledge available for quick decision making. Third, it allows employment flexibility since knowledge no longer depends on the physical presence of an employee.

*Meetings and dialogues are interventions that facilitate shared thinking, reflecting, problem solving, and decision making. Dialogues, like meetings, are interactions characterized by open-minded inquiry, active listening, and honest communication. Meetings are a method of bringing people together to collectively solve problems, share information, plan, and make decisions.

*Networks for information are related interventions that improve individual and organizational performance through rapid exchange of information among geographically dispersed performers. The Internet is a global web of computer networks that use standardized protocols to communicate in different ways, such as email, chat rooms, file transfers, and bulletin boards.

*Newsletters are a way to diminish an organization's communication problem, to publicize employee accomplishments, and to build a sense of community within the organization. They are also an important vehicle for keeping employees updated on current events within the organization and in educating employees on the marketplace surrounding the organization. Newsletters can also be used to communicate with customers, with vendors, and with other groups of people who are associated with the organization.

Policies and procedures are interventions that serve as a guide to thinking, discretionary action, and decision making for managers, supervisors, and staff personnel. Policies provide common premises for action. They help ensure coordination before decision or action and provide some assurance that recurring problems and issues will be handled with some measure of consistency throughout the organization. Procedures operationalize policies by providing specific guides for action. This includes all steps necessary for completing the task with maximum efficiency (Tracey, 1991).

*Public relations campaigns are interventions designed to promote the exchange of influence and understanding among an organization's constituent parts and the public. Public relations is a management function that helps define organizational objectives and philosophy. Public relations interventions attempt to communicate with all relevant internal and external stakeholders in the effort to create consistency between organizational goals and societal expectations (Baskin and Aronoff, 1988).

Structured text is an intervention that enhances clear and effective communication. Applied to print and electronic documents, structured text employs graphical layouts, typographic elements, and standardized formats to present different types of information (such as definitions, procedures, policies, and processes) in a consistent format.

IMPROVING HEALTH

Child-care programs are employee benefits that provide day-care facilities and personnel either on site or nearby to care for the children of employees. Other programs may provide full or partial reimbursement for such care.

Easing the burden and immense responsibility of finding good quality child care is a way of reducing stress for many employees.

*Counseling is a process by which two people come together face-to-face and one-on-one to attack a problem so that the one who has it can be helped to understand, clarify, and find a self-determined solution to it. It is essentially helping people to help themselves (Tracey, 1991).

Elder-care programs provide services to employees and their families (parents, spouses, and grandparents) who carry the burden of caring for loved ones who are unable to care for themselves. These services can include information and consultation, seminars and workshops, peer support groups, and facilities for day care. Custodial, hospice, and respite care is also included in many programs.

*Employee assistance programs (EAPs) are a benefit offered by employers that may include substance abuse counseling, mental health therapy, family crisis therapy, career counseling, financial crisis services, and many other forms of mental health services. EAPs are intended to reduce the amount of stress (and therefore the number of distractions) that are placed on employees so that they can focus on accomplishing organizational results.

*Energy management is the effective use, monitoring, and preservation of one's personal energy in order to allow the continuous achievement of goals. Personal energy consists of physical, emotional, and intellectual vigor. Energy management examines the balance of intellectual, emotional, and physical energy as it is expended on various tasks.

Exercise programs are often an element of an organization's employee health program. Exercise programs are recreational and promote fitness; they typically center on activities that improve overall physical conditioning, such as with cardiovascular and strength training. Many organizations have equipment facilities on site, whereas others offer discounted memberships to local health clubs. Exercise programs can also involve organized after-work activities such as 5k and 10k road races, ballgames, and other team sports.

Health maintenance is an intervention aimed at promoting employees' health. Health maintenance programs include activities such as health screenings (such as for blood pressure, cholesterol levels, and hearing tests), smoking cessation, weight loss, and managing stress. Health risk appraisals are also used to identify behaviors that may harm an employee's health. Examples of these include seat belt use, nutrition, sleeping patterns, and physical activity.

Nutrition programs focus on health promotion and chronic disease prevention in the workplace. This intervention is designed to supplement other wellness activities through a variety of nutrition-focused activities, such as nutrition counseling, healthy food choices in vending areas and cafeterias, heart healthy cooking classes, and weight management programs. Weight reduction, cancer prevention and control, diabetes management, and cardiovascular dietary programs are just a few of the areas that nutrition interventions focus on.

Spirituality in the workplace is a holistic approach to recognizing and appreciating employees not only for the professional roles they play, but also for their individuality, unique abilities, and overall health. Some of the techniques spiritual workplaces employ include nature programs, creative expression, open meetings, open discussions, and evolving mission statements. These workplaces encourage employee education and growth through courses on meditation, yoga, and other distinct philosophies and through practices such as t'ai chi and feng shui. Above all, perhaps, is a corporate culture that encourages getting to know one another's family, interests, community activities, and preferences.

Stress management activities and programs are conducted to eliminate or reduce the consequences of excessive stress to individual employees, their families, and the organization. Stress is often accompanied by adverse effects on physical and mental health, damage to personal and family life, increased absenteeism and tardiness, strained interpersonal relationships, substandard performance, and lower productivity. Strategies and techniques used include medical referral, exercise and fitness programs, therapy, counseling, and self-awareness training, massage, breathing techniques, and spouse and couples workshops. All of these are conducted to eliminate or reduce the effects of stress on the employee.

Well-building programs are established to provide safe, comfortable, and productive working environments. A focus of many well-building programs is on design and construction factors such as poor lighting and inadequate ventilation; environmental factors such as odor, temperature, dust, and noise; perceptual and psychological factors such as lack of privacy and claustrophobic effects due to sealed construction; and cultural and organizational factors dealing with cleanliness, maintenance, and management of the facility.

*Win-win negotiation involves *negotiation,* which is a process of back-and-forth communication with the intention to reach an agreement between two or more parties when they have shared and differing interests, and *win-win,* which refers to the goal of achieving a positive outcome for all sides with each party's seeking solutions that maximize mutual gain.

*Work-life balance is the creation of order and inner harmony between a performer's personal and professional responsibilities. It includes placing a priority and a value on all activities that a performer is involved with, and learning to let go of low-importance and low-value activities in favor of more important activities.

*Violence prevention programs help organizations assess and rectify the detrimental impact of violence on employee morale, health, safety, and productivity. The programs often include some form of training to prevent violence and mediate the impact of stress, trauma, and violence on workplace performance.

REFERENCES AND RESOURCES

Baskin, Otis, and Craig Aronoff. (1988). *Public Relations: The Profession and the Practice* (3d edition). Dubuque, IA: William C. Brown.

Berke, George B. (May 1990). "How to Conduct a Performance Appraisal." *Info-line.* Issue No. 9005. Alexandria, VA: ASTD.

Tracey, William R. (1991). *The Human Resources Glossary: A Complete Desk Reference for HR Professionals.* New York: AMACOM.

Kaplan, Robert, and David Norton. (1992). Balanced Score Card Collaborative. www.bscol.com.

ABOUT THE AUTHORS

Ethan S. Sanders is president and CEO of Sundial Learning Systems. Before founding this company, Sanders was manager of instructional design for ASTD. While at ASTD, he led the research and writing of two major competency studies, and redesigned several of ASTD's courses. Before joining ASTD, he was a senior instructional designer of management development courses in the banking industry and a training manager in the transportation industry. He is the co-author of *ASTD Models for Learning Technologies, ASTD Models for Workplace Learning and Performance,* and the ASTD course "Human Performance Improvement in the Workplace." Sanders also teaches several of ASTD's courses offered through public and corporate seminars. He holds a master's degree in applied behavioral science from Johns Hopkins University. Sanders can be reached at Sundial Learning Systems, 1805 Commonwealth Ave., Alexandria, VA 22301; phone: 703.739.4344; email: esanders@sundial learning.com.

Sivasailam "Thiagi" Thiagarajan makes a living by having fun and helping others have fun. With a Ph.D. in instructional systems and a background in cognitive sciences and social psychology, Thiagi specializes in interactive strategies for improving human performance. An author of more than 20 books and designer of more than 200 published games, Thiagi writes an online newsletter *Play for Performance* (at www.thiagi.com). As a global nomad, Thiagi has lived in three different countries and cultures (India, Liberia, and the United States) and has worked as a consultant in 27 other countries. He can be reached at Workshops by Thiagi, 4423 East Trailridge Road, Bloomington, IN 47408; phone: 812.332.1478; email: thiagi@thiagi.com.

ABOUT THE CONTRIBUTORS

Mark L. Berman is a consulting psychologist in Phoenix, Arizona. His areas of specialization include generating different approaches to personal energy management as a function of the specific occupations involved, identifying and intervening with employees who emphasize avoidance behaviors on the job, and assessing job applicants as well as existing employees in terms of their energy capabilities and probability of experiencing burnout. Prior to becoming a consultant, Berman served on the faculties of the Pennsylvania State University and the University of Washington. ASTD published his *Info-line* "Avoiding Burnout" in 1995 and his article "Be a Seeker Not an Avoider" in the April 2000 issue of Training & Development. Berman received his Ph.D. in psychology from Arizona State University in 1969. He can be reached at mark53@home.com.

Tom Devane is an internationally recognized consultant, author, and workshop leader who helps clients integrate business strategy, processes, and human factors in large-scale change efforts. His coaching assistance includes such performance levers as team-based strategic planning, business process redesign, metrics development, and the implementation of team-based organizational structures. Devane founded Premier Integration in 1988. Prior to that, he held management positions at two of the "Big Five" consulting firms and an energy company. He is co-author of *The Change Handbook: Group Methods for Shaping the Future* and a contributor to *The Organization Development and Training Sourcebook* series, the *20 Active Training Programs* series, *The Consultant's Toolkit,* and *Executive Excellence Magazine* on the topics of performance improvement and large-scale change. Devane can be reached at tdevane@mindspring.com.

Paul H. Elliott is a fellow with Saba Software of Redwood Shores, California. Elliott assists organizations in performance analysis, instructional design, product and process launch support, design of advanced training systems, and the design and implementation of integrated performance interventions. From 1995 through 2001, he was president of Human Performance Technologies, a provider of methodologies and training for performance consultants. He has served on the board of directors of ASTD and was recognized as external technical trainer of the year by that organization. In 1996, Elliott served as executive-in-residence for ASTD, where his focus was on the paradigm shift from training to performance and its implications for that professional organization. Elliott received his Ph.D. in educational psychology from the University of Illinois (1975), his M.S. in instructional technology from Syracuse University (1970), and his B.A. from Rutgers University (1970). Recent publications include the chapter on assessment in *Moving From Training* *to Performance* and on job aids in the *Handbook of Human Performance Technology*. Elliott can be contacted at Paul@hptonline.com.

Linda Beck Halliburton is the director of college and university relations at the Holmes Corporation in Minneapolis. She is responsible for overseeing a team of professionals who work with nearly 200 educational institutions to deliver high-quality continuing professional education. Prior to joining the Holmes Corporation, she worked as an associate director of continuing education, human resource manager, employee development specialist, and sales specialist. She has also taught college courses in human resource management, career development, human resource development, and small business management. Halliburton has gained broad knowledge through a background that spans business and education, the public and private sectors, and small and large organizations. She holds a B.A. in business administration from Augustana College and an M.A. in human resource development from St. Cloud State University. She has taken courses toward an M.B.A. from the University of St. Thomas. Professional memberships include ASTD, Society for Human Resource Management (SHRM), and the International Society for Performance Improvement (ISPI). She can be contacted at lindah @holmescorp.com.

Stewart Hickman is the director of the Learning Network at Georgetown University Hospital, in Washington, D.C. His department provides internal consulting and training services aimed at enhancing organizational, departmental, and individual performance. Prior to this appointment, he was the director of human resources for ASTD. His experience includes work as an OD specialist at Johns Hopkins Hospital and as an external management consultant for O'Hare Associates, working in the United States and abroad with an emphasis on international nonprofit research institutions. He has trained and consulted on a range of topics from interpersonal communications and customer service to organizational culture and appreciative inquiry. Throughout his 20-year career, he has sought to bring a wholistic approach to helping organizations become more productive and satisfying places to work and learn. He has a master's degree in education and human resource development from George Washington University. He can be reached at esh5@gunet.george town.edu.

Jennifer Homer is the director of public relations for ASTD. She is responsible for the association's internal and external communications, public relations, and media relations campaigns. Prior to coming to ASTD, she was an account executive with Cyphers Wood, an advertising agency based in Annapolis, Maryland, specializing in real estate and economic development. Her experience includes work as the manager for the Remodelors Council, a 6,500-member special interest group of the National Association of Home Builders (NAHB). Homer has been a leader in the International Association of Business Communicators (IABC), Washington, D.C., chapter for six years, serving as the vice president of communications, vice president of membership, president-elect, president, and past president. She is currently serving as treasurer for the IABC District III board of directors, which serves chapters in Pennsylvania, Delaware, Maryland, Washington, D.C., Virginia, and North Carolina. She can be reached at jhomer@astd.org.

Kathy Kelly is vice president of business development for Nforma. In this role she is responsible for helping clients use Nforma's two-dimensional assessment tool to improve their performance metrics in order to maximize the return on their investment in training. Prior to joining Nforma, she was director of learning environments for Saba and director of instructional technology for Arthur Andersen. Kelly's academic experience includes serving as associate professor and mathematics education program chair at the Florida Institute of Technology and assistant professor at Jersey City State College. She holds a doctorate in educational psychology from City University of New York, Graduate Center; a master's degree in education from Long Island University, C.W. Post Center; and a bachelor's degree in mathematics from St. John's University. Kelly (formerly Kelly-Benjamin) is also a published author and public speaker. She can be reached at kathyk@nforma.com.

Andrew Kimball is a founder and CEO of QBInternational, a performance-consulting and training firm with offices in North America and Europe. He has designed and delivered programs in more than 15 countries worldwide. Prior to founding QBInternational, Kimball held sales and executive management positions at Coopers & Lybrand, Bank of America, and Citibank. Kimball has been interviewed and has published extensively on topics as diverse as building a high-performance culture, technical team communication processes and practices, high-tech sales practices and strategies, effective instructional design for e-learning curricula, and maximizing return-on-investment in corporate universities. He is a frequent presenter at such events as the International Society of Performance Improvement Annual Conference, the North American Simulation and Gaming Association Conference, ASTD, and the Association for Quality and Participation Annual Conference. He can be reached at AKimball@qube.com.

Kat Koppett is a senior consultant with QBInternational, for whom she has designed and delivered programs in negotiation, presentation, and general communication skills. Koppett is also the co-founder of StoryNet, LLC (http://www.thestorynet.com), a consulting company devoted to harnessing the power of storytelling in business settings, and the corporate division director and a performing member of Bay Area Theatresports, an improvisational theater company on the West Coast. She is the author of *Training to Imagine: Practical Improvisational Theatre Techniques to Enhance Creativity, Teamwork, Leadership and Learning* (Stylus Publishing, May 2001), a book about the use of improvisational theater techniques in business. Koppett's clients include Cadence Design Systems, Netcentives, Oracle, Sony, Roche Molecular Systems, Price-Waterhouse, Kaiser-Permanente, Charles Schwab, and Microsoft. She holds an M.A. in organizational psychology from Columbia University. She can be reached at kkoppett@earthlink.net.

Michael J. Marquardt is a professor of human resource development and program director of overseas programs at George Washington University, in Washington, D.C. He also serves as president of Global Learning Associates, a firm assisting corporations to become global learning organizations. He has held senior management, training, and marketing positions with various organizations worldwide and has trained more than 25,000 managers in 85 countries. He is the author of 14 books and over 50 professional articles in the fields of leadership, learning, globalization, and organizational change including *Building the Learning Organization, The Global Advantage,* and *Action Learning in Action.* Marquardt's recognitions include the International Practitioner of the Year Award from ASTD and an honorary Ph.D. from the International Management Centre at Oxford, England, for his work in the field of action learning. He serves as a senior advisor for the United Nations Staff College in the areas of policy, technology, and learning systems, and is a Fellow of the National Academy for Human Resource Development and a co-founder of the Asian Learning Organization Network. He received his doctorate in human resource development from George Washington University and his master's and bachelor's degrees from Maryknoll College. He can be reached at mjmq@aol.com.

Todd Packer helps organizations grow responsibly. As an independent consultant he provides research and training in organizational development and creative problem solving to help ensure workplace peace and productivity. With over 10 years' experience with human rights and human resources, he seeks to improve performance through dynamic new approaches to creativity and communication at work. His innovative training techniques, which use finger paints, music, and crepe paper, have sparked ideas and reduced stress for individuals from corporations, universities, nonprofit institutions, and health-care facilities in the United States, Canada, and India. Packer has been actively involved with ISPI since 1993. Packer's presentations at international business and academic conferences include: "Time is a Vampire: Managing Organizational Horror, Chaos and Performance for Professional Competence and High-Speed Change," "Human Rights and Human Resources: Strategies for Empowering Communications in Organizations and Society in India and the USA," "Microscopes in Minefields: Intercultural Research, Creativity and Empowerment," and "Handling Management Mess: Finger-paint Brainstorming." He has a master's degree in social service administration from the University of Chicago. He can be reached via email at toddpacker@usa.net.

George Piskurich is an organizational learning and performance consultant specializing in e-learning interventions, performance analysis, and telecommuting. He presents workshops on self-directed learning, structured mentoring, and preparing learners for e-learning. With over 25 years of experience in learning technology, he has been a classroom instructor, training manager, instructional designer, and e-learning consultant for multinational clients and smaller organizations. He has created classroom seminars, OJT mentoring systems, and e-learning interventions. He has been a presenter and workshop leader at over 30 conferences and symposia and is an active member of both ISPI and ASTD. He has written books and articles on instructional technology, self-directed learning, instructional design, and telecommuting, and is currently editing two books on e-learning. In 1986, he was ASTD's Instructional Technologist of the Year, and won the Best Use of Instructional Technology in Business award in 1992. He can be reached at gmp1@compuserve.com.

Margo Prator is currently an HR manager at PMC Sierra, in Gaithersburg, Maryland. Prior to joining PMC Sierra, she worked in human resources, marketing, and sales at Unisys, Apple Computer, and 3Com Corporation in Silicon Valley. She has managed multiple functions within the human resource field, primarily focusing on the staffing aspects of HR. She holds a degree from

American University in Washington, D.C. She can be reached at margo _prator@pmc-sierra.com.

Matthew S. Richter is a senior consultant and trainer for QBInternational. He has consulted with such *Fortune* 500 organizations as MasterCard, Silicon Graphics, Ralph Lauren, Cadence Design Systems, Broadvision, Global Crossing, Aceva Technologies, Xerox, Guidant, and Olympus to enhance their overall productivity through the successful management of people using coaching systems, human performance technology, and training. He is a frequent public speaker, delivering keynotes and conference presentations nationally. Richter is the co-founder of StoryNet, a partnership that recognizes the dynamic nature of story and its inherent application in business and training. StoryNet is dedicated to the process of developing knowledge and understanding through activities that enhance learning. Richter has published several articles on the applications of storytelling in technical training, instructional design, and organizational development. He is the co-developer of MESA, a tool for measuring intrinsic and extrinsic motivation in the workplace, and is also the co-author of PIIE, the Program Initiative Impact Evaluation, a process for measuring the return-on-investment of strategic and organizational development interventions. Richter is working on a doctorate at the University of Rochester. He can be reached at matthew @thestorynet.com.

Lou Russell's job is to help her *Fortune* 50 clients understand that it is not about the technology—it's about what the technology does. As president and CEO of Russell Martin and Associates (a 14-year-old Indianapolis-based company), Russell teaches that in order for technology to succeed within a broader business strategy, there must be joint ownership of both its design and its expected outcomes by both business-side and IT colleagues. Russell is the author of two books on accelerated learning and writes widely for industry publications such as *Computer World, Cutter Executive Reports,* and *Network World.* A frequent and popular speaker, she has addressed such conferences as the Project Management Institute, Project World, LotuSphere, GIGA World, and the Society of Information Management (SIM). Russell holds a computer science degree from Purdue University and a master's degree in instructional technology from Indiana University. She can be reached at www.russell martin.com.

Kim E. Ruyle is manager of learning technologies for Deere & Company's Worldwide Learning and Development group. He is responsible for developing and implementing the enterprise strategy for e-learning and is involved in related initiatives in knowledge management and technical information content management. Ruyle has held positions as training manager and university professor, and he founded and ran a software company for 10 years before joining Deere. His company pioneered the implementation of industrial EPSS in a variety of industries and produced many award-winning applications. Ruyle has a rare blend of hands-on work experience (diesel mechanic, welder, machinist) and academic credentials (three master's degrees and a Ph.D.). He has written numerous articles and book chapters about learning technologies and is a frequent conference speaker. He can be reached at RuyleKimE @JohnDeere.com.

Ralph Sanders is the J. Carlton Ward Distinguished Professor at the National Defense University (NDU)/Industrial College of the Armed Forces (ICAF). He received his BSFS, MSFS, and Ph.D. from Georgetown University in 1950, 1952, and 1958, respectively. In 1958, he worked at the White House as co-author of the water development proposals contained in President Eisenhower's address to the United Nations. ICAF and the National War College gave him diplomas in 1962 and 1979. In 1967, he served on the systems analysis staff of the secretary of defense. At NDU, Sanders originated the NATO Symposium and was the co-author of the Strategy/Resources Exercise. At ICAF he taught courses in military strategy, national security, technology and the art of war, and industrial preparedness. Sanders has been awarded the Decoration for Exceptional Service (the Army's highest civilian award) and the Decoration for Meritorious Service (twice). Among his many publications are *The Executive Decisionmaking Process, Defense Industries: New Suppliers and Regional Security, International Dynamics of Technology,* and the *Politics of Defense Systems Analysis.* He can be reached at at DRRSanders@aol.com.

Patti Shank is the managing partner of Learning Peaks, LLC (http://www.learningpeaks.com), a consulting group that helps organizations and higher education institutions optimize Web-based and distance education initiatives through analysis, design, and planning. Clients include government, corporations, and higher education institutions. She is known for her independent and systems-oriented approaches to training, performance, and learning technologies and is listed in *Who's Who in Instructional Technology.* She speaks frequently at training and instructional technology conferences, is often quoted in training publications, and has contributed numerous chapters to training, instructional design, and instructional technology books. Shank teaches graduate educational technology courses for the University of Colorado, Denver, and is an award-winning contributing editor for Bill Communication's *Online Learning Magazine.* Shank has a master's degree in educational technology leadership from George Washington University and is currently working on her Ph.D. at the University of Colorado, Denver. She can be reached at patti@learningpeaks.com.

Rick Sullivan is the director of the Learning and Performance Support Office at the JHPIEGO Corporation, an affiliate of Johns Hopkins University. Sullivan and his team are responsible for the design and implementation of structured on-the-job training, instructor-led training, technology-assisted learning, and other learning interventions to improve the performance of health-care providers in developing countries. He has written several books and numerous articles in a variety of professional journals. He has presented papers and presentations at many national conferences including ASTD. Sullivan can be reached at rsullivan@jhpiego.org.

Mark Van Buren is director of research at ASTD. Van Buren oversees ASTD's primary research initiatives on workplace learning and performance involving worldwide industry trends, training for low-skill and low-wage workers, and the development of standards of measurement. His current research includes studies on learner acceptance of technology-based training and on training in the temporary staffing industry. In recent years, his research has examined the use of high-performance work systems in a number of *Fortune* 500 companies, the creation of learning organizations, and the management and measurement of intellectual capital. His particular fields of expertise are in the areas of e-learning and knowledge management. Prior to joining ASTD in 1995, he conducted research on new technologies and new forms of work at the University of North Carolina-Chapel Hill. Van Buren received a Ph.D. and master's degree in sociology from the University of North Carolina-Chapel Hill, and both a B.A. in sociology and a B.S. in computer science from the University of Dayton. He can be reached at mvanburen@astd.org.

Jacqueline B. Visnius will receive a master's in organization development and human resources from Johns Hopkins University in May 2002. Visnius is concentrating her studies and fieldwork in the areas of performance improvement and training. She is in ASTD's HPI Certificate program, which is supplemented by her graduate studies. Prior to her work in the field of performance improvement, she spent 15 years in mortgage banking. She was a project manager and team leader on many of the high-profile savings and loan closings that took place in the 1980s. Following her work in the banking industry, she was an account executive for many high-profile banks such as Bank of America and Wells Fargo. She can be reached at cjvisnius@aol.com.

ABOUT THE INTERNATIONAL SOCIETY FOR PERFORMANCE IMPROVEMENT

International Society for Performance Improvement (ISPI) is the leading international association of professionals who are dedicated to improving individual, organizational, and societal performance using a systematic and reproducible methodology known as Human Performance Technology.

ISPI members hold management and line positions in performance technology, employee training, human resource development, instructional design, organizational development, and other key management areas.

For four decades, ISPI members have been steadily improving performance for the largest, most successful organizations in nearly 40 countries around the world.

Individual ISPI members are employed by private firms and corporations (including 75 percent of the Fortune 100), leading educational institutions, non-profit organizations, and numerous city, state and provincial governments, as well as national civilian and military agencies of countries around the world.

ISPI corporate members and supporters include Andersen, CADDI, Comcast Cable, Eli Lilly, Ford Motor Company, Georgia-Pacific, Hewlett Packard, IBM, iGeneration, International Monetary Fund, Maritz, Metropolitan Life Insurance, Microsoft, Sun Microsystems, United States Coast Guard, United States Food and Drug Administration, Walgreen, Wells Fargo, and others.

ISPI offers its members outstanding performance improvement education, networking opportunities, and involvement through conferences, institutes, book publishing, professional journals, an interactive Website, research, and local chapters.

For information about ISPI:

International Society for Performance Improvement
1400 Spring Street, Suite 260
Silver Spring, MD 20910 USA
Telephone: 1.301.587.8570
Fax: 1.301.587.8573
Email: info@ispi.org
Web: www.ispi.org